Classroom interactions in literacy

Classroom interactions in literacy

edited by
Eve Bearne, Henrietta Dombey and Teresa
Grainger

Open University Press

Open University Press
McGraw-Hill Education
McGraw-Hill House
Shoppenhangers Road
Maidenhead
Berkshire
England
SL6 2QL

email: enquiries@openup.co.uk
world wide web: www.openup.co.uk

First published 2003

A catalogue record of this book is available from the British Library

ISBN 0 335 21385 5 (pb)   0 335 21386 3 (hb)

Library of Congress Cataloging-in-Publication Data
CIP data has been applied for

Typeset by Refine Catch Limited, Bungay, Suffolk
Printed in Great Britain by Bell and Bain Ltd, Glasgow

Contents

List of figures

Notes on contributors

Robin Alexander is Visiting Professor of Education at the University of Cambridge and previously was Professor of Education at the universities of Leeds and Warwick. His most recent book, *Culture and Pedagogy: International Comparisons in Primary Education* (Blackwell), won the 2002 American Educational Research Association Outstanding Book Award.

Evelyn Arizpe is a researcher attached to the Faculty of Education, University of Cambridge. After receiving her doctorate on adolescent literature and reading from this university, she has worked on research projects in the areas of literacy and gender, both in Mexico and in England, and has taught on higher education courses in children's literature. Her first book (in Spanish) is a critical analysis of literature for children in Mexico. She has just completed a second book, with Morag Styles, entitled *Children Reading Pictures: Interpreting Visual Texts* (Routledge 2003).

Eve Bearne divides her time at the University of Cambridge Faculty of Education between research and teaching. Her current research interests are children's production of multimodal texts, and gender, language and literacy. She has edited and written a number of books about language and literacy, and about children's literature. She is currently President of the United Kingdom Literacy Association.

Kathy Coulthard is Senior Schools Development Officer in the City of Westminster, having previously been an adviser for ethnic minority achievement and advisory teacher for English and assessment. She writes for journals such as *English in Education* and *Language Matters* and has contributed a chapter to *Children Reading Pictures* (Arizpe and Styles 2003). She is in demand as a speaker on inclusion, and teaching and learning in multilingual classrooms.

Henrietta Dombey started to learn about literacy teaching and learning during her years as a primary teacher in schools in inner London where she pioneered teaching reading without a reading scheme. She developed her interest in the interactions between the children, the texts and the teacher while carrying out fieldwork in a nursery class for her PhD on young children's experience of hearing stories read aloud. She is currently investigating the patterns of interaction during whole class parts of the Literacy Hour in classrooms of highly successful teachers of literacy. During the introduction of the national curriculum she chaired the National Association for the Teaching of English. She was also President of UKRA (UK Reading Association) from 2002 to 2003.

After a brief period discovering what he didn't want to do with his life, **Peter Geekie** became a teacher in 1961 and has been involved in education ever since. He taught in primary schools, highschools and a teacher's college before becoming part of the Education Faculty at the University of Wollongong in the early 1980s. He has been trying to understand, for at least 30 years, how children become literate, and is still engaged in this project. Although he has recently retired, he is still involved in teaching and research, and is currently investigating the link between literacy development and the growth of referential communication skills in 6-year-old children.

Teresa Grainger is a reader in Education at Canterbury Christ Church University College where she coordinates the MA in Language and Literacy, the PGCE English programme, facilitates a pedagogy study group for staff and undertakes research and consultancy. She was president of the United Kingdom Reading Association in 2001–02 and is Editor of the UK Reading Association journal *Reading Literacy and Language*. Teresa has published widely on literacy and the language arts, on drama, storytelling, literature and poetry and most recently has edited a Routledge/Falmer *Reader on Language and Literacy*. Her current research projects include: investigating children's voice, verve and creativity in writing; exploring the relationship between drama and writing; and examining the nature of creative teaching and learning, the links between the development of spirituality and literacy, and the teacher as a creative artist in the language classroom.

Charmian Kenner is a researcher and lecturer on bilingualism and biliteracy, and Research Fellow at Goldsmiths College, London. She has recently completed an Economic and Social Research Council (ESRC) funded research project at the Institute of Education, University of London, about 6-year-olds becoming biliterate. Her previous work on creating a multilingual literacy environment in early years classrooms is described in the book *Home Pages: Literacy Links for Bilingual Children* (Trentham Books 2000).

Trinka Messenheimer (Dr) is currently the Undergraduate Coordinator for Intervention Services at Bowling Green State University, in Bowling Green, Ohio, USA. Her teaching is in the area of literacy instruction for students with disabilities. Her main research has been focused on students' writing and instruction as she has been a participant observer in a 5th grade (10–11-year-olds) classroom for three years.

Angela Packwood (Dr) is a senior lecturer in the Education Department at Keele University. Her interest in literacy stems from her training as an English teacher and her connection with the National Oracy Project. Over the past three years she has engaged in research with Dr Messenheimer to investigate children as writers in UK and US classrooms.

Louise Poulson is a senior lecturer in Education at the University of Bath, UK. Her research interests are in the area of literacy and education policy and reform. She co-directed the Effective Teachers of Literacy in Primary Schools project in the UK; and has also researched family literacy provision in local communities for the Basic Skills Agency in England and Wales.

Sandra Smidt was born and educated in apartheid South Africa. She came to the UK in 1964 and lived and taught in inner city schools in Manchester before moving to London in 1978. During this time she developed interests in language and literacy, in education and diversity, and in the arts. After a stint as headteacher of a school in Hackney she moved on to working in local authorities and her professional interests broadened to include early childhood education. She developed and led the first graduate programme in England for those working with young children in any setting, both as a face to face degree and as a distance learning programme. In 1996 she returned to South Africa and for three years, lived and worked there, leading a national pilot programme on early childhood education. In 1999 she returned to the UK and currently works at the University of East London where she is the director of the undergraduate programmes in the School of Education and Community Studies.

Ilana Snyder is an associate professor in the Faculty of Education, Monash University. *Hypertext* (Melbourne University Press 1996), *Page to Screen* (Routledge 1998), *Teachers and Technoliteracy* (co-authored with Colin Lankshear) (Allen & Unwin 2000), and *Silicon Literacies* (Routledge 2002) explore changes to cultural practices associated with the use of new media.

Morag Styles is a senior lecturer in the Faculty of Education, Cambridge, and a Reader in Children's Literature at Homerton College, Cambridge. She has written and lectured widely on children's literature (especially poetry and picturebooks), reading and writing. She is the author of *From the Garden to the Street: 300 Years of Poetry for Children* (1998) and *Children Reading Pictures: Interpreting Visual Texts* (with Evelyn Arizpe) (2002). She has co-edited several volumes of essays with Eve Bearne and Victor Watson and was an advisory editor for the latter's *Cambridge Guide to Children's Books in English*.

Sam Twiselton is the programme leader for the primary PGCE at St Martin's College. She also lectures in primary English and recently completed her PhD thesis. This involved research into the development of understandings and beliefs about English in student teachers as they learn in the primary classroom.

Gordon Wells (Dr) is currently Professor of Education at the University of California, Santa Cruz, where he researches and teaches in the fields of: language, literacy and learning; the analysis of classroom interaction; and sociocultural theory. Before emigrating to North America in 1984, he directed the Bristol Study of Language Development. From 1984 to 2000, he was a professor at the Ontario Institute for Studies in Education of the University of Toronto where, in addition to teaching and research, he was involved in several collaborative action research projects with educational practitioners in Canada.

Professor Wells has lectured and acted as consultant in Europe, Latin America, Asia and Australia, as well as in Britain and North America. His most recent, co-edited, book, *Learning for Life in the Twenty-first Century: Sociocultural Perspectives on the Future of Education* has just been published by Blackwell (2002).

Introduction

The inspiration and impetus for this book came from the United Kingdom Reading Association (UKRA) International Conference, 2002. However, it is not a book of 'conference proceedings'. While some of the chapters are written by contributors to the conference, other educationists who are nationally and internationally recognized in their fields have been invited to join in constructing an agenda for future language and literacy teaching. For some time now books about education have been written in response to imposed initiatives. Such books are necessary but can distract attention from educators' own research and reflection since they feel they must address other people's concerns before their own. This book sets out to give individual writers the space to express their own convictions about language, literacy and pedagogy in the current context and the chance to look towards the future. Some chapters draw on recent research, while others give a more reflective overview of educational practice in a particular domain of language and literacy. All of them bring a distinctive quality to the theme of classroom interactions. Overall, the intention is to challenge some current restrictive thinking and contribute to a more open and expansive agenda.

In the 1980s and 1990s there were many studies in Australia, the United Kingdom and the US about classroom interaction. In particular Douglas Barnes, Jerome Bruner and Gordon Wells were influential in prompting close attention to the role of language in group interactions. At that time, the idea of learners being encouraged to shape and build meanings for themselves, scaffolded by their teachers, indicated a particular stance towards pedagogy. Since that era, in which rich contributions to educational thinking were made, the term 'interaction' has gone underground; recently, however, it has been resurrected to denote a particular view of pedagogy. 'Interactive teaching' has currently come to have a new stipulative definition, one which assumes that the teacher controls the interaction and that teaching will be organized through whole class arrangements. Rather than describing a dynamic exchange between partners in education, interactive teaching has taken on the flavour of transmissional teaching. Greater attention to talk and learning is welcome but tends to sideline the important interactions between, for example, reader/writer and text, or child and child. The contributors to this book are responding to a new sense of urgency as teachers and others involved in educational policy and practice are realizing that transmissional teaching doesn't equal good learning.

If even such an apparently dynamic term as interaction has a more restricted definition, others, notably pedagogy and literacy itself, have also taken on new stipulative meanings. It is time to re-examine terminology about classrooms, language, literacy and learning. This book tackles assumptions about shared meanings, exploring and unpicking some of the complexities, tensions and debates about language, literacy and learning in the twenty-first century. It also relates classroom concerns to the wider realm of cultural and social relationships which are fundamental elements in learning. In acknowledging such breadth of scope, this book explores interactions between: children and teachers; children and children; children and texts of all kinds; language, literacy and learning in schools and homes; and institutions, governments and the teaching profession. Any of these interactions can operate with or without symmetry and in critiquing present arrangements and in setting an agenda for the future it is crucial to examine the power relations implicit in pedagogic settings. It is equally imperative to examine the understandings and assumptions of all partners in the process of teaching and learning. Common terminology does not necessarily denote common principles, common understanding or common practice.

Interaction should have the dynamic to move thinking and learning on. In this book the individual and convinced voices of experienced educators reinvigorate the quest not only for definitions of current educational terminology or debates about the principles underlying teaching and learning, but for refreshing and rejuvenating classroom practice.

In accord with the belief of ideas developing best through interaction, the book has been arranged so that the chapters offer complementary points of view. Each section, except the first, is made up of pairs of chapters which tackle similar issues and through their juxtapositions extend the debates which are their focus. Each chapter contributes a strand to the interwoven texture of a book which sees critical thinking and critical pedagogy as central to language, literacy and learning. Part 1 sets the frame as Ilana Snyder explores current terminology and considers the nature of a contemporary pedagogy of literacy which acknowledges the shaping influence of new media. While the experience of rapid worldwide change can prompt insecurity, Ilana is optimistic and sees opportunities and possibilities for new pedagogical frameworks which move faster and more surely towards an informed and assured critical literacy.

Part 2 starts to sketch out the elements of a critical pedagogy. Beginning with an outline of his large scale international research Robin Alexander offers a comprehensive analysis of the cultural and historical roots of different class-room practices, suggesting ways in which the findings can contribute to more productive classroom discourse. In contrast with this wide range perspective, Henrietta Dombey puts one teacher and her pupils under the microscope to examine the patterns of interaction between teachers, pupils and text in a whole class literacy session. This close attention to literacy teaching acts as a bridge between policy and practice.

In Part 3 Louise Poulson and Sam Twiselton consider questions of teachers' knowledge and expertise. Louise Poulson points out that, in the UK at least, education policies over the past decade, particularly in relation to primary school teachers, have emphasized the importance of strong subject knowledge to teach literacy. However, it is important to examine critically assumptions about the relationship between subject knowledge and pedagogy in literacy in the primary phase. In her study of student teachers' perceptions of literacy teaching, Sam Twiselton presents research findings from the period directly before the introduction of the National Literacy Strategy in England and three years after implementation. By the end of initial teacher education some student teachers were able to see the Strategy as a flexible tool for facilitating effective learning in literacy while others were still caught in a more instrumental position of 'delivery'. However, she also distinguishes between literacy and English teaching, arguing, like Poulson, that subject knowledge alone is not enough. Professional expertise means knowing something about the ends of education as well as its means.

Extending the theme of critical pedagogy, in Part 4 Kathy Coulthard, Evelyn Arizpe and Morag Styles describe how pupils and teachers work collaboratively to negotiate meaning in responding to picturebooks. Acknowledging children's cultural and text knowledge is an important element in such negotiations. Charmian Kenner outlines ways in which researchers and educators have engaged with bilingual children's home knowledge, arguing that a successful interactive pedagogy begins by supporting and developing bilingual children's existing knowledge in the mainstream classroom. Such a pedagogy integrates cultural and text knowledge bringing two more important elements of professional knowledge into focus – knowledge of learners and knowledge of educational contexts within and outside schools.

The theme of teachers' professional knowledge is extended – and challenged – in the next section, Part 5. Teresa Grainger suggests a move away from 'certainties' in the classroom, which can often be restrictive, towards acceptance of uncertainty. She argues that through drama, teachers can create a community of collaborative learners whose interactions raise questions, offer alternative perspectives and reflect the ambiguity of living. She shows how 'dramatic literacies' can support a pedagogy which explores, interprets and reflects upon learning. Dramatic activity allows children to engage with the transformative possibilities of literacy. Sandra Smidt also argues that the purpose of education is about developing people who can 'read' their world, interpret and challenge it. Examining the role of play in early years education, she questions some western notions about play which relate to choice, child-centredness and some sort of 'freedom'. Millions of children throughout the world learn effectively and efficiently in cultures and communities where our notions of play are not held. Sandra Smidt argues for a redefinition of play and its role in learning and in literacy, since play by its very nature allows control to pass from the adult to the learner.

In Part 6 Eve Bearne argues that multimodal, multidimensional texts have changed the ways in which young readers expect to read, the ways they think and the ways they construct meaning. Showing how children play with the possibilities of the texts they know, Bearne suggests that teachers are prevented from giving these texts their full value in the classroom because of institutional arrangements for assessment. Both chapters in this section look to the future of a pedagogy which can appreciate and sustain the many dimensions of children's text knowledge and text production and which encourages critical thinking about those texts. Angela Packwood and Trinka Messenheimer continue the debate about restrictive practices around writing offering an alternative to the approach emerging from recent reforms on both sides of the Atlantic which have narrowed the pedagogical focus and required increased accountability. Such practices not only devalue what young learners know and can do, but importantly close down future possibilities.

The final section of the book Part 7 integrates views about children's text knowledge drawn from outside school with a critical pedagogy within the classroom. Both Peter Geekie and Gordon Wells consider the social and cultural influences on literacy education, arguing for an integrative pedagogy. Geekie argues that good teaching does not involve a highly structured programme of skill development, but rather collaborative involvement in tasks that are culturally significant. Gordon Wells also emphasizes collaboration between learners, and interaction between all the language modes as children and teachers shape learning. Wells emphasizes that learning involves others and that literacy gives access to social and cultural knowledge and understandings. These are not things to be added on after children become literate.

This concluding chapter echoes the principles expressed by all contributors to the book. In setting their agenda for the future of language, literacy and learning they emphasize the importance of explicit and wide-ranging professional knowledge informed by a critical pedagogy. The book represents a welcome move from restrictive certainties to the potent possibilities of uncertainty. A move from security which looks more like fixity, towards greater risk accompanied by an integrative rather than fragmented view, offers a professional challenge. At the same time, it gives an invigorating picture of the future for language, literacy and learning.

PART 1
Revisiting the Web of Meaning

Twenty years ago Janet Emig introduced a book about the texture of language, literacy and learning, *The Web of Meaning*. It was a precursor to what is now termed critical pedagogy, which ended with a call for views about literacy which would be 'subtle and humane and tough enough for these times' (Emig 1983: 178). The century has turned but teachers, children, their families and communities still need a view of literacy which, as Emig urged, provides access, sponsors learning, unleashes literal power and activates 'the greatest power of all – the imagination' (Emig 1983).

This book opens with much the same spirit but places the web of meaning in the twenty-first century with questions about current definitions. In the opening chapter, starting with 'pedagogy', Ilana Snyder examines educational terminology. She argues that while there is increasing recognition among literacy educators of the need to devise pedagogies to meet changes in communications which use new media, there has not been much alteration in teaching practices and classrooms. In this introductory chapter, Snyder considers what a literacy pedagogy designed to take account of the new media might look like. Such an approach to teaching and learning would provide students with opportunities to learn how to communicate effectively when using the new media. It would also encourage students to respond critically to the changing material and cultural conditions in which literacy education – both formal and informal – is situated. Through the study of texts, both print and electronic, a subtle, tough and humane pedagogy would aim to provide learners with a sense of their place in the world, and with the capacity to develop strategies for making it a better place.

Discussing the tensions in literacy education between the forces for continuity and those for change, Snyder draws on her research in literacy and technology studies to suggest a pedagogical framework which takes account of critical thinking. Such a framework implies a new way of seeing teachers' professional knowledge and role. A rigorous examination like this could tend towards a sense of destabilization and disjunction from some of the safer ground of classroom practice but Snyder outlines the attraction of the challenges of the twenty-first century. Such a hopeful and challenging starting point sets the tone for the rest of the book.

1 Keywords: a vocabulary of pedagogy and new media

Ilana Snyder

In this chapter I ask an apparently simple pair of questions, what do we mean by the ugly word 'pedagogy'? And, more importantly, what do we mean by pedagogy in the age of the Internet? These questions are critical for, while there is increasing recognition among literacy teachers of the cultural significance of digital technologies, classrooms and ways of teaching have not altered very much since personal computers first entered educational institutions in the late 1970s. It seems that new media are used far less in the classroom than at home and much classroom use is uninspired. And there is a somewhat prosaic explanation for this: in the main, literacy teachers are not trained to use new media nor are they given real opportunities to devise imaginative ways to exploit their possibilities.

This pair of questions also has profound implications for the effective design of new curriculum frameworks and teachers' inservice and preservice programmes that take account of new media. Classroom change is more likely if teachers understand the nature of the new media for themselves, share, even if imperfectly, the language with which to talk about them and have real opportunities to consider how best to reorganize their classrooms and their approaches to teaching and learning in creative ways when they are used.

The meaning of pedagogy

In *Keywords: A Vocabulary of Culture and Society*, Raymond Williams (1976) points out that when some people see a word they think the first thing to do is to define it. Dictionaries are produced and, with authority, a meaning is provided. For words such as 'desk' and 'blackboard', this kind of definition is effective. But for words such as 'pedagogy', which involves ideas and values, 'it is not only an impossible but an irrelevant procedure' (Williams 1976: 17).

Dictionaries provide a number of current meanings for 'pedagogy'. For example, *Webster's Dictionary* (1975: 1320) defines it as:

1   'the profession or function of a teacher; teaching'
2   'the art or science of teaching; especially, instruction in teaching methods'.

The first is an instrumental definition which emphasizes the process of teaching, the activity itself, the second, the acquisition of skills to do it. Both may be taken to assume that teaching how to teach and acquiring the skills to teach are not only possible but also unproblematic. These definitions do not entertain the idea that teaching is connected to learning and the production of knowledge. They also imply a transmission model of teaching.

By contrast, historical dictionaries, argues Williams, go beyond such limited and limiting meanings. For example, the *Shorter Oxford Dictionary on Historical Principles* (Little, Fowler & Coulson 1973: 1537) explains that 'pedagogue' comes from the Greek *paedagogus*, a 'slave who took a boy to and from school':

1   'A man having the oversight of a child or youth; an attendant who led [*or* leads?] a boy to school. Obs. exc. in ref. to ancient times. 1483.'

Later, the *Shorter Oxford Dictionary* continues, 'pedagogue' was used to describe:

2   'A schoolmaster, teacher, preceptor, (Now usu. hostile, with implication of pedantry, dogmatism, or severity.) late ME.'

We can contemplate the irony of a pedagogue characterized as someone who leads a student to school but is in no way responsible for what happens once the student is there. And as for the emergent association between teacher and pedantry, dogmatism and severity, that understanding, sadly, continues to linger. But even the historical 'definitions' don't get us very far in understanding what 'pedagogy' means today, at the beginning of the twenty-first century, a time of immense change much of which is mediated by the rapidly increasing use of the new information and communication technologies.

For Williams there are difficulties in any kind of definition because the meaning of a word such as 'pedagogy' is embedded in relationships and in processes of social and historical change. No word ever finally stands on its own; it is always an element in the social process of language. Thus his extraordinary book, *Keywords*, is neither a dictionary nor a glossary: it is a record of an inquiry into a vocabulary, a shared body of words and meanings concerned with the practices and institutions described as 'culture' and 'society'.

Although Williams's focus was different, we can usefully apply his method in *Keywords* to the central concern of this chapter: exploring the notion of 'pedagogy' when new media are used. Taking my lead from Williams, I identify a shared body of words and their meanings foundational to a potentially illuminating and generative discussion of literacy in a world increasingly mediated by the use of new electronic technologies. Each word that I have included has somehow demanded my consideration because the problems of its meaning seem bound up with the problems I have used it to discuss. Of course, the complex issues surrounding teaching and technology cannot be understood simply by analysing the words used to discuss them. But at the same time, the issues can't really be thought through unless we're conscious of the words as elements of the problems.

What follows is a first cut at which words should be included and how we might begin to explain them. The body of words and their meanings represents, however, a work in progress which is unashamedly idiosyncratic and not exhaustive because of the constraints of the chapter's prescribed word limit. The emphasis is on current use. As the project develops, more attention will be given to changes in the meaning of the words over time, and to their interconnections.

Pedagogy in the age of the Internet: keywords

In alphabetical order, the words I've selected are: communication, critical, culture, database, equity, hypertext, information, interface, knowledge, literacy, narrative, new media, pedagogy and technology. Although someone else might have come up with a different cluster, this does no more than affirm Williams's insight that each of us has different immediate values and that we use language differently – especially when strong feelings or important ideas are in question, as they are here. Although the group of words chosen is somewhat arbitrary, I hope that the selection will be encountered critically – a process fundamental to the development of language. The words offered have meanings that are to be tested, confirmed, asserted, qualified and perhaps changed.

Communication

'Communication' represents a practice or a process. It encompasses communication for information and ideas, in print and electronic media. It is also commonly applied to non-human systems such as animals, canals, roads and railways. At one extreme, 'communication' means the unidirectional transfer of meaning from one to another. Alternatively, it can signify the sharing of common meanings, activities and purposes, a mutual process. 'Communication' as sharing is to do with having the capacity to convey to others the nature of individuals' unique experiences.

'Communication' is more strongly associated with media studies than with literacy studies. Computer mediated 'communication', however, is increasingly used to distinguish between print-based literacy and screen-based literacy practices. In the context of new media, 'communication' is a word that could be used to destabilize the close association so often made between literacy and the printed word (Snyder 2001).

Critical

'Critical' is a difficult word because its predominant sense is of disapproval and denigration. In literary studies it tends to refer to commentary and judgement, but in literacy studies, it is often used in association with 'literacy' or 'pedagogy' to highlight the complex relationships among language, power, social groups and social practices (Knobel and Healey 1998). Like 'communication', 'critical' represents a practice or a process. Concerned with the development of social awareness and active, responsible citizenship, a 'critical' approach to literacy or pedagogy argues that meanings of words and texts cannot be separated from the cultural and social practices in which they are constructed. It recognizes the non-neutrality of texts and is concerned with the politics of meaning: how dominant meanings are maintained, challenged and changed.

As the use of the Internet expands, attention increasingly turns to the promotion of 'critical' digital literacy practices. 'Critical' digital literacy is about recognizing and valuing the breadth of information available and learning how to evaluate, analyse and synthesize that information. It is also concerned with the construction of new meanings and knowledge with technology and with the capacity to communicate in a variety of media for different audiences and purposes. Moreover, it focuses on understanding the ethical, cultural, environmental and societal implications of the use of new media (Faigley 1999).

Culture

Possibly one of the most complicated words in the English language, 'culture' represents an abstract process. Long associated with being cultivated, even as a synonym for civilization, 'culture' has acquired a number of other meanings. When pluralized, it refers to national and traditional cultures, but is also used to distinguish between human and material culture. More recently, it has come to be used in three principal senses: the general process of intellectual, spiritual and aesthetic development; as a particular way of life, whether of a people, a period, a group or humanity in general; the works and practices of intellectual and especially artistic activity (Williams 1976). A distinction is often drawn between high 'culture' and popular 'culture'. In his early works, Williams ([1958] 1983) developed the concept of a common culture. He conceived of culture not as the domain of a special elite but rather as something all could share through education. Bruner (1996) also makes the link between 'culture' and education. He proposes that the mind reaches its full potential only through participation in the culture – not just its formal arts and sciences, but its ways of perceiving, thinking, feeling and carrying out discourse. A central goal of education thus becomes one of equipping individuals to participate in the culture on which life and livelihood depend.

'Cultural' practices are characterized as regular and repeated ways of doing things – constituted over time. The meaning of different 'cultural' practices is established by the shared purposes, values and beliefs of those participating in the 'cultural' practice (Lemke 1995). Computer 'culture' refers to the 'culture' of a distinguishable group, a 'subculture' of people, who engage in a set of 'cultural' practices surrounding the use of new media. Visual 'culture' represents the internal organization, iconography and viewer experience of visual sites in contemporary life: advertising, fashion, supermarkets, billboards, television, websites and so on. Information 'culture' (Manovich 2001) includes ways in which information is presented in different 'cultural' sites and objects: road signs, displays in airports and train stations; television onscreen menus, layout of books, newspapers and magazines; interior designs of banks, hotels and other commercial and leisure spaces; the interfaces of planes and cars; and the interfaces of computer operating systems. There are also what Manovich (2001) calls 'cultural' interfaces: the ways in which computers present and allow users to interact with 'cultural' data. 'Cultural' interfaces include the interfaces used by designers of websites, online museums and magazines, computer games and so on.

Database

A 'database' is a structured collection of data organized to maximize fast search and retrieval by a computer. It represents an abstract process of organizing information. There are different types of 'databases' – hierarchical, network, relational and object orientated – and each uses a different model to organize data. No matter how they are organized, 'databases' appear to users as collections of items to view, navigate and search. The experience of using such a collection of information is different from reading a narrative or watching a film. Like a narrative, a 'database' presents a particular model of what a particular world is like and in this sense represents an independent cultural form.

Some argue that the 'database', examples of which include multimedia encyclopaedias and commercial CD-ROM or DVD, is the dominant cultural form in new media (Manovich 2001). Indeed, multimedia works that have cultural content, such as the CD-ROM virtual tour through a museum collection, favour the 'database' form. Instead of a constructed narrative, the user is presented with a 'database' of texts that can be navigated in a variety of ways. As a cultural form, the 'database' represents the world as a list of items and it does not order that list. By contrast, a narrative creates a cause and effect trajectory of items or events. However, in the context of new media, these two dominant cultural forms are not necessarily competing or oppositional: rather, most often, there is a complex interplay and exchange between them. For example, when users access a museum 'database', the objects in themselves are meaningless: they have to be framed in narrative terms to become meaningful. This might be achieved by a web developer or by the users, who create their own narrative 'exchanges' (Reid 1992) as they choose which links to activate and thus which elements to juxtapose and connect.

Equity

The social sense of equity involves the notion of equivalence of position or status. Integral to its meaning are the processes of equalization (that all people are equal although not necessarily in particular attributes) and the removal of inherent privileges (that all people should begin equally but may become unequal in achievement or condition) (Williams 1976). The notion of the 'digital divide' builds on these ideas about 'equity', arguing that because access to the new technologies is unequally distributed, there is a growing divide between the haves and the have-nots (Castells 2001). Intrinsic to this notion of the digital divide is the cachet society accords access to the new media. It is also widely understood that the overriding factor in determining who gets access and who does not is wealth: the per capita funding of particular educational institutions and the income level of students' family/caregivers determine the likelihood that particular students will have access, at school and/or at home, to the new technologies.

Hypertext

'Hypertext' provides a means of arranging information in a nonsequential manner with the computer automating the process of connecting one piece of information to another. It differs from printed text by offering users multiple paths through a body of information: it allows users to make their own connections and to produce their own meanings (Snyder 1996). In 'hypertext' systems, individual media elements (images, audio, chunks of written text) can be connected by hyperlinking. Elements connected through hyperlinks can exist on the same computer or on different computers connected on a network, as in the case of the web. Critical digital literacy theorists alert 'hypertext' users to the non-neutrality of hyperlinks: they do not just happen to be there. Rather, they are put there (or omitted) by someone to achieve particular purposes.

'Hypertext' is the literacy model of the electronic world of the web. On the web, sequential reading is supported by non-linear connections to alternative ideas; the journey through the labyrinth of 'texts' is replete with choices. And because the journey through text is full of choices, developing navigational skills is a basic capacity (Gilster 1997).

Information

'Information' comprises data that have been organized and communicated; it represents what is essentially a static resource. While recognizing that the categories cannot be absolutely separate and that the relationships are fluid, there are important distinctions between 'information' and knowledge. To convert 'information' into knowledge requires 'an active, purposeful process of selection and interpretation' (Reid 2001: 4).

The Internet demands a comprehensive and necessarily sceptical approach to 'information': knowing how to manage 'information' thoughtfully is more important than ever. 'Information' literacy involves three generic skills: acquiring 'information', evaluating 'information' and using 'information'; it is essential to the process of shaping 'information' into knowledge. Becoming 'information' literate involves ensuring that students at all levels of education can locate, retrieve, decode, appraise and apply information in a range of contexts and media. 'Information' literacy underpins the development of knowledge (Reid 2001).

As the Internet rapidly becomes more broadly established, with hyperlinks connecting users to vast amounts of 'information' on any subject, questions arise: does the act of access change the ways in which users regard 'information'? Does the fact that 'information' appears on a screen give it more or less weight than its counterpart on a printed page? Further, does the packaging of 'information' in a cohesive format, as in a CD-ROM, preclude the student user from an important part of the learning process – the act of acquiring 'information'? On the other hand, it may be that some users are drawn to these texts precisely because of their availability and persuasiveness.

Interface

The term human–computer 'interface' describes the ways in which users interact with a computer. The 'interface' includes physical input and output devices such as the monitor, the keyboard and the mouse. It also includes the metaphors used to conceptualize the organization of computer data. For instance, the Macintosh 'interface', introduced by Apple in 1984, uses the metaphor of files and folders arranged on a desktop. Since Microsoft adopted the same icon driven 'interface', the desktop metaphor has become more or less ubiquitous. Further, the 'interface' includes ways of manipulating data: copy, rename and delete a file; list the contents of a directory; start and stop a program; set the computer's date and time (Manovich 2001). As more and more forms of culture become digitized, computer 'interfaces' allow more interaction with cultural data: hence the notion of cultural 'interface'. And the language of cultural 'interfaces' largely comprises elements of other, already familiar, cultural forms such as painting, photography and film.

Knowledge

'Knowledge' is a set of facts or ideas, presenting a reasoned judgement, which is communicated to others in a systematic form. As it involves the acquisition of some degree of understanding, 'knowledge' entails considerably more than the gathering of information. Nor is 'knowledge' produced in the intentions of those who believe they hold it: it is produced in the process of interaction, for example, between writer and reader at the moment of reading, and between teacher and learner at the moment of classroom engagement (Lusted 1986). Knowledge isn't what's offered so much as what is understood.

'Knowledge' has several forms all of which require a critical focus if they are to lead to true learning. 'Knowledge' about facts is just information: 'know-what' as distinct from 'know-why' (explanatory science), 'know-who' (socially related understandings) and 'know-how' (skill in managing practical processes) (Lundvall and Johnson 1994).

'Knowledge' assembly is the ability to collect and evaluate information, both fact and opinion (Gilster 1997). Effective information gathering can be represented as a balancing act. Used skilfully, networked information possesses unique advantages. It is searchable. It can be customized to reflect users' needs. Moreover, its hypertextual nature connects with a wide range of information sources, allowing users to consider different points of view and to make informed decisions about their validity. The process of using these tools and evaluating the results is 'knowledge' assembly.

Literacy

Moving beyond narrowly conceived explanations of 'literacy', rendered simply as encoding and decoding language, more recent versions take account of social phenomena. They also critique inadequate views of 'literacy' which fail to look further than pedagogy and the classroom (Barton 2001). 'Literacy' studies investigates reading and writing in diverse areas including everyday life and the workplace. It covers a range of cultures and historical periods, as well as multilingual contexts, and is concerned with the use of new technologies, including the Internet. Further, 'literacy' studies recognizes that 'literacy' is not fixed but is always changing: successive advances in technology extend the boundaries of what was previously possible. And each technological advance has seen a corresponding change in how literacy is practised and its social role understood (Lankshear and Snyder 2000).

Digital (or silicon, electronic and technological) 'literacy' is the capacity to access networked computer resources and use them (Snyder 2002). It is the ability to use and understand information in multiple formats from a wide range of sources when it is presented via computers. The Internet can broaden the 'literacy' experience from the world of print by incorporating video, hyperlinks to archival information, sound clips, discussion areas, supporting databases and related software. Talk of technological or digital 'literacy' seems to arise from the fact that the technologies integral to conventional 'literacy' practices have become invisible, but when new technologies come along, they stand out in relief from conventional practice and notions of applying them strike users as introducing a technological dimension (Lankshear and Knobel 1997).

Acquiring digital 'literacy', or information 'literacy', for Internet use involves becoming proficient with a set of important skills. The most essential of these is the ability to make informed judgements about the information that is found online, for unlike conventional media much of the Internet is unfiltered by editors. This capacity for critical thinking – critical digital 'literacy' – governs the judicious use of what is found online. Developing the habit of critical thinking might be considered to be the most significant skill of all: if it is achieved, other skills fall into place; if it is ignored, the Internet remains a seductive, perhaps deceptive, space. Despite the speed of change in the digital world, core 'literacies', at least for the moment, include: Internet searching, hypertextual navigation, content evaluation and knowledge assembly (Gilster 1997).

Narrative

'Narrative' has been described as 'a primary act of mind transferred to art from life' (Hardy 1977: 12). The most effective techniques for achieving a strong storyline in the print medium are linearity, plot, characterization, textual coherence, resolution and closure. In the context of new media, these qualities are diminished in varying degrees by exploiting the electronic medium's capacity to create open-ended stories with multiple narrative strands, a form often referred to as interactive 'narrative' (Snyder 1996). 'Narrative' created with new media represents a significant cultural form, the principal purpose of which, like its print counterpart, is to make meaning of the world.

If creating a 'narrative' work in new media can be understood as 'the construction of an interface to a database' (Manovich 2001: 226), then the user of the narrative is traversing a database, following links between its records as established by the database's creator. An interactive 'narrative', then, can be understood 'as the sum of multiple trajectories through a database' (p. 227). To qualify as a 'narrative', however, a cultural object has to satisfy a number of criteria: it should contain both an actor and a narrator; it should contain three distinct levels consisting of the text, the story and the fabula; and its content should be a series of connected events caused or experienced by actors (Bal 1985). Thus not all cultural objects are 'narratives'. Just creating trajectories is not enough – the creator also has to control the semantics of the elements and the logic of their connections so that the resulting object will meet the criteria of 'narrative' as outlined above. It also cannot be assumed that by creating their own paths, users construct their own unique 'narratives'.

Regardless of whether new media objects present themselves as linear 'narratives', interactive 'narratives', databases or something else, underneath, on the level of material organization, they are all databases (Manovich 2001). In new media, the database supports a variety of cultural forms that range from direct translation, that is, the database remains a database, to a form that is closer to a 'narrative'. Importantly, databases occupy a significant if not the largest territory of the new media landscape.

New media

The categories commonly discussed under the label 'new media' include: the Internet, websites, computer multimedia, computer games, CD-ROMs and DVD, and virtual reality. But the explanation might also include: a television programme shot on digital video and edited on computer workstations; feature films that use 3-D animation and digital compositing; as well as images and text-image compositions – photographs, illustrations, layouts, adverts – created on computers and then printed on paper. Popular understanding of 'new media' identifies it with the use of a computer for distribution and exhibition rather than production so that texts distributed on a computer (websites and electronic books) are considered to be 'new media', whereas texts distributed on paper are not. Similarly, photographs that are put on a CD-ROM and require a computer to be viewed are considered 'new media'; the same photographs printed in a book are not (Manovich 2001).

This explanation, however, is too limiting. There's no reason to privilege the computer as a machine for exhibition and distribution of media over the computer as a tool for media production or as a media storage device. All have the same potential to change existing cultural practices and all have the same potential to leave culture as it is (Manovich 2001).

In education, and in the social sciences more broadly, the terms 'information and communication technologies' or simply 'new technologies' are more commonly used than 'new media'. 'New media' seems particularly useful as it accommodates a greater range of technologies. If indeed we are in the middle of 'a new media revolution' – the shift of culture to computer mediated forms of production, distribution and communication – then an all-encompassing term is appropriate.

Pedagogy

'Pedagogy' is a key 'concept-framing word' which indicates how teaching is to be grasped as a complex activity, in terms of 'an extensive understanding of educational theory interrelated, in practice, with a wide range of classroom management skills' (Levine 1992: 197). Pedagogy brings together theory and practice, and art and science, conventionally and commonly understood as separate and distinct.

More specifically, Green (1998: 179) suggests that 'pedagogy' refers to the structured relationship between teaching and learning, that is, 'pedagogy' refers to teaching *and* learning, as dynamically interrelated. Further, explains Green, 'pedagogy' is best conceived as 'teaching *for* learning', with teaching understood not as the *cause* of learning but rather as its *context*. This view of teaching as contextual rather than causative with regard to learning leads to a semiotic view of pedagogy and curriculum, rather than one that is mechanistic in nature.

Thus the concept of 'pedagogy' draws attention to the process not only through which knowledge is transmitted or reproduced but also to how it is produced. It poses the question: under what conditions and through what means do we come to know? As Lusted argues: 'How one teaches is therefore of central interest but through the prism of pedagogy, it becomes inseparable from what is being taught and, crucially, how one learns' (1986: 3). What 'pedagogy' addresses is the 'transformation of consciousness' that takes place in the interaction of three agencies – the teacher, the learner and the knowledge they produce together (Lusted 1986: 3).

Such an understanding of 'pedagogy' denies notions of the teacher as neutral transmitter of knowledge, the learner as empty vessel and knowledge as immutable material to impart. Instead it foregrounds exchange, recognizes the productivity of the relationships and renders the participants as active, changing and changeable: in essence, it's transactional (Lusted 1986). Significantly, it is probably a pointless exercise to try to describe a general 'pedagogy'. As 'pedagogy' is always tied to an historical moment, 'it is necessary to clarify the nature of particular pedagogies in particular instances of theory and teaching' (Lusted 1986: 10).

'Pedagogy' implies that it is teachers who take responsibility for what and how students learn. It is teachers who take responsibility for creating the conditions in which understanding is possible; it is the students who take advantage of opportunities for coming to know (Laurillard 1993). Since the advent of new media, a vision of learning with growing currency is of young people pursuing their own objectives towards knowledge, inspired but not necessarily directed by their teachers. When students take responsibility for their own learning, they can use the classroom as offering a set of resources which are largely under their control.

What should pedagogy in the age of the Internet aim to achieve? To deepen and refine students' capacity for significant response to cultural change, so that the changes can be constantly criticized and their implications understood. To raise the level of literacy in its full sense to ensure that 'the technical changes which have made our culture more dependent on literate forms are matched by a proportionate increase in training in literacy in its full sense' (Williams [1958] 1983: 310). Although writing before the advent of the web, Williams' admonition continues to resonate. Despite the widely held belief that teachers will become less important as students become more independent, engaging in self-directed learning, teachers are needed more than ever because critical digital 'literacy' practices are cognitively and socially demanding.

Technology

It is still common for teachers to think of 'technology' in terms of tools, implements and applications. Although this is not wrong, it is limiting; it impedes understanding of 'technology's' social and cultural dimensions. Like literacy, 'technology' is widely recognized as social practice. It represents not just the need to acquire certain skills: 'technology' is 'an expression of the ideologies, the cultural norms, and the value systems of a society' (Bruce 1999: 225). This means that talk about 'technology' and its effects is inadequate if it remains in the realm of the technical.

It's easy to produce a list of the technical things teachers perhaps should know: how to operate a multimedia system; how to use certain software; how to use tools such as word processing, databases and spreadsheets; and how to explore, evaluate and use a range of computer applications. Just as important, however, are the underlying pedagogical values 'which might inform decisions about whether this option is appropriate for particular students in a given context, how it should be used, and how one might judge its success' (Bruce 1999: 226). A set of questions needs to be asked: On what basis should teachers judge software? What kind of instruction is required to support it? What do teachers want the tools to help produce? A list of the technical requirements fails to connect with the fundamental issues of teaching and learning. Finding answers to these questions is a central part of everyday teaching: thinking primarily about learning is paramount, but thinking critically about the technologies that support it is also important (Lankshear and Snyder 2000).

Endnote

Philip Roth opens *I Married a Communist* (1998: 1–2) with a description of Murray Ringold, highschool English teacher. He is remembered by Nathan Zuckerman, Roth's alter-ego:

He was in those days, a crusty, brash, baldheaded guy . . . rangy and athletic, who hovered over our heads in a perpetual state of awareness. He was altogether natural in his manner and posture while in his speech verbally copious and intellectually almost menacing. His passion was to explain, to clarify, to make us understand, with the result that every last subject we talked about he broke down into its principal elements no less meticulously than he diagrammed sentences on the blackboard. His special talent was for dramatising inquiry, for casting a strong narrative spell even when he was being strictly analytic and scrutinizing aloud, in his clear-cut way, what we read and wrote.

Along with the brawn and the conspicuous braininess, Mr Ringold brought with him into the classroom a charge of visceral spontaneity that was a revelation to tamed, respectablized kids who were yet to comprehend that obeying a teacher's rules of decorum had nothing to do with mental development. There was more importance than perhaps even he imagined in his winning predilection for heaving a blackboard eraser in your direction when the answer you gave didn't hit the mark. Or maybe there wasn't. Maybe Mr Ringold knew very well that what boys like me needed to learn was not only how to express themselves with precision and acquire a more discerning response to words, but how to be rambunctious without being stupid, how not to be too well concealed or too well behaved, how to begin to release the masculine intensities from the institutional rectitude that intimidated the bright kids the most.

Zuckerman runs into Ringold in July 1997 for the first time since graduating from high school in 1950 (p. 2):

In every discernible way still the teacher whose task is realistically, without self-parody or inflating dramatics, to personify for his students the maverick dictum 'I don't give a good goddam,' to teach them that you don't have to be Al Capone to transgress – you just have to *think*. 'In human society,' Mr Ringold taught us, 'thinking's the greatest transgression of all.' 'Cri-ti-cal think-ing,' Mr Ringold said, using his knuckles to rap out each of the syllables on his desktop, '– there is the ultimate subversion.'

For Zuckerman,

hearing this early on from a manly guy like him – seeing it *demonstrated* by him – provided the most valuable clue to growing up that I had clutched at, albeit half comprehendingly, as a provincial, protected, high-minded high school kid yearning to be rational and of consequence and free.

Although Ringold, the 'pedagogue', immortalized in Roth's masterpiece, worked in a post-Second World War classroom in which the most complex literacy technology was a blackboard, his approach to teaching and learning, his keen understanding of the key to effective knowledge production, embodies the critical pedagogy promulgated by theorists such as Freire, McClaren and Giroux. Improving the material and cultural conditions of the world – subverting what is less than desirable – can only be facilitated if students are given opportunities to develop their capacity for 'critical thinking'. If students themselves want 'to be rational and of consequence and free', and if their teachers want something similar for them, then the capacity for 'critical thinking' is fundamental.

In the final analysis, attention needs to be given in classrooms to what Roth calls 'critical thinking', or what some literacy educators call 'critical digital literacy'. It represents the most significant goal of literacy education in the age of the Internet, and it cannot be reached just by giving students more access to computers. If, however, teachers and their students begin to develop shared understandings of the keywords intrinsic to the promotion of effective literacy teaching and learning, predicated on the critical use of new media, then the process required to achieve this important goal has already begun.

PART 2
The Detail of Classroom Discourse

Careful examination of the texture of classroom language and learning reveals the complexities involved. The two articles in this section allow both a wide-angle view as well as a very close focus on classroom interactions, particularly on the role of talk. Observations of classroom discourse have shown the different ways in which spoken language contributes to the construction of learning. Cognitive psychology has explained the dynamic relationship between thought and language and ethnographic studies have shown the importance of culturally developed ways of communicating knowledge and meaning. There seems little doubt that talk in all its forms is fundamental in helping the young shape and transform their experience into understanding. However, there are important differences between the ways in which adults and children exchange ideas within school settings, and in homes and communities.

Much of the discourse surrounding classroom talk uses the term 'dialogue' to indicate collaborative construction of meaning between children and adults. However, just as there is ambiguity about what 'interaction' means in terms of pedagogy, there are different shades of meaning attached to 'dialogue'. Certainly, it implies some exchange of views between two or more speakers; there is also an assumption that such encounters will move thinking further. In the classroom there is an added ingredient – the relative power of the contributors – and this is accompanied by the sense that the teacher's professional knowledge will guide the dialogue towards a pre-selected end. In taking the wide view and presenting the findings of international research, Robin Alexander identifies some conditions for dialogic teaching. In close-up detail, Henrietta Dombey presents a fine grained portrait of teacher-directed interchanges. Both of these research perspectives reveal the layers and complexities of interaction and dialogue.

In any dialogue there are pauses and silences. It would not be dialogue otherwise. Both Alexander and Dombey draw attention to the spaces in the teachers' interactions with their pupils which create opportunities for thought. In their own way, too, these two chapters can be seen as a dialogue between conclusions drawn from a cumulative analysis of many classrooms across the world and several sessions with one class seen through the magnifying lens of close study. The connections and gaps between the two perspectives allow pause for thought. Where Alexander traces connections and dissonances between language and literacy pedagogy across several countries, Dombey shows how the nature of teacher–pupil exchange alters during the course of a literacy session in relation to the teacher's aims for learning. She offers a careful description of the difference between what appears and what is, between the surface features of classroom interactions and the teacher's deeper learning intention.

The emphasis in these two chapters is not only on the teachers' talk, however. Alexander points out that the children's answers should not be seen as the end of a learning exchange but 'its true centre of gravity'. In Dombey's chapter, the 'active, textured discussion' shown in the transcripts, where children ask questions, give examples, hypothesize, explain and justify their ideas, extends the sense that the children's side of classroom dialogues also deserve to be treated gravely and seriously.

2 Oracy, literacy and pedagogy: international perspectives

Robin Alexander

The central proposition which I want to explore here is this. English primary education has long claimed to give high priority to fostering talk for learning, communication and social development. Yet from an international standpoint the educational place of talk in our primary schools seems ambivalent, and its dynamic and content belie the rhetoric of pedagogic and curricular reform and set the oral culture of English primary classrooms sharply apart from the continental European mainstream. The idea which is advanced here as a corrective to these tendencies is that of 'dialogic teaching'.

The chapter draws mainly, though briefly and very selectively, on data from a comparative study of primary education in England, France, India, Russia and the United States whose first phase culminated in a detailed comparative analysis of classroom talk, though it explored much else besides (Alexander 2000). Talk featured prominently in the study not just because of its ubiquity as a teaching tool and its demonstrable impact on children's learning and understanding, but also because the study's main purpose was to explore the relationship between culture and pedagogy, and the spoken word is at the heart of both.[1]

The place of talk in the curriculum

We need look no further than Calais for a striking first dimension of international difference. On this side of the water we have England's persistently atavistic account of the educational 'basics' as reading, writing and calculation, but emphatically not speaking. On the other, French schools celebrate the primacy of the spoken word. Here, literacy: there, language. In fact, *l'alphabétisation* in France is no less important an objective than literacy in England, but while literacy is defined here as a 'basic skill', *l'alphabétisation* is embedded in a more comprehensive account of language which transcends its etymologically narrow focus and confers not just instrumental skills but also identity. Language teaching in France reflects a confident nexus of linguistic skills, literary knowledge, nationalistic values, civic virtues and high cultural aspirations.

What then is the relationship, within the national curriculum's attainment targets for English, between En1 (speaking and listening), En2 (reading) and En3 (writing)? Has it been properly articulated? Have we indeed moved beyond the view that in English classrooms 'talk is the medium of instruction rather than its object?' (Cameron 2003). How far do we still subscribe to the 'literacy myth' which attributes an impressive array of personal qualities and social and economic advantages to literacy, only a few of which can be empirically demonstrated (Graff 1991); or to the 'grand dichotomy' which portrays writing not only as different from speech but also superior (Goody 1993)? Much of this country's educational discourse suggests that both the literacy myth and the grand dichotomy are alive and well, and that oracy is at best a poor relation. Recent advocacy of 'communication skills' may appear to raise the status of talk: in fact, by restricting its focus to the instrumental and detaching it from the exploration of language, literature and culture, it does the opposite. (Cameron 2003).

In contrast, our data show how in Russian teaching oracy and literacy are viewed by teachers as inseparable and are transacted accordingly: there, talk is both a medium of instruction (the main one, in fact) and, within a comprehensive definition of literacy, its object. In France, policy no less than practice underlines a similar position: *'L'apprentissage de la langue orale et celui de la langue écrite'* proclaims the Ministry of Education in Paris, *'s'articulent étroitement'* (Ministère de l'Education Nationale 1995). Our American data also seemed to signal the importance of talk, but for a different purpose. There, teachers prioritized the social function of talk in developing the pupil's confidence, and its democratization through appropriate attitudes and classroom procedures – 'caring', 'sharing', 'teacher conference', 'peer conference' and 'author's chair' – rather than its content, about which rather less was said.

So the oracy/literacy dichotomy is by no means universal. Here, Ron Carter's suggestion that speech and writing should be viewed as a continuum provides one helpful corrective (Carter 1997). Another is Shirley Brice-Heath's observation that for most adults 'there are more literacy events which call for appropriate knowledge of forms and uses of speech events, than there are occasions for extended reading and writing' (Brice-Heath 1983). Going beyond Carter, she postulates not a single speech-to-writing continuum, but two continua, the oral and the written, which are overlapping rather than discrete. This makes sense when we contrast the colloquial, conversational register of both talk and writing in American and English primary classrooms, and the formal, speaking-as-if-written talk which one so frequently hears in Russia and France.

Teaching, learning and social relations: the framing values

Let us turn now from the place of talk in the curriculum to the use of talk in teaching. Once again, it is to the values that we should attend first. Our international evidence shows how, within the wider context of values and beliefs which inform public schooling, ideas about how people should relate to each other are paramount within the more specific domain of teaching. Teachers in our study chose from, articulated and enacted – or steered an uncertain path between – three versions of human solidarity: individualism, community and collectivism.

- *Individualism* puts self above others and personal rights before collective responsibilities. It emphasizes unconstrained freedom of action and thought.
- *Community* centres on human interdependence, caring for others, sharing and collaborating.
- *Collectivism* also emphasizes human interdependence, but only in so far as it serves the larger needs of society, or the state (the two are not identical), as a whole.

Within the observed classrooms, a commitment to individualism was manifested in intellectual or social differentiation, divergent rather than uniform learning outcomes, and a view of knowledge as personal and unique rather than imposed from above in the form of disciplines. Community was reflected in collaborative learning tasks, often in small groups, in the concern given to developing a climate of caring and sharing rather than competing, and indeed in an emphasis on the affective rather than the cognitive. Collectivism was reflected in common knowledge, common ideals, a single curriculum for all, an emphasis on national culture rather than pluralism and multiculture, and on learning together rather than in isolation or in small groups.

These values were pervasive at national, school and classroom levels. In the latter context it seems not at all accidental that so much discussion of teaching methods should have centred on the relative merits of whole class teaching, group and individual work. In France this debate reaches back to arguments at the start of the nineteenth century about the relative merits of *l'enseignement simultané, l'enseignement mutuel* and *l'enseignement individuel* (Reboul-Sherrer 1989). As a post-revolutionary instrument for fostering civic commitment and national identity as well as the efficient teaching of literacy, *l'enseignement simultané* won. Only recently, in conjunction with the decentralizing movement of the 1980s and the rising tide of individualism, has the hegemony of whole class teaching in France begun to be questioned.

Individualism, community and collectivism – or child, group and class – are the organizational nodes of pedagogy not just for reasons of practical exigency but because they are the social and indeed political nodes of human relations. This proposition underlines the gulf between two currently competing standpoints in English educational discourse: pedagogy as a manifestation of the wider culture versus pedagogy as a value-neutral sequence of pragmatic decisions about 'what works'.

Alongside these three primordial values there emerged from our data a second set which related more specifically to the educational context. Where individualism, community and collectivism speak to the human condition generally, the six pedagogical values below reflect views on the purposes of education, the nature of knowledge and the relationship of teacher and learner.

- *Teaching as transmission* sees education primarily as a process of instructing children to absorb, replicate and apply basic information and skills.
- *Teaching as induction* sees education as the means of providing access to, and passing on from one generation to the next, the culture's stock of high status knowledge, for example, in literature, the arts, humanities and the sciences.
- *Teaching as democracy in action* reflects the Deweyan idea that teachers and students jointly create knowledge and understanding rather than relate to one another as authoritative source of knowledge and its passive recipient.
- *Teaching as developmental facilitation* guides the teacher by principles which are psychological (and, more specifically, Piagetian) rather than social or epistemological. The teacher respects and nurtures individual differences, and waits until children are ready to move on rather than pressing them to do so.
- *Teaching as acceleration*, in contrast, implements the Vygotskian principle that education is planned and guided acculturation rather than facilitated 'natural' development, and indeed that the teacher seeks to outpace development rather than follow it (Vygotsky 1978).
- *Teaching as technique*, finally, is relatively neutral in its stance on society, knowledge and the child. Here the important issue is the efficiency of teaching regardless of the context of values, and to that end matters like structure, the economic use of time and space, carefully graduated tasks, regular assessment and clear feedback are more pressing than ideas such as democracy, autonomy, development or the disciplines.

Without wishing to oversimplify, I draw on this pair of value frameworks to offer two observations. First, whereas English primary education traditionally leans towards individualistic and communal values and practices, the collective principle is much more prominent in French and Russian pedagogy (and indeed in that of many countries of continental Europe). Second, English primary teaching is an uneasy and unadmitted amalgam of transmission (the abiding legacy of the elementary system), developmentalism (the progressive reaction against this) and induction (imported from the grammar/public school tradition via the first version of the national curriculum, though now rather weaker). Although Deweyan ideas about democratic education infiltrated the Hadow and Plowden reports and Vygotsky's work is currently adduced to legitimate both 'social constructivist' and 'dialogic' teaching (on which more later), his principle of acceleration makes little headway here because it is seen to conflict not just with developmentalism but also individualism. The same can be said for the principles of structure, gradation, economy, pace and collective learning, which began to influence continental European teaching as long ago as 1657, when Comenius first formulated them in his *Didactica Magna*, but have had relatively little impact on teaching in England.

Talk in individual, group and whole class contexts

Let us consider where values such as these inform classroom talk. First, in our data the collective ambience of Russian and French classrooms was buttressed by the very public nature of teacher–pupil exchanges there, which contrasted with that quintessential and prominent mode of interaction in English classrooms, one to one monitoring, with its private, intimate and often whispered exchanges. Talk being very much a collective and public affair in the Russian and French classrooms, children are expected to talk clearly, loudly and expressively, and they learn very early to do so. They expect to hear and be heard.

Although there is one to one monitoring in these settings too, the dominance of whole class interactions means that the full gamut of teacher–pupil exchanges is in the public domain, whether children and teachers like it or not. In our English classrooms, public exchanges tended to focus on the need to provide answers which would be judged *correct*; while problems and mistakes tended to be dealt with privately and discreetly, in one to one monitoring. Teachers strove to avoid exposing children to the embarrassment of making a public mistake, and in that eventuality their feedback could be decidedly ambiguous ('Ye-es', meaning 'No, but I don't want to discourage you by saying so') rather than genuinely diagnostic. In the Russian classrooms, problems and mistakes were no less open to collective scrutiny than were correct answers. There, sooner rather than later, children learn that the difficulties they encounter are genuinely grist to the pedagogical mill. Teachers will ask children confronted by an apparently insoluble maths problem, say, to bring it to the board so that all can join in the task of working out how it can be tackled. This collectivizing of responsibility for the learning task reduces the fear of giving a wrong answer, and the high premium set on providing only the right answer, which are such prominent themes in British and American classroom research (Edwards and Westgate 1992). But in this very public context Russian teachers must also formulate their questions with care and precision if they are not to expose children to needless insecurity. In Doyle's terms, teacher questions in such a setting may promote the necessary ambiguity for children to engage cognitively with ideas rather than merely parrot set piece responses, but at the same time they must minimize interpersonal risk (Doyle 1983).

The superordinate commitment to 'the class' was reflected in both the proportions of class/group/individual interactions in Russia and France, and the way talk was pitched. In Russia especially, the ideal was collective, public learning. I have contrasted this with the way that although talk in English and American classrooms is individualized, the fact that it takes place in what is in other respects a collective setting makes for ambiguities. In English whole class teaching children talk back to the teacher, sometimes barely audibly; in Russia they talk to the rest of the class. However, in our English and American classrooms the group was also important, and teachers there, especially in the American classrooms, made some use of collaborative tasks, though here again contradictions surface, as Galton and Simon first noted in the 1970s, between children working everywhere *as* groups but rarely *in* groups (Galton *et al.* 1980). And as one of our English teachers warned her class: 'I don't mind if you co-operate, as long as I can't hear you . . .'

Conversation and dialogue

Talk in the American classrooms had a markedly conversational ambience and tone. The teachers themselves defined it thus, usually by reference to 'democratic' pedagogy and the importance of 'sharing', whereas Russian teachers explicitly distinguished conversation from dialogue and highlighted their role in fostering the latter.

Yet was what we recorded in American and English classrooms conversation in the strict sense, that is, a form of discourse in which control is 'locally managed'? (Edwards and Westgate 1992) As in so many aspects of the American and English teaching which we observed, conversational talk was hedged by ambiguity and dissonance, and talk might be conversational in lexis and syntax but not in conduct and control. Both dissonances could hamper the discourse of learning. In contrast, in the French classrooms talk could be conversational in tone, but it was never other than firmly directed by the teacher, and subject-specific referents kept it on its intended epistemic track.

However, the critical question here concerns not so much the *tone* of the discourse as where it leads. I want to suggest a stipulative distinction for the classroom context between 'conversation' and 'dialogue' (most dictionaries treat these words as synonymous). Where conversation is – or purports to be – locally managed, classroom dialogue is teacher-managed. Where the end point of conversation may not be clear at the outset in classroom dialogue, for the teacher at least, it is. Conversation may go nowhere. Equally, it may spectacularly open up the unexpected. Classroom dialogue in contrast steers a safer course. Where conversation may consist of a sequence of unchained two-part exchanges, as participants talk at or past each other (although it *can* be very different), classroom dialogue explicitly seeks to chain exchanges into a meaningful sequence. This, I admit, is an overtly Bakhtinian version of dialogue. Here it is the act of *questioning* which differentiates conversation from dialogue, and the critical issue is what follows from *answers*: 'If an answer does not give rise to a new question from itself, then it falls out of the dialogue' (Bakhtin 1986: 168).

One of the most significant demarcation lines in our international discourse data, then, was between those questions and responses which were chained into meaningful and cognitively demanding sequences, and those which were blocked by the repetitive initiation–response (IR) exchange of rote, by the ambiguities and vagaries of quasi-conversation (as in the United States), and/or by an emphasis on participation at the expense of continuity and cumulation (as in England).

In their exegesis of Bakhtin's concept of dialogue in the context of small group discussion, Barnes and Todd identify six features: a shared acceptance of difference of perspective; a commitment to mutual attention; speculation and the use of hypothetical cases; tentativeness in offering views and the absence of prior roles and authority by right; mutual support; and lack of closure (Barnes and Todd 1995). On this basis, much of the interaction which we recorded in English primary classrooms might be neither conversation nor dialogue. Whether it was conversational in lexis and syntax or more formally structured:

- interactions tended to be brief rather than sustained, and teachers moved from one child to another in rapid succession rather than developed individual lines of thinking and understanding;
- teachers asked questions about content, but children asked questions mainly about points of procedure;
- closed questions predominated;
- children concentrated on identifying 'correct' answers, and teachers glossed over 'wrong' answers rather than using them as stepping stones to understanding;
- there was little speculative talk, or 'thinking aloud';

- the child's answers marked the end of an exchange, and the teacher's feedback formally closed it;
- feedback tended to encourage and praise rather than inform.

In these respects, such talk may lack the formal structures of classic 'recitation' teaching (Dillon 1990), but in its fundamental asymmetry it is closer to recitation than to either conversation or dialogue. Further, contrary to confident claims from official sources about the transforming power of the national literacy and numeracy strategies, independent research suggests that features such as those listed above are remarkably resistant to centralized reform (Hardman *et al.* 2003; Moyles *et al.* 2003; Skidmore 2002). This replicates earlier comparative studies of primary teaching before and after the introduction of the national curriculum and national testing, undertaken by Alexander and Galton (Alexander *et al.* 1996; Galton *et al.* 1999). Habits of classroom talk, and the thinking that goes with them, are deeply embedded, historically and culturally.

Social and cognitive purposes

Cameron warns us not to polarize the 'social' and 'cognitive' purposes of classroom talk (Cameron 2003). Yet in our study teachers themselves emphasized this distinction, and it was clearly manifested in their teaching. The need to build children's social confidence is a major theme in the British primary pedagogical tradition which was dominant between the 1960s and 1990s and for many older teachers it remains one of their bedrock beliefs. At a more banal level this emphasis characterized those many assessment checklists from that period which made 'participation' the main criterion for assessing children's talk. It is this concern which produces that quintessentially English mix of classroom discourse which is warm and inclusive but cognitively undemanding, and which prefers bland and eventually phatic praise to focused feedback, for fear that children might be discouraged by the latter. The tendency was even more marked in some of the American classrooms, where it was reinforced by the ubiquitous posters listing '101 Ways to Praise a Child' ('Neat!', 'Wow!', 'Nice job', 'Beautiful sharing!', 'Way to go!' etc.). It is also worth asking what the constant reiteration of the words 'confident' and 'confidence' in the national curriculum EN1 framework ('pupils talk and listen with confidence') signals about the perceived balance of the social and the cognitive.

The cognitive dimension of talk in English classrooms has been somewhat sharpened by the recent popularization of the work of Vygotsky, Bruner and to a lesser extent Luria, and if there is now a tendency to emphasize the cognitive potential of talk at the expense of the social, then this must be understood as a necessary corrective. But of course this, like the polarizing of oracy and literacy, is a false dichotomy. First, because at a commonsense level there is little point in promoting cognitively rich talk if children are too inhibited or reserved to participate in it. Second, because it misses the very point that Vygotsky was making, which is that learning is fundamentally a *social* process. Having regard to the three underpinning versions of human solidarity we considered earlier, it might be suggested that the Marxian, collectivist context of Vygotsky's work may have been reconfigured in terms of the more palatable, 'lone scientist' tradition of British Piagetianism.[2]

Every lesson in our project was videotaped and transcribed. Some British teachers who have watched samples of the Russian teaching have found it intimidating or even autocratic. True, the Russian (and French) teachers did not use the special teacherly voices, circumlocutions and oblique control devices deployed by many English early years teachers. Yet we found no more evidence of timid or inhibited responses among Russian than English primary pupils. In fact, by making talk and learning strongly collective activities, the Russian teachers effectively reconciled the social and the cognitive.

Communicative competence

Although in the real world communicative competence may be defined by reference to the Gricean maxims of *quantity*, *quality*, *relation* and *manner* (Grice 1975), in classrooms the unequal power relationship of teacher and taught may produce a very different set of rules which for pupils are dominated by listening, bidding for turns, spotting 'correct' answers and other coping strategies which anywhere outside a school would seem pretty bizarre (Edwards 1992).

Since this has much in common with ideas first put forward on the far side of the Atlantic by Philip Jackson nearly 40 years ago (Jackson 1968), one might suppose that this is the way, everywhere, that classrooms inevitably are. It isn't. Our international data show that the Edwards rules of communicative competence (which were based on observation in English secondary classrooms) can be subverted *either* by genuine discussion of the kind advocated by the National Oracy Project (Norman 1992) or by a version of whole class teaching rather different from classic British recitation. Indeed, we have become so used to the British version of whole class teaching that there seems to be a tendency to assume that only through small group discussion can dialogic teaching be promoted.

Again, France and Russia provide useful counterpoints. The English tradition emphasizes the importance of equal distribution of teacher time and attention among all the pupils, and participation by all of them in oral work, in every lesson. So with only one teacher and 25 to 35 pupils in a class it is inevitable that competitive bidding and the gamesmanship of 'guess what teacher is thinking', and above all searching for the 'right' answer, become critical to the pupil's getting by and maintaining face. But in Russia, in a given lesson, only a proportion of children are expected to take part, and some of those will be pupils who have made mistakes and talk about them to the class. This is because instead of eliciting a succession of brief 'now or never' answers from many children the teacher will construct a sequence of much more sustained exchanges with a smaller number. And because the ambience is collective rather than individualized or collaborative, the child talks to the class as much as to the teacher, and is in a sense a representative of the class as much as an individual. This reduces the element of communicative gamesmanship; but it also – crucially – may be a much more powerful learning tool.

Towards dialogic teaching

The differences provoke an important question. From what pattern of exchange do pupils learn more: questioning involving many children, brief answers and little follow up, or questions directed at fewer children which invite longer and more considered answers, which in turn lead to further questions? In the one scenario, children bid for turns if they know the answer, or try to avoid being nominated if they do not; in the other, they listen to each other. In the English approach, communicative competence is defined by whether, having been nominated for or bid for what is probably one's sole oral contribution to the lesson, one provides the answer which the teacher judges to be correct, acceptable or relevant. In the Russian approach (which is also replicated across much of central and Eastern Europe) communicative competence is judged by how one performs over the whole transaction rather than whether one gives the single 'right' answer; and on the *manner* of the response – clarity, articulateness, attention to the question – as well as its substance.

The matter of communicative gamesmanship apart, I suggest that if we are interested in enhancing the learning potential of classroom talk we would do well to attend to the psychological dimension of the differences I have briefly sketched out. For extended, low-stakes exchanges – in which children are able to speculate and develop their thinking, in which teacher questions have a probing or indeed a scaffolding rather than an inquisitorial function, and which pivot on the constructive handling of answers as much as the careful conceptualizing of questions – come rather closer to meeting the conditions for cognitively challenging talk.

Like Barnes and Todd (1995) I find myself drawn to Bakhtin's version of dialogue and hence to *dialogic teaching*. There are other resonances. Jerome Bruner has demonstrated 'the use of language in the growth of concepts and the developing structure of the mind', and the importance not just of 'interaction' (which – as in 'interactive teaching' – can mean anything) but of the kind of interaction which bridges old and new understandings, facilitates the 'handover' of the latter, and is 'premised on a mutual sharing of assumptions and beliefs about how the world is, how mind works, what we are up to, and how communication should proceed' (Bruner 1987). Gordon Wells uses 'dialogic inquiry' to encapsulate his updating of Vygotsky's ideas for today's classrooms (Wells 1999). His idea of teaching as the promoting of a 'community of inquiry' is close to Neil Mercer's use of 'interthinking' to convey the idea that talk in learning is not one way linear 'communication' but a reciprocal process in which ideas are bounced back and forth and on that basis take children's thinking forward (Mercer 2000). Similarly, Barnes and Todd stress the importance of fostering both the spirit and the procedures of a 'joint enquiry' through which learners can construct shared meanings from the different frames of reference which each of them brings to the common learning task (Barnes and Todd 1995).

Bakhtin's axiom about answers and questions, quoted earlier, should give us pause for thought, for if we accept that dialogue is a necessary tool of learning then we may need to accept also that the child's answer is not the end of a learning exchange (as in many classrooms it tends to be) but its true centre of gravity. Important though questions are – and they certainly need to be formulated with care – we could profitably pay at least equal attention to children's *answers* and to what we do or don't do with them. Put more bluntly, if we want children to talk to learn – as well as learn to talk – then what they say actually matters more than what teachers say. So it is the qualities of *continuity* and *cumulation* which transform classroom talk from the familiar closed question/answer/feedback routine of the classic IRF exchange (Sinclair and Coulthard 1975) into purposeful and productive dialogue where questions, answers, feedback – and feedforward – progressively build into coherent and expanding chains of enquiry and understanding.

From all this we can crystallize four criteria or conditions of dialogic teaching. It should be:

- *collective*: pupils and teachers address learning tasks together, whether as a group or as a class, rather than in isolation;
- *reciprocal*: pupils and teachers listen to each other, share ideas and consider alternative viewpoints;
- *cumulative*: pupils and teachers build on their own and each other's ideas and chain them into coherent lines of thinking and enquiry;
- *supportive*: children articulate their ideas freely, without fear of embarrassment over 'wrong' answers; and they help each other to reach common understandings.

Extending the teaching repertoire

Across our five countries we observed teachers drawing on a basic repertoire of three kinds of teaching talk:

- *Rote* (teacher–class): the drilling of facts, ideas and routines through constant repetition.
- *Recitation* (teacher–class or teacher–group): the accumulation of knowledge and understanding through questions designed to test or stimulate recall of what has been previously encountered, or to cue pupils to work out the answer from clues provided in the question.
- *Instruction/exposition* (teacher–class, teacher–group or teacher–individual): telling the pupil what to do, and/or imparting information, and/or explaining facts, principles or procedures.

These three approaches provide the familiar bedrock of teaching by direct instruction. Less universally, we observed some teachers, but by no means all, also using:

- *Discussion* (teacher–class, teacher–group, pupil–pupil): the exchange of ideas with a view to sharing information and solving problems.
- *Scaffolded dialogue* (teacher–class, teacher–group, teacher–pupil, or pupil–pupil): achieving common understanding through structured and cumulative questioning and discussion which guide and prompt, reduce choices, minimize risk and error, and expedite 'handover' of concepts and principles.

Only discussion and scaffolded dialogue are likely to meet the four conditions of dialogic teaching set out above, and while I am not arguing that rote should disappear (for even this most elemental of techniques has its place) I would certainly suggest that teaching which is limited to the first three modes – drilling, questioning for recall and telling – is unlikely to offer the kinds of cognitive challenge which children need or which a broad and balanced curriculum requires.

Learning from comparing: a cautionary note

Comparative analysis shows how classroom talk reflects assumptions about the nature of teaching and learning and the place of language, and especially spoken language, in the curriculum as a whole; and how it is shaped by more general ideas about how the individual should stand in relation to others and to society.

Talk being a cultural artefact, it is not surprising that the character of classroom talk is very different in countries which are as diverse culturally and politically as are England, France, India, Russia and the United States.

So, notwithstanding the current vogue for pedagogical transplants, in the realm of classroom talk we should be especially cautious about importing the practices we admire. Thus, we should not seek to emulate the strongly dialogic qualities of some of the talk we hear in continental European classrooms without first acknowledging the extent to which this is underpinned by a collective ethic, unambiguous teacher authority, epistemic structure, learning viewed as accelerated development, and an account of pupils' progress which focuses more on effort than on fatalistic assumptions about innate ability.

Such a framework for oracy cannot readily be accommodated to an educational tradition which celebrates individualism, differentiated learning tasks and divergent learning outcomes; which until recently has resisted structure, boundary and predictability in the curriculum, in the use of time and space, and in language itself, as somehow incompatible with children's unique potentialities and ways of making sense; which yet remains influenced by the determinist legacy of the IQ, intelligence testing and 'innate' ability; and which has seen the function of talk more in relation to the development of confidence than cognition and the teacher as a facilitator or co-learner rather than an authority.

If we are impressed by such practices as we see them elsewhere, we should try first to discover the values and pedagogical principles which shape them. Having done so we can then examine how far these can accommodate to our own, and how far our own ideas are capable of being changed. Out of this accommodation will come not a culturally-disembedded aping of others' practices but something which by being psychologically tenable, philosophically coherent and culturally compatible may stand a chance of making a long-term difference. In this light, the candidacy of dialogic teaching seems definitely worth considering.

Notes

1   The study's analysis of classroom talk has two parts: a quantitative account (*Culture and Pedagogy*, pp. 391–426) of the management of interaction, placed in the contexts of time, pace and lesson structure, which deploys the full dataset; and a more fine grained sociolinguistic analysis of transcribed discourse extracts from 17 sample lessons (*Culture and Pedagogy*, pp. 427–528). It will be understood that this paper is not an account of the research so much as a reflection on issues arising from one aspect of it.

2   The 'lone scientist' phrase is Jerome Bruner's (1987).

3   Moving forward together

Henrietta Dombey

Some years ago, over the period of a school year, I spent many mornings in the nursery class of a primary school in a bleak housing estate on England's south coast, trying to find out about the children's experience of hearing stories read aloud (Dombey 1988). I knew that the teacher in this class had many years of successfully engaging children from non-bookish homes in books and reading. I gradually came to understand that what I was witnessing was not a one way transmission from book via teacher to child, but a complex interaction between these three participants, in which the children were taking significant roles. Since then my interest in interaction in literacy learning has grown, and with it the conviction that, if we are to make significant improvements in children's literacy learning, we need to learn more about the kinds of transaction that operate in successful classrooms.

Recent studies have told us much about common classroom practice in literacy teaching in England (Galton *et al.* 1999; Mroz *et al.* 2000; English *et al.* 2002; Skidmore *et al.* 2003). The picture they paint is depressingly consistent. In both whole class and small group situations, the kind of interaction that predominates is very much a one way affair. Children play little part in initiating topics or sustaining them, and teachers rarely expand on children's responses to their questions. There is need for change. Intervention studies have much to tell us (for example, Mercer 2000; Warwick and Maloch 2003), but there is much also, I would claim, to be learned from studying what actually goes on in the classrooms of highly effective teachers of literacy.

Donna, a highly effective teacher of literacy

Donna has been nominated by the advisory service of her local education authority and by her headteacher, as a particularly effective teacher of literacy. The children in her Year 3 class did well in their English standard achievement tests (SATs) last year, the tests that all children in English primary schools take at about the age of 7. They are eager and relatively experienced readers and writers. This is their second year with Donna, so they are all familiar with each other. Their school is a small primary in an unremarkable area of an English south coast town. There are a few children for whom English is an additional language and a small proportion on free school dinners. The homes of most of the children are not particularly bookish. It is at school that they are learning to talk about texts – those they write and those they read.

Donna's class is one of five that I have been studying in an attempt to find out something about the nature of interaction in the classrooms of highly effective teachers of literacy. I would like to examine three extracts from a transcript of a videotape of a literacy hour lesson taught by Donna in February, well into the school year. I should say at this point that Donna and the children are used to being videotaped. This is the third time since September that I have recorded one of their literacy hours. My intention is to examine what is happening between the teacher, the children and the text in these three extracts and to relate it to what we know of classroom interaction in general and to current ideas on literacy teaching. The extracts have been selected to demonstrate something of the variety of interactive styles operating during whole class sessions in this classroom.

What is not apparent from the transcript, but is immediately evident from the video is the keen involvement of the children and the absence of fidgeting, time wasting or other forms of 'off-task' behaviour. The children all appear to be interested in what is going on, from the start of the lesson.

A lesson on traditional tales

They have just started a unit of work on traditional tales. A big book version of *Cinderella* stands on an easel by Donna's chair, and a child stands by her, holding the Cinderella doll she has brought in. Here then is the first extract, taken from the beginning of the lesson. It has not been possible to identify all the children by name.

Extract 1		
1	Teacher	You've all got good ideas to offer.
2	Teacher	And if we put our heads together and our ideas together, then what we come up with is often pretty fantastic isn't it and you do all your ideas, every single one of you.
3	Teacher	We often say two heads are better than one, well thirty-one heads is a lot better than one,
4	Teacher	Shall I just pop it in the (unclear)

5	Teacher	Right, okay, we're going to tell (unclear)
6	Teacher	And who can tell me what we've been learning about in our literacy lessons, what kind of, texts have we been reading, what kind of texts have we been reading?
7	Teacher	Now remember there are two particular kinds of texts we learn about in literacy, two particular kinds, and then this is a special kind of that, isn't it,
8	Teacher	We call that, new word for you,
9	Teacher	You will forget this word won't you,
10	Teacher	It's a new word, it's quite, sounds really horrible and hard and it actually sounds like a French word, that's because it is,
11	Teacher	Shall I tell you what it is?
12	Teacher	Okay, if you can tell me which of the two kinds this is, then I'll tell you that new word in a minute, which of the two kinds of texts is this, there's two kinds of texts, something and something, which one is this?
13	Teacher	Jess?
14	Jess	Is it fiction, and it's fairy tales sort of like it's not made up.
15	Teacher	It is, it, it, is it made up or is it not made up?
16	Jess	It's not made up.
17	Child	Some are made up as well.
18	Child	Stories are made up as well.
19	Teacher	You, so you think, who thinks it is made up, made up story, that we really get pumpkins turning into coaches and probably, probably we don't really get those things and it probably is made up?
20	Teacher	Who thinks it really actually happened, it's fact fact that that pumpkin turned into a carriage, coach,
21	Teacher	OK, so fiction means, made up, doesn't it, invented, somebody's invented that.
22	Teacher	Shall I tell you the new word,
23	Teacher	OK, we're learning about, all about traditional tales aren't we, and traditional tales are fiction, they're a kind of fiction, what we say, a kind of fiction is a word called genre,
24	Teacher	Can you say that?
25	All	Genre.
26	Teacher	Ooh, that's a funny word isn't it,
27	Teacher	You will forget that word, won't you,
28	Teacher	What was the word?
29	All	Genre.
30	Teacher	Genre, genre, French,
31	Teacher	I would, I would imagine Peter can pronounce it beautifully for us, can you?
32	Peter	Genre.

33	Teacher	Genre, said better than me,
34	Teacher	So genre just means kind, kind of fiction, genre, so you could get traditional tales, you could get myths and legends, all different kinds of fiction, adventure, you could get thriller, horror stories, okay.
35	Teacher	So you will, you have forgotten that new word, kinds of fiction haven't you,
36	Teacher	What was it?
37	All	Genre.
38	Teacher	Genre,

Relationships

Quite obviously Donna is doing very nearly all the talking in a way that is depressingly consistent with the findings of classroom studies over the last 30 years (Flanders 1970). Only one child, Jess, at 14, asks a question and this is a tentatively expressed answer to a question from Donna, the teacher, rather than a request for information.

Donna asks a number of 'display-questions' – five in all – questions to which she already knows the answer. She starts with 'What kinds of text have we been reading?' at 6 and ends this extract with 'What was it?' at 36. She clearly wants the answers 'fact and fiction' for one and 'genre' for the other. In asking these and the other display questions she seems to be positioning herself as interrogator (although kindly) and the children as her subjects. But is that all?

Before she asks any questions, Donna praises the 'good ideas' the children all have to offer, implying that learning is a matter of sharing such ideas. And these display questions could be seen as concerned at least as much with teaching as they are with interrogation. As Mercer points out, display questions often have an important function in steering children's thinking (Mercer 1995). Here the question at 6 'What kinds of text have we been reading?' appears to be intended to call to mind previous work through a term that will permit them to 'move up the ladder of abstraction' as Moffett (1968) puts it. However, there is no response from the children, perhaps because they are unsure whether the term requested is 'fiction' or 'fairy tales'. As Donna presses on, Jess hedges her bets at 14, further covering herself by presenting her answer in the form of a question, and adding, puzzlingly, 'sort of like it's not made up'. Perhaps she means that traditional tales are not the product of identifiable authors. No one individual makes one up. However, Donna still wants to know if fiction is made up or not. Jess sticks to her view, but two other children jump in with answers more along the expected lines. So then Donna asks what the other children think, steering the question to elicit the appropriate response which most of them duly give her. The remaining display questions are concerned with the word 'genre', which is reintroduced, explained and rehearsed.

The other eight questions are rather different. Three tag questions follow statements as in 'You will forget that word, won't you?' at 9. These serve to reinforce the preceding statement. But in the case of two of these tag questions, the previous statement asserts that the children will forget or have forgotten the key term just introduced. Donna seems to be appealing to the children's contrariness. By saying they will forget she is implicitly challenging the children to prove her wrong. This implies a more playful and less straightforward relationship between teacher and class than that of interrogator and test subject.

Two further questions such as 'Shall I tell you what it is?' at 11 appear to function as discursive gambits to whet the children's curiosity about information she is about to deliver. Two more can be classed as pseudo-questions, in that they operate as softened instructions, so that 'Can you say that?' clearly invites the children to pronounce the word 'genre' rather than to reply to the affirmative. The other, at 20, appears to be an open request for information: Donna is asking who thinks 'we really get pumpkins turning into coaches' and who thinks that stories like this are made up. This could be construed as another kind of pseudo-question: in posing her enquiry in this way, Donna is implicitly directing the children to agree with her that such stories are made up.

So these questions show that the relationship between teacher and children is not simply a narrow interrogatory one. Donna, the teacher, holds the power. She does nearly all the talking and asks nearly all the questions. But the relationship she has established with the children is not confined to the interrogatory: it involves challenge and playfulness and steering them towards certain interpretations.

Getting ready to move forward

Although the children have made only a limited contribution, this opening section of the lesson has reminded them of earlier thinking, introduced them to a conceptually challenging term and challenged them to examine the relation between 'reality' and text, even if the process of constructing the genre of traditional tales has not been as fully explored as perhaps Jess would like. The children are being helped to re-assemble at the arrival point of yesterday's lesson, which Donna sees as the starting point of today's part of the journey.

First they need to look at the map, to know where they are going. So Donna points the children to today's learning objectives, taken from the text level objectives for Year 3 Term 2 in the National Literacy Strategy (NLS). They all read out the NLS formulation 'to identify and discuss main characters and justify our views'. The children join Donna in providing explanations of these terms, after which they are given a minute to identify, in pairs, the kinds of main characters who crop up in traditional tales. This they do eagerly, after which Donna reminds them of yesterday's topic: 'theme' – another difficult abstraction which she tries to make comprehensible by likening it to 'the messages from that story . . . underneath it all the time'. Now we move into the second extract from the transcript.

		Extract 2
73	Teacher	And yesterday, we made a list on the board which unfortunately we haven't got today, we've rubbed it out, but we had a whole list, if you can visualize it on the board yesterday, we had a whole list, we had traditional tale there, and then we had the kinds of theme.
74	Teacher	Can you remember?
75	Children	Yeah.
76	Teacher	Can anybody remember one of the special themes that we put down on the board, there were two that we particularly identified weren't there, and if I can just put that on the board, let me see, two themes weren't there,
77	Teacher	What were the main two themes, Craig?
78	Craig	Good over evil, and
78	Teacher	Good, you had good, versus evil, we said often that the good overcame in the end didn't it, in a traditional tale.
79	Teacher	What was the other one,
80	Teacher	Daniel.
81	Daniel	Trials and forfeits.
82	Teacher	Fantastic, you can have a smiley later,
83	Teacher	Fantastic because they were tricky words and we had to think of, get our heads round what exactly what they meant didn't we, what they,
84	Teacher	We sort of decided it was like a challenge didn't we.
85	Isobel	Sometimes we said it was a challenge.
86	Teacher	Yeah.
87	Rachel	And sometimes it, it was a challenge, but sometimes it, it doesn't always start off as a challenge, it starts off normal and then it turns into a challenge.
88	Teacher	Right, right

89	Teacher	And we said things like Rumpelstiltskin, can you remember, that he gave the girl a challenge, she had to,
90	Rachel	Figure out his name.
91	Teacher	That's,
92	Rachel	Rumpelstiltskin said if you figure out my name then I'll let, then I'll do everything else for you.
93	Teacher	Yes, that's right,
94	Teacher	And we said the *Princess and the Pea*,
95	Teacher	What was the challenge in the *Princess and the Pea*, Craig?
96	Craig	If she could feel the pea through in twenty mattresses she's a true princess.
97	Teacher	Exactly, and did she meet that challenge?
98	Children	{Yeah.
99	Teacher	{Yes, OK.
100	Children	*******
101	Daniel	I don't understand but that, that is a fairy tale because that's a, it's erm twenty mattresses,
102	Daniel	I can't I can't understand how that would happen.
103	Teacher	{You can't
104	Rachel	{No she has, such skin, she had such skin, she had such delicate skin.
105	Craig	Don't try it at home.
106	Rachel	You see, a princess has such delicate skin, she could feel it right through twenty mattresses.
107	Teacher	Yeah, but Daniel doesn't understand how that could happen.
108	Child	{I don't
109	Rachel	{It could happen
110	Child	{If you try it at home.
111	Teacher	You seem to have a lot of ideas.
112	Rachel	It's only a tale, {right.
113	Child	{It could happen.
114	Teacher	OK Rachel, go on then, very quickly.
115	Rachel	It's only a fairy tale, it, it, sometimes it could, it might not be, it might not be tr, it might not happen in real life, but it's just a, it's just a story, it can not be true.
116	Child	They just made it up.
117	Child	It's your imagination.
118	Teacher	Anything.
119	Child	Anything can happen.
120	Teacher	That's true. You're quite right Rachel,
121	Teacher	So we've got good versus evil and we've got trials, and, forfeits.

Here we see immediately that participation is rather more evenly distributed than in the first extract. Children speak more often and they tend to speak at greater length. About half the utterances are theirs, with only two of these being single word utterances and several taking the form of multiclause utterances. There are some similarities with the earlier extract in that Donna asks four 'display questions'. As before these appear to focus the children, cueing them in to what she wants them to think about. But again more is going on than would appear at first sight.

As she recaps on yesterday's lesson, getting them all to today's starting point, Donna appears to be concerned to elicit from the children merely the brief phrases listed in the NLS framework. 'Good over evil' and 'Trials and forfeits', much as she elicited the term 'genre' at the start of the lesson. Craig volunteers the former and Daniel the latter and both are rewarded with a positive evaluation. Thus far these seem to be classic IRF (Sinclair and Coulthard 1975) exchanges with the Initiation by the teacher followed by a Response from the children, evoking in turn Feedback from the teacher. This takes an evaluative form, as is so frequently found in classrooms. And the knowledge being elicited appears to be formulaic. But Donna is doing more than this. In her feedback moves she extends the children's responses, recalling relevant explanatory points from yesterday's discussion, helping them to relive the thinking that brought them to this point.

And here the exchanges between teacher and children change quite markedly, as the children no longer wait for Donna to prompt them, but instead recall yesterday's discussion by themselves and contribute without waiting to be asked. At 85, uninvited, Isobel modifies what Donna has just said and is rewarded briefly with a 'Yeah'. Then at 87, again uninvited, Rachel extends what Isobel has said. Donna's response rewards her for this. Unlike the adjacent child utterances in the earlier extract, these are not two consecutive responses to a question asked by the teacher, but here the second child's utterance is an elaboration on what the first child has just said. They are even syntactically connected: Rachel's four clause utterance at 87 opens with the conjunction 'and', connecting it explicitly to what Isobel has just said. This has something of the texture of discussion. These children have moved out of the role of passive responders to their teacher and are taking instead the role of active initiators and responders to one another.

When Donna neatly takes back the initiative, it is to make a contribution similar in kind to those of Isobel and Rachel, thus tactfully validating the mode and content of their contributions. She cites the tale of *Rumpelstiltskin* and moves towards specifying the challenge at its centre. But in this she is interrupted and pre-empted again by Rachel at 90, who states the challenge succinctly and then, in a second interruption, expands on this. Donna responds positively to these interruptions, and then turns to another tale, to ask another 'display question' about the challenge contained in it.

Donna is in control of the discussion in that she is introducing all the topic changes, but, rather than waiting to be asked, the children are volunteering their own observations on these topics, sometimes interrupting her as they do so. However, when at 101 Daniel expresses his puzzlement about the physical impossibility of the event central to the story – feeling a pea through 20 mattresses – it is the children who respond to him. Donna steers this response initially, but gives way to the children only re-asserting herself to conclude the discussion by approving Rachel's view. The episode closes with Donna taking the classic role of teacher as evaluator, as she sums up the discussion in terms of the topic she introduced initially: the themes found in traditional tales.

Changes in direction

Now she draws two headings: 'Good' and 'Evil' on the board, with a vertical line between them, inviting the children to nominate 'kinds of main character' and agree on which heading to place them under.

One child observes, unasked, in a six clause utterance, that princes and princesses are sometimes evil and sometimes good and should therefore be placed under both headings. However, guided by Donna, the children decide to categorize them as good, because most of the time they are.

After deciding on where to place princes, princesses, kings, queens and stepmothers, at the beginning of the third extract, Tom raises 'the two sisters' who Donna classes as the ugly sisters.

Extract 3		
176	Teacher	Any other characters that we find in traditional tales, we've got, prince, princesses, queens, stepmother, erm, Tom?
177	Tom	The two sisters?
178	Teacher	Right, so, ugly, yeah, ugly sisters,
179	Teacher	Ooh, do you know, I didn't ask you where you put them, I'm automatically putting them in there, do you think that's the right place?
180	Child	Yes.
181	John	It's evil because they're evil.
182	Child	Yeah, because at the, at the end, they did something at the erm end.
183	John	They're evil too.
184	Child	Ugly stepsisters.
185	Isobel	They might be ugly but it doesn't mean they're horrible, but they are.

186	Peter	No, you don't know, you don't know if they're good or evil cos they don't say it.
187	Teacher	Ah, so shall we
188	Peter	So you don't know.
189	Teacher	Shall we have a think about that in a minute, cos that's the next thing I want to do.
190	Peter	They're not usually, but they're not, not, there aren't usually ugly sisters in books because it's only really in Cinderella that there are ugly sisters.
191	Child	They're not in like Snow White.
192	Teacher	I'm very pleased that some of you are listening to what Peter's got to say, would you like to say that again?
193	Peter	Well there are not usually Ugly Sisters in traditional tales, they're only really in Cinderella.
194	Teacher	Right, so if we don't say ugly sisters then what can we say?
195	Child	Just stepsisters.
196	Teacher	Stepsisters, what does that mean stepsisters, or stepbrothers?
197	Teacher	What does that mean Emma?
198	Emma	Does it mean that, they're not your real brother {or sister?
199	Jess	{Cos I've got a half brother, two sisters and a brother, cos we've got different dads.
200	Teacher	Right so it means that you've got the same {dad, but, the same, dad, the
201	Child	{The same dad but a different mother.
202	Teacher	But a different mum.
203	Child	Like we've got the same mum.
204	Teacher	Your dad's remarried.
205	Emma	It's mostly like the mum's died or they don't, ***** they separated and the mum just goes with another and dad gets a girlfriend, but erm, it's mostly, it's not like, it's not like your real mum it's mostly just your stepmum.
206	Teacher	So we do, we see stepsisters or stepbrothers in other traditional tales?
207	Children	No.

Again, as in Extract 2 there is a more even distribution of participation than there is in Extract 1. Indeed, although Donna's utterances tend to be longer than the children's (with a mean of 15 words to the children's mean of 8.5), she produces only 7 utterances to their 13. So, the children speak slightly more words (111) in this extract than does the teacher (105). Of course, there are 27 of them to only one of her, but this almost balanced ratio is very different from the 2:1 ratio typically found in classrooms (Flanders 1970). While they continue to discuss characters in traditional tales, the rest of the lesson continues in a similar pattern.

The significance of this pattern is not just numerical: the children are not merely speaking more than they did at the start of the lesson they are also responding both to one another as well as to their teacher, and introducing new ideas such as the idea that being ugly doesn't necessarily mean being horrible. Peter even questions the validity of including ugly sisters in a list of 'main characters', arguing that they appear only in Cinderella. This perceptive point is accepted by Donna who then recognizes the need to change what she was putting on the board, asking for a new term with more general application.

If we look at the questions in this extract we can see that, like those in Extract 2, they are also more evenly balanced between teacher and children than those of the first extract: the children ask two to Donna's four. Donna invites the class to nominate 'any other characters that we find in traditional tales' to which Tom responds with a question which, like Jess's question in Extract 1, is a tentative answer. To another question from Donna, Emma produces a similarly tentative response, also in question form. The children appear to be using questions to protect themselves against commitment to the propositions they contain.

Of Donna's four questions, two are pseudo questions, which seem intended as softened instructions, as in the one where she asks the children to think about whether the text says the two stepsisters are good or evil and in the other where she asks Peter to repeat what he has just said. But one question takes the form of an invitation to the children to evaluate her actions, as she asks them whether they think she is right to have placed the ugly sisters in the 'bad' column. It is this question that produces a chain of seven consecutive utterances from the children who interpret it as indicating that their views and reasons for these are being sought. Donna's last question, which opens with the discourse marker, 'Right', indicating that a point has been established from which they can now move forward, can be thought of as a display question, but it is one apparently intended to move their thinking on. It is an appeal for a higher order abstraction, a term which will have applicability beyond the specific instance of *Cinderella*.

Learning and teaching in Donna's classroom

Partly thanks to the playful relationship established between them, Donna's students are learning to listen to her with interest, to take up the challenges offered, to review yesterday's learning thoughtfully and to make it today's starting point. They are also learning how to ask their own questions, how to build and modify their own understandings and how to extend and challenge the understandings of others. This is achieved partly through Donna's careful elicitation of the key points of yesterday's lesson and partly through her extensions of their responses to her questions. But perhaps a more important part is played by her readiness to invite the children to make judgements on her actions, and to listen to the children's extensions and amendments of what she has said. When Peter raises a reasoned objection to the inclusion of ugly sisters in a table of main characters in traditional tales, Donna urges all the children to listen. By her acceptance of Peter's challenge, she both models for them how to listen to reason, and also makes it clear that it is legitimate and even praiseworthy for the children to question what she says. Through her actions she demonstrates the value of her words at 2 in the first extract 'And if we put our heads together and our ideas together, then what we come up with is often pretty fantastic'.

Interactive whole class teaching – the wider picture

Since the report of the Three Wise Men (Alexander *et al.* 1992) primary teachers in England have been urged to make greater use of whole class teaching. A substantial proportion of whole class teaching is built into the Literacy Hour, recommended for all primary pupils in England's National Literacy Strategy (Standards and Effectiveness Unit 1998). But research on classroom interaction has tended to focus on small groups as providing at least the best context for active participation by children in their learning (Mercer 2000; Skidmore *et al.* 2003; Warwick and Maloch 2003). Whole class teaching has been seen as the context for transmissional teaching, where the teacher informs the children on the one hand and interrogates and evaluates them on the other (Sinclair and Coulthard 1975). Indeed in two studies 20 years apart, of interaction in English primary classrooms, and working with two different teams, Galton found a shift towards whole class teaching, accompanied by a more transmissional style, with the vast majority of exchanges initiated by the teacher, most taking the form of Teacher Initiation Pupil Response and Teacher Feedback (Galton *et al.* 1980, 1999).

However the data, even for the later Galton study, were gathered before the introduction of the NLS. Examining the whole class interactions in Literacy Hour lessons of effective teachers, after the introduction of the NLS, with its heavy emphasis on whole class interactive teaching, Mroz *et al.* (2000) found an intensification of this tendency. English *et al.* (2002) found that the very many lessons they analysed were only 'superficially interactive'. So is it just unrealistic to expect primary children to take anything other than a passive responding role in whole class literacy sessions?

Such whole class sessions are now an essential part of the almost universally adopted (but not mandatory) Literacy Hour in England's primary schools. But despite enjoining teachers to make lessons interactive, the NLS provides little guidance on what this might mean in practice. However, as I argue in a recent article (Dombey 2003: 37–58) some of its own video demonstration material is implicitly endorsing the narrowest kind of transmissional teaching, with the teacher never straying from the role of interrogator and the children penned into their role as test subjects. The epithet 'superficially interactive' seems entirely appropriate.

By the nature of its prescriptive framework, by the weight of the objectives included in the termly programmes for each year group, and by the detailed planning required over a fortnight, an implicit message appears to have been sent to England's primary teachers that teaching is transmission, and that deviation from a planned lesson is not to be encouraged.

The predominance of a transmissional approach to classroom interaction is not confined to classrooms in England. The work of Nystrand and colleagues investigating secondary school English lessons in the US would certainly suggest that it is usual to find whole class sessions in which teachers nominate all topics, initiate virtually all exchanges and rarely extend students' responses (Nystrand *et al.* 1997). Yet in a small minority of Nystrand and colleagues' classrooms a different pattern was found in which the lessons took the form of textured discussion, with the students actively exploring a topic and responding to one another rather than passively listening or continually taking the second slot in an IRF exchange. The students in these classrooms achieved significantly higher mean scores on an English literature test than did students in classrooms matched for socioeconomic situation. Certainly at secondary level, active participation in whole class discussion appears to be both possible and productive.

So where are we?

Donna and her children show us that active participation in whole class discussion is also possible and productive in primary school. But, as in the rare US highschool English classrooms where Nystrand and colleagues found active, textured discussion, it is certainly not a matter of 'anything goes'. Donna's lessons are not aimless or unprepared. She has a close knowledge of the Framework of the National Literacy Strategy (Standards and Effectiveness Unit 1998) and is concerned to meet its objectives. As she says in discussion with other teachers in this project, 'You've got to prepare. You've got to have a starting point.' But then she adds: *'But what I always hope is that the children will take me somewhere I hadn't thought of going.'*

We need to help other teachers develop something of the confidence, understanding and skill that have allowed Donna to construct a rather more collaborative, open-ended approach to literacy learning, and in the process given her students a greater degree of autonomy and a greater sense of participating in a shared endeavour.

PART 3
Professional Knowledge and Understanding

The issue of professional knowledge and understanding, a prevalent zeitgeist, is the focus of the chapters in this section. Policy initiatives over the past decade have focused heavily upon teachers' knowledge about language, have assessed and critiqued it, and developed training programmes to increase levels of naming and knowing. However, subject knowledge on its own, itself a complex issue, is only part of the picture, since such knowledge is applied in practice through the use of pedagogical knowledge, informed intuition, experience and understanding.

Both Louise Poulson and Sam Twiselton resolutely refuse to be beguiled by the purportedly simple notion that increasing teachers' knowledge is the key to effective literacy teaching and examine the nature of this knowledge, its construction and application. Research is used to support the position that there is no clear relationship between formal academic knowledge of language and literacy and effective literacy teaching in the primary phase, and both writers insist such knowledge is pedagogically situated. It is important to understand why this issue has come to occupy such a central role on the contemporary educational stage and how the deficit model of primary teachers' knowledge developed; these chapters offer insights in this regard. Poulson argues, for example, that current models tend to take a psychological stance and assume that knowledge is located in the minds of individuals. She suggests a reconceptualization of teachers' knowledge and understanding based on more recent ideas about thinking, learning and knowing, which emphasize its socio-cultural nature. In addition, she recognizes the problematic nature of subject knowledge in relation to the contested concept of literacy, which for the purposes of policy and politics is seen as an apparently singular set of assessable skills. Teachers' knowledge about literacy needs to encompass an understanding of its provisional nature and what counts as literacy in the lives of the children they teach.

Trainee teachers likewise, need to be aware of the literacy demands of the twenty-first century and be knowledgeable about the literacy practices of their learners, and the expectations of schooled literacy. Twiselton shows how the ways in which student teachers view themselves as teachers interacts with the beliefs and values they hold about literacy, and demonstrates that these factors are just as important as their knowledge and skills. In her research, the students' competence in the classroom and ability to apply their knowledge and understanding related closely to their sense of identity as teachers. Her data reveals that immediately after the implementation of the NLS, most of the students in the study viewed themselves as 'curriculum deliverers', and were unable to move beyond this and transform their knowledge of the curriculum in interaction with the learners. This emphasis on curriculum knowledge and delivery, allied to a concern to cover the objectives and ensure targets are met, is part of everyday discourse in the currently directive culture of teaching in England. If curriculum knowledge, knowledge of the 'tools of the trade' and subject knowledge continue to dominate the agenda, then potential practitioners may not be the only ones who emerge disabled. Such 'professionals' may merely become classroom operatives, capable only of parcelling out their curriculum/content knowledge in regularized chunks, and being the bricklayers, not the architects of children's learning (Mortimore 1999).

Despite the considerable challenge of the current context, both writers suggest ways forward, and focus on the process of weaving, combining threads from different knowledge bases in order to make connections between the learner, the subject and the curriculum. Knowledge about learning deserves to be profiled and once again come out of the shadow into the light.

4 The subject of literacy: what kind of knowledge is needed to teach literacy successfully?

Louise Poulson

There is a growing acceptance that successful pedagogy involves not only what teachers do, but also what they know and how they think. The apparently simple idea that teachers who know more teach better has underpinned various attempts to improve education through policy, research and practice (Cochran-Smith and Lytle 1999). It has also been recognized that teachers' knowledge and thinking may be a key element in sustaining innovation and reform efforts in various parts of the world (see for example Earl *et al.* 2001). Consequently, there has been a strong policy focus on increasing teachers' knowledge in various ways. Although the idea is deceptively simple, it has been a rather more complex task to identify what kind of knowledge is needed to improve teaching; and also, how and in what contexts it is best developed. Within policy discourses about teacher education and development, it has become almost taken for granted that the main concern should be with teachers' *subject* knowledge. In Britain, education policies over the past decade have ensured that the acquisition and development of subject specific knowledge has become a key element in initial training and teacher development for the primary (elementary) phase (for see example DfEE 1998c). An argument underpinning this tendency is that strong subject knowledge is necessary to teach the core national curriculum subjects and, more recently, to implement the National Literacy and Numeracy Strategies. Policies promoting subject specific knowledge have also claimed to be underpinned by research evidence from the US, the UK and elsewhere. However, the notion of subject knowledge is not unproblematic: particularly in relation to primary school teachers, and to literacy. This chapter has a number of aims: the first is to examine critically prevalent assumptions about the relationship between subject knowledge and pedagogy in literacy in the primary phase. The second is to consider how teachers' knowledge – particularly subject knowledge – came to have a position of such prominence in educational research and policy. The third aim is to examine the nature and focus of a range of research studies addressing primary teachers' subject knowledge, and how they have influenced policy. The chapter then discusses issues arising from attempts to apply the notion of subject knowledge in relation to literacy teaching. Finally, it considers how new ideas about knowledge and learning, derived from socio-cultural theory, might inform the ways in which we conceptualize the kinds of knowledge that successful teachers of literacy develop, and how they use it in the classroom.

The nature and role of primary teachers' knowledge: evidence from empirical research

Since the mid-1980s when Shulman (1986) identified it as a missing paradigm in educational research, interest in teachers' knowledge and thinking has expanded to such an extent that Connolly *et al.* (1997: 666) describe it as having exploded. One explanation put forward for its growth was that while the idea of a knowledge base for teaching was often promoted rhetorically, its character was rarely specified (Shulman 1987: 4), thus some researchers sought what they regarded as a scientific basis for teaching and teacher education (Korthagen and Lagerwerf 1996). However, there have been a number of different approaches and models informing studies of teachers' knowledge and thinking. Fenstermacher (1994) identified two major strands: one which was largely concerned with teachers' formal knowledge – conceptualized as a knowledge base; and another which was concerned more with teachers' experience-based, practical knowledge. A key aim of both strands was to conceptualize adequately the often implicit knowledge, beliefs and values of teachers. Shulman (1987) had argued the need for teachers to make explicit what they did, and their reasons for what they were doing, to students, other teachers and the wider community. He proposed that researchers should work with practitioners 'to develop codified representations of the practical pedagogical wisdom of able teachers' (1987: 11).

In the intervening years, the work of Shulman and his associates at Stanford (see Shulman 1986, 1987; Grossman *et al.* 1989) has had a strong impact on both research and policy: particularly in conceptualizing subject knowledge and its pedagogical application. The model of subject content knowledge developed by the Stanford Knowledge Growth in a Profession projects, and widely adopted in subsequent research, was based upon a structure of the disciplines approach, derived from Schwab (1978), among others. A basic proposition was that subjects were structured according to the ways in which their content was organized (substantive structures), or according to the accepted ways of adding to that knowledge (syntactic structure). The Stanford researchers were particularly interested in the processes by which teachers selected and represented aspects of a discipline to students; and how they developed subject specific pedagogical knowledge. This they termed *pedagogical content knowledge* and claimed it as a distinctive part of the teacher's knowledge base (Shulman 1986). Since then, considerable attention has been given to elaborating pedagogical content knowledge, and, as Fenstermacher (1994: 14) observed, the concept has spawned an extensive set of research studies. However, an underlying assumption of the Stanford research was that in order to develop pedagogical content knowledge, teachers already had a strong understanding of the content and accepted modes of enquiry within a discipline. While this condition was probably applicable to the majority of secondary school subject specialists, it was less likely to be fulfilled by primary class teachers.

Even though the Knowledge Growth in Profession research projects focused on the knowledge bases of subject specialist secondary school teachers, this work also influenced many studies of primary teachers' knowledge – particularly in Britain in the late 1980s and 1990s. However, many of the specific assumptions underpinning the investigation of subject knowledge were not necessarily applicable to primary school teachers. Indeed, the Stanford researchers had themselves cautioned against attempts to apply their model of knowledge bases directly to teachers in primary schools (Shulman 1987: 4; Wilson *et al.* 1987: 121–2; Grossman *et al.* 1989: 28). As Shulman (1987: 4) pointed out, the notion of subject knowledge and its pedagogical application was considerably more complex when a teacher had numerous subjects to deal with, thus they warned that 'the implications of this research for elementary school teaching should be drawn cautiously' (Grossman *et al.* 1989: 28). In spite of the reservations outlined above, a number of research studies did attempt to identify the extent of primary teachers' subject knowledge, and in some cases the relationship between knowledge and classroom practice (for example Wragg *et al.* 1989; Bennett 1993; Aubrey 1997). There were also other investigations of the role of subject knowledge, which viewed application of the Stanford model more critically (for example Furlong and Maynard 1995; Maynard 1997; Edwards and Ogden 1998).

A deficit model of primary teachers' knowledge

Many of the initial studies of primary teachers' subject knowledge tended to contribute to what has been identified more recently as a deficit model of teachers' knowledge, highlighting what they appeared not to know, and deducing that increasing teachers' own subject knowledge would lead to better teaching (see for example Askew *et al.* 1997b). For example, a survey of teachers in 400 primary schools in Great Britain, reported by Wragg *et al.* (1989) indicated that many appeared to have limited knowledge of some subject areas and did not feel confident to teach them in the national curriculum, science being identified as particularly problematic, followed by mathematics. A second study in the same research programme (Bennett 1993) found trainee teachers' subject knowledge across a range of subjects to be limited when they were tested at the beginning and end of their training. Aubrey's research (1997) on early years' teachers claimed that their knowledge of mathematics was often not extensive. A conclusion drawn in much of this work was that these apparently low levels of subject knowledge were problematic: teachers could not teach what they did not understand (Bennett 1993), therefore subject knowledge in initial training, professional development and in-service courses should be enhanced and prioritized. This body of work lent support to education policies in Britain that were already moving in the direction of giving a higher profile to separate subjects in primary schools through a compulsory national curriculum. They also seemed to support a stronger focus on subject study in primary teacher education. Thus the expansion of interest in researching primary teachers' knowledge bases in Britain in the late 1980s and throughout the 1990s coincided with, and was partly fostered by, the prevailing political and policy context.

In many respects, the research findings related to primary teachers' subject knowledge were unsurprising given the generalist academic background and training of many of them. Teachers for the primary phases, particularly those qualifying before the late 1980s, in Britain, were unlikely to have well developed knowledge of a single academic discipline; and few of them would constitute their knowledge and professional identity in terms of a specific subject. Largely because of the class teacher system in primary schools, the organization of the curriculum and classification of knowledge into discrete subjects has long been problematic.

However, from the late 1980s there was a deliberate, ideologically motivated attempt to shift the culture in primary schools towards a stronger subject orientation. This entailed a move away from a primary curriculum based on integration of subjects and problem-based enquiry, both of which were seen as central to progressive pedagogy. At the time, progressive ideas and practices in primary schools were blamed for a perceived failure of the maintained education system. A common argument, although based on little real evidence, was that such ideas had led to badly managed classrooms and poor teaching. The establishment of a prescriptive, subject-based national curriculum in primary schools, enabled a case to be made for strengthening subject knowledge among primary teachers (Alexander *et al.* 1992), which, in turn, appeared to be supported by research on teachers' knowledge.

Challenges to the deficit model of primary teachers' knowledge

More recently, researchers have begun to question the assumptions and conclusions of many of the earlier British studies of primary teachers' subject knowledge. For example, Brown and colleagues (see Askew *et al.* 1997a,b; Brown *et al.* 1998) highlight two important issues: first that ways of identifying, and quantifying teachers' knowledge of a subject have been problematic and, second, that the knowledge required to teach primary school pupils effectively may not be the same as that needed at advanced secondary school or degree level. Reporting findings from their own study of the knowledge, beliefs and practices of 90 primary teachers of numeracy, who were identified as effective in relation to pupil outcome measures, they suggest that a sound grasp of the content to be taught, along with the ability to represent this to pupils, and to make conceptual connections between different aspects of a topic or content – in short, what Shulman (1987) and others have referred to as pedagogical content knowledge – may be more important than knowledge of subject content on its own. They also argue that despite the concerns about weaknesses in teachers' mathematical and scientific knowledge, expressed in official reports from school inspections (for example Ofsted 1994), in 84 lessons observed in their study, no teachers made significant mathematical errors. In only two lessons were there occasions when teachers were clearly limited by their knowledge. Askew *et al.* (1997a: 59, 64) conclude that: 'It is therefore clear that some teachers of younger children have real problems over subject knowledge, but it is not clear how much this affects their effectiveness'; and that although there were gaps in teachers' subject knowledge, these did not seem to be especially damaging or difficult to retrieve.

A parallel study in which I and my colleagues investigated the knowledge, beliefs and practices of a sample of 225 teachers in England identified as effective in teaching literacy also concluded that there was no clear relationship between teachers' formal academic knowledge and their success in teaching literacy (see for example Medwell *et al.* 1998; Poulson *et al.* 2001; Wray *et al.* 2002; Poulson and Avramidis 2003). This research found that academic qualifications in English, or related subjects, were not extensive among effective literacy teachers: only a minority of them had degrees in any discipline; most had qualified as generalist primary teachers with a Certificate in Education more than 20 years previously. More detailed examination of the content knowledge of a smaller sub-sample of teachers was also undertaken. This involved completion of a test on aspects of linguistic and literary content related to teaching literacy, including items on morphology, phonology, syntax and sociolinguistics. The results of the test (reported in detail in Medwell *et al.* 1998; Wray *et al.* 2002) indicated that effective teachers of literacy did not appear to have particularly high levels of knowledge about the formal aspects of language structure such as sentence grammar, aspects of text cohesion and coherence, phonology and the use of linguistic terminology. Overall, their results differed little from those of a comparison sample of teachers representing the full range of effectiveness. However, the effective teachers performed much better on items which were related to knowledge of children's literature;

and those which were contextualized in practical classroom situations – such as commenting on the errors and strategies in examples of children's reading and writing. Prior to completing the test, lessons had been observed, and one of the things we noted was that several teachers who struggled to answer items in the test had been observed, only a short time before, dealing with the same content competently and confidently in the classroom. When concepts in language or literacy were decontextualized from classroom practice, and presented more formally, the teachers appeared to find them much harder to identify. Several individuals articulated the problem they were experiencing, exemplified by the following comments by two teachers taken from interview data:

> I did know all this stuff [grammatical items] . . . but I just don't use it so of course it's gone. I don't know that I *do* need it, but if I do I can look it up.

> It's impossible to remember everything. I really believe that it's because it simply isn't how we do it in class . . . if do use it regularly it's fine, but this detail is not the sort of thing I'd use in class.

One conclusion might be that these individuals appeared to be teaching what they did not understand themselves. However, analysis of lesson observations indicated that they were able to present content to pupils and make conceptual connections between different aspects of language and texts. They explained and exemplified particular aspects of language use. Their knowledge was functional: they appeared to know about and teach the features of language *in use*; but their knowledge of *language as system* appeared not to be well developed, nor did they use high levels of linguistic terminology. A model in which teachers' prior knowledge of subject content and structure was then transformed into pedagogical content knowledge to make it accessible to pupils, seemed not to be applicable. Knowledge of literacy appeared to be pedagogically situated. Even so, the teachers taught effective lessons and maintained higher than average pupil gains on standardized tests from year to year.

The message indicated by the studies outlined above is that subject knowledge, and its pedagogical transformation and articulation is, as Shulman predicted, much more complex in relation to primary class teachers. There appears to be little evidence of a clear relationship between well developed formal academic knowledge of particular subject content and effective teaching in the primary phase of schooling. While it might be argued that teachers who were already effective might have become even more so had they had greater knowledge of linguistic terminology or sentence structure, the issue is less than clear cut. It is apparent that the nature of the relationship between teachers' knowledge and successful pedagogy in literacy, and other curriculum areas in the primary school, is still not well understood. Thus the wider implications of suggestions (Earl *et al.* 2001) that primary teachers' subject knowledge needs to be boosted in order to implement and sustain reforms such as the National Literacy Strategy in the UK, need to be considered very carefully. Although claims for a distinctive knowledge base for teaching fitted well with policies in Britain and elsewhere that aimed to raise the profile of teaching and set standards of entry to the profession, a closer look at relevant research does, in fact, reveal a much more complex picture. It is one that raises many questions about the direction of recent policies for primary teacher education and professional development that emphasize the acquisition of atomized knowledge in the form of competences and standards. It would appear that the promotion of primary teachers' knowledge of subject content, and subject specific pedagogy, while appearing to be underpinned by research, has, in fact, been driven as much by ideology as by empirical evidence. In Britain, the obsession with primary teachers' subject knowledge has also obscured the importance of other aspects of the teacher's knowledge base identified by Shulman. In particular, knowledge of learners and of the curriculum; and additionally, other implicit forms of knowledge. It is worth reminding ourselves that Shulman (1987: 4) proposed that researchers and teachers should work together to make explicit, and codify, the often implicit practical wisdom of able teachers. For British teachers, knowledge of the curriculum has come to mean knowing the content of an externally devised and prescribed national curriculum and Literacy Strategy framework of objectives. There also has been some ambiguity about the importance of teachers possessing knowledge of learners. On the one hand, this kind of knowledge has been implicitly associated with progressive ideas and practices in primary schools: characterized by the once common assertion that primary school teachers taught children rather than subjects. Ideologically, from the late 1980s onwards, this became unacceptable, as indicated earlier in this chapter. A further concern highlighted by Filer and Pollard (2000) relates to the ways in which teachers' knowledge of pupils and their capacity for learning and achievement can be affected by issues of social class, gender and ethnicity. To a large extent, teachers' knowledge of pupils has been reframed to focus more closely on knowing about pupils' learning strategies and misconceptions within a subject.

The problem of 'subject' knowledge in relation to literacy

The concern with primary teachers' subject knowledge poses particular problems in relation to literacy. This issue arose in the British effective teachers of literacy study, outlined earlier in this chapter. From a review of existing literature on successful or effective teachers in general, and literacy teachers specifically, it appeared likely that successful literacy teachers would have a coherent belief system about literacy and its teaching. Also it was likely that they would have well developed knowledge about literacy and its pedagogy. However, defining what constitutes subject knowledge in literacy is far from straightforward. Literacy is not a subject in the usual sense, with an accepted body of knowledge and a range of organizing principles: it is in fact a concept with a relatively short history. Literacy has neither clear semantic nor syntactic structures. Nonetheless, this has not prevented it from being treated as though it were a subject in the conventional sense, particularly in relation to teachers' knowledge and the school curriculum. In fact, successful literacy teaching draws on a range of disciplinary knowledge including literature, linguistics, the psychology of learning and child language development; and it also draws upon an understanding of how people use, mediate and produce written texts in various aspects of their lives. Even as a term to describe part of the primary school curriculum, literacy is a relatively recent phenomenon in Britain. From the 1970s to the late 1980s – until the introduction of a national curriculum – the term language, or language development would have been more familiar in British primary schools. The national curriculum brought with it a change of terminology: from language to English, which previously had been associated with the secondary school curriculum. Since the late 1990s this has changed again as a result of the policy focus on literacy and numeracy: English lessons have been replaced by literacy and the Literacy Hour.

A further point is that there is no universally agreed way of defining literacy. It is a contested concept and there are multiple understandings, informed by different theoretical perspectives, of what constitutes literacy. For example, literacy may be conceptualized as practice embedded within particular social and cultural contexts – a perspective which underpins what is widely known as New Literacy Studies (see for example Street 1995; Gee 1996; Barton and Hamilton 1998). Work within the New Literacy Studies theoretical perspective is largely based on a number of key premises (Baynham and Prinsloo 2001: 83). First, that literacy is primarily a set of practices, embedded in particular forms of social and cultural activity. Second, there are different forms of literacy (or literacies) associated with different domains of life: a key issue is what people *do* with literacy. Third, that literacy practices – as with all forms of language and discourse practice – are also shaped by power relations, both formal/institutional and informal, and that they are also historically situated. An alternative way of conceptualizing literacy is more functionally orientated, and regards it as consisting of a largely portable set of skills and competences that are acquired by individuals primarily in formal education settings. These skills and competences are regarded as necessary for success in achieving credentials within the education system; in the labour market; and, more generally, are believed to be fundamental to developing a high skills, knowledge-based economy. From this perspective, reading and writing are regarded as fundamentally singular, individual and externally determinable processes (Freebody and Freiberg 2001: 222). These two alternative ways of constructing literacy are not easily reconciled and the latter has tended to dominate in terms of literacy policy relating to school age students, adult learners and home–school initiatives. It is certainly apparent in policy texts such as the British national curriculum for initial teacher training, which specifies the knowledge, competences and standards to be achieved by entrants to the profession. Barton (2001: 94–5) points out that while the New Literacy Studies has been influential, and has provided a powerful research paradigm, it is difficult to detect much influence in relation to current policy.

Reconceptualizing teachers' knowledge and learning

Equally, new ideas about learning, thinking and knowledge also appear to have had little influence on policy and research connected with teachers' knowledge. A key assumption underpinning almost all policy, and much research, is that teachers' knowledge is located primarily within the minds of individuals and can be subject to valid examination or testing outside a specific context of practice. Much of the research on teachers' knowledge and thinking has had a psychological orientation. It has been largely concerned with finding out what individuals know, how they acquire or develop that knowledge, and identifying the thought processes in which they engage. A key metaphor in the teacher knowledge and thinking literature has been 'getting inside teachers' heads' (Feiman-Nemser and Flodden 1986: 506). The metaphor implies a simple and direct relationship between thought and language: that teachers' language acts as a mirror or conduit for their thought and merely reflects or conveys ideas which lie within individuals' minds. This assumption implicitly ignores the complex and dialectical nature of the relationship between thinking and language highlighted, for example, in the work of Vygotsky (for example Vygotsky [1962] 1986). It also fails to acknowledge that language is a social institution (Volosinov 1973), and that utterances are often multifaceted (Bakhtin 1981) with individual meanings inserted alongside those of others, both past and present. Feldman (1997: 759–62) argues that much of the work in this field – particularly the strand concerned with formal knowledge, or knowledge bases has been underpinned by what Bruner (1990) has termed a computational model of the mind. According to this model, knowledge is seen as something to be accreted, stored and then transmitted to others. Thus teachers learn the structure and content of a subject themselves, and then develop ways of transforming and representing it to pupils.

Few of the studies concerned with teachers' knowledge bases, and their cognitive processes, appear to have examined the structure of the disciplines approach critically, considering its development as a powerful ideology

(Cherryholmes 1987). Instead it has tended to be assumed that all disciplines have clear syntactic and semantic structures, and that subjects in the school curriculum can be equated with disciplines. In many respects this represents a more restricted conceptualization of knowledge, and its organization and structure within disciplines, than that found in Schwab's own writing. For example, Schwab (1978) maintained that the structure of disciplines was not fixed, and that within some disciplines there were numerous ways of organizing and structuring knowledge. A further issue, highlighted by Young (1998), is the failure to distinguish between what are generally regarded as fundamental forms of knowledge, and school curriculum subjects. The notion of fundamental and relatively unchanging forms of knowledge and understanding, which shape people's experience and understanding of the world, can be traced back to Kant and beyond; school subjects, as Hirst (1974) recognized, are socially constructed ways of organizing knowledge. Furthermore, the nature of school subjects may change, not only across time, but also according to the particular context in which that subject is taught, and the values and assumptions of those who teach it. By narrowing the focus in this way, an unproblematized and somewhat rigid conceptualization of knowledge and teachers' knowledge bases has come to dominate.

Like Feldman (1997), Putnam and Borko (2000: 4) point out that, so far at least, more recent ideas about the nature of knowledge, thinking and learning which emphasize its social and situated nature have yet to make much impact on research and policy relating to teachers' knowledge. Most discussions of these ideas and their implications for educational practice, they argue, have taken place in relation to student learning. Yet, the sociocultural, or 'situative', perspective has considerable potential in understanding teacher learning and development. Putnam and Borko (2000) identify three conceptual themes that are central to this perspective: first that thinking and knowledge are primarily social in nature; second, that they are situated in particular physical and social contexts; and third, that they are distributed across individuals, systems and tools. Sociocultural theory focuses on interactive systems that include individuals as participants, interacting with each other and with materials and representational systems (in other words, material and symbolic tools). Individuals also participate in discourse communities over time that help to shape ideas, theories and concepts that individuals then appropriate and internalize through their own efforts to make sense of experience (Ball 2000). Rather than considering cognition and knowledge as the property of individuals residing within the mind, sociocultural theories posit that they are distributed across persons, contexts and physical and symbolic tools. Outside formal educational settings, intelligent activity often depends on resources and knowledge beyond individuals themselves. Thus distributing cognition across persons, tools and contexts expands a system's potential capacity for knowledge and innovation (Putnam and Borko

2000). In many respects, a sociocultural perspective on learning, thinking and knowledge complements and parallels the concerns of the New Literacy Studies, highlighted earlier.

Theoretical understanding derived from both sociocultural perspectives on learning and knowledge, and the New Literacy Studies has considerable potential to help understand better how successful literacy teachers in primary schools think, know and act. In relation to the effective teachers of literacy study discussed earlier in this chapter, it provides a possible explanation of the paradox identified there: why some teachers who were observed successfully teaching aspects of literacy, had neither high levels of formal academic credentials in related subjects, nor achieved high scores on decontextualized tests of 'subject' knowledge for literacy. The study concluded that rather than having an in-depth knowledge of a model of language in which there were interconnected levels (such as word sentence text), the teachers tended to represent their knowledge in terms of what students could do. They were less able to show knowledge in the abstract, such as in identifying particular linguistic forms and structures. Knowledge appeared to be highly embedded within the teaching context (Wray *et al.* 2002: 80–1). Thus teachers' knowledge often appeared to be distributed and contextualized, rather than carried around in individual minds. This aspect of the research findings was also consistent with other work in the US and the UK on the relationship between primary teachers' knowledge and practice (see for example Calderhead 1988; Leinhardt 1988). The explanation also makes intuitive sense as it would be difficult, if not impossible, for individual primary school teachers to internalize all the knowledge needed to teach the range of subjects within the school curriculum. Instead, successful literacy teachers appeared to draw upon interactive systems (Greeno 1997), which included not only themselves, but also interaction with students, other teachers and classroom assistants, and parents or carers. Their knowledge base was also distributed or stretched across themselves, other people and artefacts, such as texts and physical and symbolic tools (Lave 1988). For example, the classroom observations highlighted the importance of the literacy environment created within classrooms and schools, which was frequently used as a tool in literacy teaching. Examples of different text types were displayed and a wide range of literacy practices (both macro- and micro-level) were encouraged within and outside formal teaching sessions. Teachers often drew upon the shared activities and specific literacy practices of teacher and students, and of practices outside the classroom, to demonstrate and exemplify aspects of reading, writing and their relationship with spoken language. The effective literacy teachers also tended to have well developed theoretical models of literacy and language development which guided their practice. Analysis of teachers' beliefs about literacy and its teaching had indicated a strongly positive orientation to holistic theoretical models of literacy, with a strong emphasis on helping learners to understand texts; the use of authentic texts and activities in teaching reading and writing; and a strong focus on developing students' engagement with, understanding and production of a range of textual forms and structures (Poulson *et al.* 2001: 288). Observations of practice were also consistent with teachers' theoretical beliefs about literacy and its teaching. However, these theoretical models and beliefs may not always be consonant with current models informing prescriptive policies related to how literacy should be taught in the primary school.

5 Beyond the curriculum: learning to teach primary literacy

Sam Twiselton

How do the beliefs, values and understandings that student teachers hold impact on their understanding of the National Literacy Strategy and their teaching of English? This chapter investigates the differing understandings of literacy and teacher identity that student teachers hold as they learn to teach primary English. In particular, it looks at the interaction between their view of their role in the classroom and their understandings, values and beliefs about the subject they are teaching. The research on which the chapter is based leads to the conclusion that the interactive relationship between student teachers' learning away from school and how they see themselves in the classroom is fundamental to their effectiveness as teachers. The study took place over a period of five years (1996–2001) and included time before, during and up to three years after the implementation of the National Literacy Strategy. In each year of the study a sample of student teachers were observed and interviewed.

It emerged from the data that student teachers could be crudely categorized into one of three categories: task managers, curriculum deliverers and concept/skill builders (Twiselton 1999, 2000). Typically student teachers belonging to the task manager category would be near the beginning of Initial Teacher Education (ITE), at a point where survival to the end of the lesson was the primary concern. However, the findings suggest that the sequence of progression is not necessarily as straightforward as might be predicted. The way student teachers view themselves as teachers, how they understand the curriculum (the National Literacy Strategy in particular) and the beliefs and values they hold in relation to the subject have a direct impact on the ability of student teachers to effectively support children's learning in literacy.

The need to develop more effective ways of supporting student teachers' learning has been both refined and intensified by recent curriculum developments. The implementation of the National Literacy Strategy (NLS) (DfEE 1998a) has provided a welcome emphasis on subject knowledge and a fresh impetus for re-examining the content of the literacy curriculum for both children and student teachers. However, it could also be argued that the highly detailed and prescriptive nature of these curricula has also resulted in an even more urgent need to consider the role of the curriculum in relation to learning. Consideration needs to be given to ways of developing the understandings needed to transform what is prescribed by the curriculum into a transferable 'generality of knowing' (Greeno 1997) that can be applied and adapted to contexts both inside and outside the classroom.

Categories of student teacher

Task managers

These were student teachers who were very product orientated, in other words, concerned with completing the task rather than developing the learning it was supposed to promote. The student teachers judged whether the lesson was successful by the children apparently being on task during it. Examples of comments made by student teachers in this category include:

> I didn't want them to start being silly, that was really the main thing I was thinking about

> Really I was just concentrating on getting it done.

Curriculum deliverers

These student teachers did reveal an understanding of the purpose of the task beyond simply wanting to get it done, but this was conceived within the restrictions of an externally 'given' curriculum. Typical examples include:

> We needed to cover the comprehension bit before going on to the next one.

> The school wanted me to do story writing so that's why I was looking at that really.

> I thought that would be the sentence level bit before doing the word level.

> It was in the scheme . . . that was what was next.

Concept/skill builders

These student teachers were far more focused on the subject and the concepts and skills needed to become proficient within it. They were able to articulate their learning objectives in a sense that linked to a broader understanding of the subject and its importance for children. Examples include:

> They need to consolidate and apply it to their own writing and see how the process works, backwards and forwards. I wanted them to get the information and then convey the information, because so much work they do depends on being able to do that.

> I wanted them to think about story structures – that would help them with their prediction.

> It was the adjectives that brought the text to life . . . they needed to see that.

> I wanted to show them in different ways – help them see what it was all about.

Previously published findings (Twiselton 2000) demonstrated that pre-National Literacy Strategy there was a fairly even spread between the groups that crudely reflected the stage of progression student teachers had reached in ITE. Immediately after it was implemented there was a clustering around the curriculum deliverer category, with less task management but also less concept/skill building. The National Literacy Strategy appeared to have helped even student teachers near the beginning of ITE to avoid an exclusive focus on tasks. However, in these early stages it also appeared to have restricted student teachers' ability to reflect on the skills and concepts they were teaching in a wider sense.

The very last stage of the study involved student teachers who were the best placed to have moved beyond being curriculum deliverers – English specialists who had just completed their final school placement. I wanted to re-examine the impact of the National Literacy Strategy on student teacher learning long enough after its implementation in schools for it to have started to feel familiar to both student teachers and the people they had been working with in school. These student teachers appeared to have found ways of using the National Literacy Strategy as a catalyst for thinking about the curriculum in a way that connected to the subject that underpinned it. Particularly strong themes included:

- The importance of developing a child oriented response and the need for flexibility in time, planning and pedagogy, for example:

  > It all depends on what you're trying to cover and what you want to get out of the children. You have to have that in mind and

take an approach which is more effective – not tick boxes all the time.

. . . and I went though a phase where I thought 'Oh the literacy hour is terrible because teachers just do that and they're all doing the same thing and no one's got any individual qualities or anything' but I've kind of grown out of that a little bit because you find different ways to do it and it's funny how you see things differently.

Be flexible in the discussion so you haven't like got a set of questions that you just . . . like a script – so be flexible so you can respond . . . go with the flow.

- Making connections with underlying structures:

With the NLS – they can see how everything is important if we want our English to be good and it's helped me to see it that way too. Before we just used to see it all separately. This way is much better.

I've seen it in some schools now where it's 15 minutes of horrible stuff and then we'll get on to the nice bits. But it should be 'well we have to do this in order for the next bit to make sense. So it's cyclical – it goes from one place to another and it all connects.

When teachers don't understand . . . when it comes down to it they've probably covered the objectives but not as wonderfully as another school. Not as deeply and in a way that is as grounded. I think it would be a lot easier for children to forget those lessons that have been done with old texts and the teacher has been a little bit 'oh well, it'll do'.

- The role of values and beliefs about the subject:

I live with 3 girls that aren't specialists and they amaze me sometimes because I do really strongly believe in English and its importance and I could fight for it and everything and be really enthusiastic. And I think that's probably what really comes across in the classroom and I feel more kind of able to say 'YES this is good!'

By the end of the study there was a great deal of data, from which many themes, patterns and questions had emerged. One of the most pressing, from a personal perspective, centred around the potential impact of the National Literacy Strategy on student teachers' understanding of the subject.

Types of teacher knowledge

To some extent the mental images of teaching held by the different categories of student teacher identified in this study can be equated to Shulman's (1987) definitions of teacher knowledge.

Task managers

These student teachers appeared to be mainly relying on a limited version of one type of knowledge – *knowledge of educational contexts*. As they begin their ITE, student teachers have what are often superficial models of what it is to be a teacher, involving authority, order and 'busyness'. The data shows that, in fact, pre-ITE influences remain an important factor throughout (and no doubt beyond) ITE, but that these usually become refined by other experiences as student teachers progress.

Cole's (1996) model of 'scripts' is useful here. He describes scripts as event schema that specify the people who appropriately participate in an event, the roles they play, the objects they use and the sequence of causal relations that applies. The scripts used by the task managers were based on a cultural under- standing of teaching that originated from their experiences as pupils. As D'Andrade (1995) claimed, once a person has a crude script they can enter the flow of a particular event with partial knowledge. For task managers the obvi- ous script to hand involved their interpretation of classrooms from being pupils themselves. This crude and simplistic script allowed them to participate in the practices of teaching very early in their ITE.

Curriculum deliverers

As the name suggests, curriculum dliverers appeared to focus a great deal on *curriculum knowledge*. Shulman defines curriculum knowledge as a grasp of the materials and programmes that serve as 'tools of the trade'. These tools have now been presented for student teachers in such detail that they can be very clear about the content of their lessons. This possibly also explains why the number of student teachers in the task manager category was reduced after the implementation of the National Literacy Strategy.

However, it is clear that the given curriculum cannot fully define the knowledge base required in being an effective teacher. It is illuminating to consider two of Shulman's other categories in relation to the curriculum deliverers, and what they appear to lack. These are *content knowledge* and *pedagogical content knowledge*.

Shulman claims that the *content knowledge* of the teacher should go well beyond what is to be taught. That is to say that in order to teach the subject effectively, the teacher must have knowledge of its underlying structures and organizing principles. This knowledge will enable them to structure learning experiences so that they will be revealed, in a more basic way, to the learner. A number of studies (for example Larkin *et al.* 1980; Chi *et al.* 1982) show that it is not mainly the amount of knowledge that the expert possesses that is important but how it is organized in the memory. Sternberg and Horvath (1995) suggest that expert teachers possess knowledge that is thoroughly integrated in the form of propositional structures and schemata. This definitely did not appear to be the case with the curriculum deliverers. For example, one of the curriculum deliverers taught about verbs and followed a clear lesson structure, but his main concern was not focused on the applications of this knowledge, but merely on 'ticking off' the objectives listed in his lesson plan.

These student teachers appeared to have a grasp of the content but not of how the content connected within the subject and the ways of knowing that are intrinsic to the subject. Consequently the literacy knowledge that the curriculum deliverers were operating with (and seeking to develop in children) was a narrow, restricted version.

It can be claimed that *pedagogical content knowledge* is very closely related to the syntactic level of knowledge, seemingly lacking in the curriculum deliverers. To operate responsively within the subject and to engage learners within the content, student teachers need to develop a command of how the subject is structured and how an expert in the subject thinks and uses it. This contrasts with the expert literacy teachers studied by Medwell *et al.* (1998) who embedded their teaching in wider, meaningful contexts and made explicit and implicit links between concepts and contexts.

Concept/skill builders

Concept/skill builders were arguably beginning to demonstrate understanding that was broader and deeper than the knowledge revealed by the curriculum deliverers. One concept/skill builder's teaching had moved beyond the 'script' to a position where she understood what she was doing so well that she could scaffold the children's learning on a moment by moment basis. Teaching like this requires an ability to read the situation and develop a course of action based on that reading. This links with the 'insight' Sternberg and Horvath (1995) associate with expert teaching.

Student teachers in relation to context and beliefs

It could be argued that within the contexts in which the student teachers operated there were a number of influencing factors. Taking the notion of context as that which surrounds, the context can be represented as a series of concentric circles representing different levels of physical immediacy. This

Figure 5.1 Concentric circles representing the multilayered contexts of the study

form of representation is developed from Cole's model (Cole *et al.* 1987) (see Figure 5.1).

The model has been adapted so that student teacher behaviour is the unit in the middle and the levels that surround it represent the factors that potentially shape it. It is important to note that Cole *et al.*'s (1987) model makes use of the notion of a 'weaving together' (Cole 1996: 135), in which the boundaries between layers are not clear cut and static but ambiguous and dynamic.

The differing ways in which the categories of student teachers appear to conceive their role in the teaching of literacy can be explored here (in a crude and simplified way) in relation to this model. By using the frameworks to compare each category of student teachers, clear differences in their terms of reference are illuminated (see Figure 5.2).

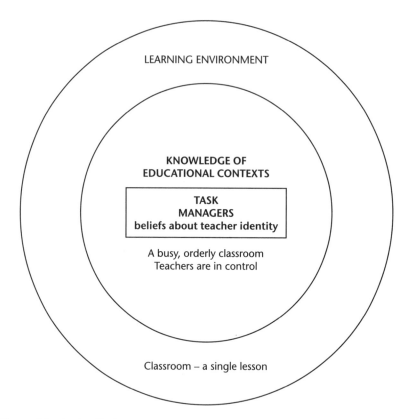

Figure 5.2 A simplified representation of the perceived professional context for task managers' conception of teaching

In Figure 5.2 the task manager's main object – to maintain an orderly and busy classroom – confines the student teachers' thinking within the limits of that particular classroom, on that particular occasion. If a lesson comes to an end and these roles and relationships have been maintained, the experience is judged by the student teacher as successful.

In Figure 5.3 the main purpose is conceived, for the curriculum deliverers, as the need to cover the curriculum. The curriculum (and those who present it to the student teacher) underpins individual lessons and provides a wider frame of reference. Coverage is seen as an end in itself, rather than as a means of something beyond it. This means that literacy learning is still conceived within the confines of the classroom and schooling and does not relate to the authentic discourse of the subject as it exists beyond schools and classrooms.

Figure 5.4 shows that the concept/skill builders' model has added a crucial extra level in the form of the broader context of the subject. Lesson plans and curricula are vehicles for authentic participation in the subject rather than as

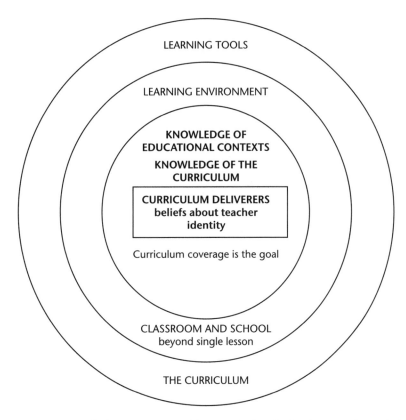

Figure 5.3   A simplified representation of the perceived professional context for curriculum deliverers' conception of teaching

ends in themselves. This increases the potential for children to be able to transfer learning and develop a 'generality of knowing' that extends beyond individual lessons and the boundaries of an awareness of literacy that is confined only to school. The outer circle is thus represented as an unlimited boundary – a broken line – to show that understandings developed in this way can be generalized to infinite situations.

When the three analytic models are compared, the contrast in the scope of the frames of reference between each of the student teacher categories becomes clear. Task managers see themselves as working within a very limited set of boundaries. Curriculum deliverers extend these boundaries to include the curriculum in a sense that is broader than an individual lesson, but this is still a closed frame, with limits clearly defined by the scope of the curriculum. The concept/skill builders have a greatly extended frame of reference, which has the next level of the authentic discourse of the subject as the ultimate goal.

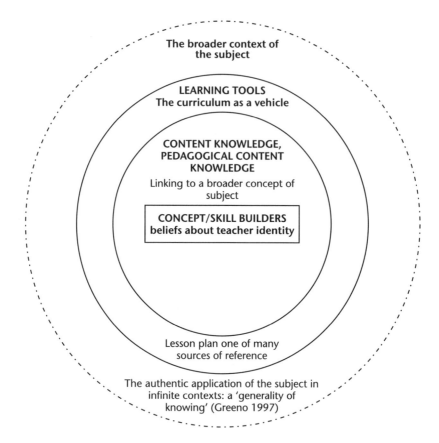

Figure 5.4 A simplified representation of the perceived professional context for concept/skill builders' conception of teaching

This opens up the frame of reference in a way that has no limits, as authentic activity within the subject is infinitely possible. It is only in this model that the subject as a set of specialized understandings has a genuine place.

Conclusions and implications

It has long been recognized that there is a huge framework of specialized knowledge that teachers need to have developed in order to teach literacy effectively. However, the findings from this study suggest that the belief systems through which such knowledge is accessed, channelled and shaped are as important as the concepts and skills themselves. This understanding is inextricably bound up with teacher identity. The ability to see connections and to help pupils to make them centres on how teachers see their primary role in the classroom and how this influences the actions they take. If their main principles for action are bound up with notions of task management and keeping children busy, these connections will not be made. Teachers need to see their primary role in the classroom as a catalyst for learning – the link between pupil, curriculum and subject, task and learning, classroom and the world beyond it.

Implications

The role of teacher identity in initial teacher education
The consideration of teacher identity needs to be a central factor in initial teacher education. All parties involved in the training partnership need to be involved in asking questions about the role of the teacher in ways that include but go beyond the practicalities of how to behave in the classroom. Student teacher educators need to be themselves considering the ultimate goals of education, and the role of the teacher in achieving them, in order to help student teachers extend their thinking and challenge their preconceptions. This is a sizeable task, when the often overwhelming external demands lead us in a direction that is mainly concerned with performance and accountability and leave us very little time for philosophical analysis.

The importance of the school context for student teachers' learning
The school context is very important for student teachers' learning. Only within this context can the essential connections be made between learner, curriculum, subject and context. The findings from the study have clearly demonstrated the importance of context in learning and decontextualized experience can have limited value in helping student teachers to fully understand the complex processes involved in scaffolding children's learning in literacy.

The need to help student teachers to make connections
School-based mentors also need to be helped to see the importance of making these connections explicit to student teachers. This means ensuring that they themselves can make such connections between learner, subject and curriculum. This is difficult for one person, when there are so many subjects to consider. There may well be an important role for subject coordinators to help in rationalizing time and expertise.

Student teachers' learning away from school
The importance of school-based learning does not mean that there is no place for learning away from school. The findings suggest that student teachers need

time and space to be able to distance themselves from the practicalities of the school setting, which can be overwhelming in the immediacy of their demands. Connections need to be made with the subject beyond the curriculum and the world beyond the classroom. Time and effort needs to be given to developing beliefs and values about the subject that will help give validity to the importance of these connections. In Bruner's (1966) terms, the core of the subject needs to be explored and valued. There is a case to be made for doing this in intense, focused episodes away from school, before using these ideas back within the school context. Taking the sociocultural approach that has underpinned the study, this needs to happen in a continuous, iterative process, so that connections can be constantly made, strengthened and reinforced in both places.

The impact of the curriculum

All those involved in supporting the learning of student teachers need to be aware of the potential impact of detailed curricula on their thinking and learning. Both in school and in university settings we need to be wary that we do not ourselves become so involved in meeting the demands of the curriculum that we lose sight of the broader purposes it is supposed to serve. As I have already suggested, this is an enormously demanding expectation for one school mentor, who has to do this with all subjects of the curriculum. Specialized use of subject leaders in supporting student teachers in the relevant area seems a logical way ahead.

Shared language

ITE training partnerships need to ensure they develop a shared language and frameworks for understanding how student teachers develop and the forms of support and types of understanding that are needed. Developing a shared language must be a two way process evolving over time, and with a commitment of effort, time and resources from both university institutions and schools. In practical terms this is likely to involve systematic opportunities for sharing of expertise in the form of mentor training (for both ITE tutors and school-based mentors, with input from both sides of the partnership) and other channels of genuine communication.

PART 4
Children's Knowledge and Teachers' Interventions

Recent emphasis on 'effective teaching' has led to careful observation of class-room exchanges with specific attention being given to what teachers know and do (Shulman 1998; Wray *et al.* 2002). Professional knowledge, often character-ized as including general and specific pedagogic knowledge, is revealed through teaching practices; content and curriculum knowledge, described in the UK as subject knowledge; and knowledge of the ends of education, expressed through the belief systems of teachers of literacy. These different aspects of professional experience are recognized through teachers' ability to talk about them – their meta-cognitive knowledge. However, such studies of effective teaching almost inevitably omit two important areas of teachers' professional capital: their knowledge of learners, and the cultures which surround the learning.

The two chapters in this section are carefully drawn examples of the importance of these areas of teacher knowledge. Kathy Coulthard, Evelyn Arizpe and Morag Styles show how children's ability to read and discuss images in picturebooks led to a thoughtful analysis of teacher interventions in reading. The researchers' contributions to the discussions about picturebooks were analysed as carefully as the children's comments and the insights from this analysis led to questions about the classroom as a site for a genuine 'community of enquiry'. From this research it became clear that 'teacher knowledge' includes speculation and toleration of uncertainty – qualities not usually associated with 'knowing'. Indeed, part of such professional expertise lies in 'not knowing' and in presenting a model of 'speculative thought and language as a tool for dealing with ambiguity'. The research carried out by Coulthard, Arizpe and Styles emphasizes children's thought and text experi-ence; it also poses challenges for teachers 'in acquiring the expertise to under-stand the complex language of the visual'. However, this chapter argues that both teachers and children can extend their ability to talk about picturebooks through participating in group interaction.

Charmian Kenner also emphasizes the knowledge about language and texts which children bring to the classroom. She describes the two added ingredients of professional capital mentioned above as 'recognition of the "whole child" as a complex and multifunctional person with an already established history in their home and community'. Her chapter outlines some findings from research with young bilingual learners, arguing like Coulthard and colleagues that teachers are crucially the 'active facilitators of linguistic and cultural creativity'. The young bilingual learners of Kenner's study demonstrate an impressive array of language and text knowledge. She goes on to show how this knowledge can be energized in the classroom for everyone's advantage by detailing the elements of an interactive pedagogy for bilingual pupils. Much of this pedagogy depends on teachers once again wanting to extend their knowledge (in this case of children's home and community learning) and being prepared to include such knowledge explicitly in regular classroom exchanges and curriculum activities.

In drawing out the threads of their research, both Kenner and Coulthard and colleagues, emphasize that acknowledging children's language and literacy knowledge leads to informed interventions so that acknowledgment of children's linguistic and cultural experience adds to teachers' professional expertise.

6 Getting inside Anthony Browne's head: pupils and teachers asking questions and reading pictures

Kathy Coulthard, Evelyn Arizpe and Morag Styles

Reading and talking pictures

A new research course on visual literacy has been introduced at the Faculty of Education in Cambridge. It is based on the Reading Pictures project, which resulted in the publication of *Children Reading Pictures: Interpreting Visual Texts* (Arizpe and Styles 2003) and is aimed at teaching students to undertake qualitative research, investigate how children interpret pictures, and analyse how such research can contribute to our understanding of the slippery concept of visual literacy. The tutors asked the students, most of whom were aspiring teachers, to prepare a list of questions about a specific picturebook for an informal individual interview with pupils aged between 4 and 11. As we were helping students to revise some of the proposed questions, it struck us again how difficult this apparently simple task was. How do you formulate questions that open up the picturebook rather than close it, that are not limited to formulaic comprehension skills, that lead to productive interactions between teacher/researcher and learner and that engage readers in the construction of meaning – questions that inspire and that you know children will keep thinking about long after they have left the classroom?

It reminded us of the beginning of the Reading Pictures project three years ago when we set ourselves the same task: finding challenging questions that would enable us to discover what children knew about how to read pictures, what impact other skills and experiences brought to bear on their facility with visual texts, and how word and image work together. Despite years of teaching and research experience we did not always succeed, but through the children we soon learned where our instincts were right.

The thrust of our initial research was about looking and thinking, but the medium through which learning took place was talk and we found ourselves returning to the insights of Michael Halliday (1975), Lev Vygotsky (1986), Gordon Wells (1986, 1999, this volume Chapter 13) and others to make sense of the interactions between children, teachers, books and pictures. Drawing on these theories, we will argue in this chapter that it is through the interaction of the young readers with the researcher and with their peers that their interpretations of text, especially visual text, becomes more precise, more sophisticated and more mature. Through examining the role of language in understanding the visual, we will attempt to show how children (and the teacher/researcher) can move towards a more thorough understanding of multimodal texts.

The aim of the Reading Pictures project was to explore how children responded to complex, multilayered picturebooks by the well known artists, Anthony Browne (*The Tunnel* and *Zoo*) and Satoshi Kitamura (*Lily Takes a Walk*). Each book was read to children of different ages in seven different schools in areas in the east and south of England with widely divergent catchment areas. We then individually interviewed 12 pupils from each school who were also asked to draw in response to the text. Finally, we set up semi-structured group interviews. Overall we talked to 126 pupils, including bilingual learners, pupils with reading difficulties and pupils with special needs.

Some of our questions ended up being very simple, such as 'Tell me about this picture' or 'How does this picture make you feel?' Others were more challenging, dealing with issues like the artist's intentions, the ironic gap between word and image and the interpretation of visual metaphors. All of the questions were open and did not have objective, correct answers. Although the researchers tried to do this without imposing their opinions, they inevitably contributed to the construction of meaning. We all set out with the same list of questions for the individual interviews and attempted to stick to the schedule but the pupils' answers influenced the way the interviews proceeded. The agenda for the researcher-led group discussion (which was held later on the same day as the individual interviews) was to follow the children's leads, focusing on particular aspects of the book that they had struggled with during the interviews, or issues that the researcher thought were interesting, or attempts to tease out a more summative response to the book as a whole. This led to some fascinating discussions where the children's thinking often moved on significantly from their individual interviews.

Learning through talk

The role of dialogue in the acquisition of language has been extensively demonstrated in the seminal works of Bruner (1983, 1986), Vygotsky (1986), Wells (1986 and 1999) and, as we shall see, Halliday:

The child's task is to construct the system of meanings that represents his [sic] own model of social reality. This process takes place inside his own head; it is a cognitive process. But it takes place in contexts of social interaction, and there is no way it can take place except in these contexts. As well as being a cognitive process, the learning of the mother tongue is also an interactive process. It takes the form of the continued exchange of meaning between the self and others. The act of meaning is a social act. The social context is therefore not so much an external condition on the learning of meanings as a generator of the meanings that are learnt. And part of the social context is the language that is used by the interactants – the language the child hears around him.

(Halliday 1975: 139–40)

Most children enjoy looking at picturebooks and their intimate inter-action with the authors and artists provide new ideas and understandings. However, if the meaning making process is going to develop more fully, it is advantageous if it occurs within social settings involving other participants such as parents, teachers or peers. In our study, we found that the enjoyment of the picturebooks increased and was significantly enriched as the children shared their understanding of narrative, symbols, artistic intentions and even their own cognitive processes, by looking and talking with others.

The work of Wells (1986, 1999 and this volume) extends the implications of Halliday's work by stressing that if children are going to be able to com-municate beyond the basic needs of everyday life, they require exposure to other kinds of experiences as well as support in order to do so. It is usually at school where this support should be forthcoming, but this is the point where questions need to be asked about the quantity, quality and ownership of the oracy experiences provided for young learners. In the 'partnership model' pro-posed by Wells, the teacher aims to facilitate learning and 'enrich their mean-ing making' (1986: 222) rather than direct it and ensure its reproduction. This entails a responsiveness to the discoveries children are making about the sym-bolic nature of language and allowing time and space for talking, listening and sharing these discoveries. Wells refers to research, such as that of Barnes and Todd (1995), that has shown how groups of children – even those with difficul-ties in reading and writing – can use discussion to solve problems, arguing that pupils learn more effectively as they turn discussion into real conversations.

However, the work of Mroz *et al.* (2000) suggests that such opportunities are still not being provided in many classrooms. The emphasis during the Literacy Hour, for example, is on simple recitation questions and recent research by Mroz and Wall (2002) reveals that 82 per cent of the interactions during this time are coming from the teacher. Opportunities for students to contribute are lost as well as time for extended answers or probing questions.

Asking questions about visual texts

Summing up the work of language theorists in his book, *How Children Think and Learn*, Wood concludes:

> Human nature may ensure that most children learn how to talk. Social experience and schooling . . . play a central role in determining both what they have to say and how they are able to express what they mean.
>
> (Wood 1988: 143)

But how does this apply to visual literacy? If we consider Wood's comment in terms of the visual, we could paraphrase his statement as follows: 'Human nature may ensure that most children can see, but social experience and schooling play a central role in determining both what they look at and what they have to say about what they see.' Following this line of thinking, we would argue that although most children can arrive at a basic understanding of visual texts by themselves, they need support to develop their visual literacy just as they do with other literacies. As Averignou and Ericson (1997: 280) argue 'the superficiality of pupil's comprehension of much of what they view, suggest that higher order visual skills do not develop unless they are identified and "taught".'

The question we addressed as researchers is the same as that posed by teachers in a classroom context: how do we teach these higher order visual skills? Can children learn these skills if the questions about the texts always come from the teacher, as in a traditional Literacy Hour format? Again, like other literacies, one needs to begin with texts that are both challenging and inviting like quality picturebooks – and then provide the support for under-standing them in more depth. As we have already indicated, real conversations such as the ones our researchers held during the group discussions, can elicit profound and insightful responses, even from children who are not aca-demically gifted or who are still learning to speak English. An exploration into the nature of the verbal interaction that takes place in these exchanges shows how children and the teacher/researcher build on each other's responses to make meaning and thus create a 'community of inquiry' (Wells 1999) where knowledge is co-constructed. This is especially apparent in the child/adult interactions around picturebooks, given that many adults, bombarded with images in daily life, have forgotten how to look closely and at length at a picture.

Barbara Kiefer, who also analysed children's responses to picturebooks, based her description of the verbal data from her research on Halliday's lan-guage functions: informative, heuristic, imaginative and personal. However, she points out that although one can identify these categories for research purposes, the children's discussion 'demonstrates the fluid and dynamic ways in which children use language; one function quickly gives rise to another as one child supports or extends the understanding of another' (Kiefer 1995: 34). Like us, Kiefer is convinced that picturebooks provide opportunities for talk which deepens children's response to books and to art in general, but she emphasizes that it is not only the picturebooks themselves that are important for stimulating meaningful discussion, but also the teachers 'who directed their eyes and their ideas' (Kiefer 1995: 44). She describes two different approaches to reading Maurice Sendak's outstanding, yet strange and troubling, *Outside Over There*. In one group, the typical pattern was teacher initiation, child response and teacher evaluation of the response. In the other group, the teacher invited prediction and reflection, and let the children speak more than she did. Questions that invited speculation, reflection and serious thought led to rich collaborative talk and deeper understandings than the first group managed.

Another useful approach we encountered during our research was to help the children make explicit the processes by which they had arrived at their ideas about the meanings in the picturebook – what you might call metacognitive awareness. Helen Bromley points out how teachers need time to become acquainted with a book and to think about the questions they are going to ask beforehand in order to have 'quality conversations'. She also suggested that the 'discussions about the picturebook provided the children with a meaningful context to reflect not only on what they knew, but most significantly on how they knew it' (Bromley 2003: 162).

Heather Mines (2000) describes the processes by which the children she interviewed in a separate study, about Browne's *The Tunnel* (two-thirds of whom were children of ethnic minority origin – like several in our sample), arrived at their understanding of the book. She reports on the 'sheer amount of language practice' involved; as the children became more engaged in the discussions, their conjectures led them to support and collaborate with each other and their language became more tentative and exploratory, including many uses of 'think', 'might', 'because', 'probably'. The use of these words which we also found in the responses to our study – showed that there was an 'increase [in] their tolerance of uncertainty', a willingness to accept alternative meanings (Mines 2000: 202).

We also found that during the group discussions the children grappled with many different language functions in their attempts to express their responses. The crucial interventions of the teacher/researchers scaffolded their learning and enabled them to work through their zone of proximal development into deeper understanding. In the following example Kathy Coulthard demonstrates how, by providing a sensitive context, children's answers were listened to and taken into account and where the contributions of each member of the group helped transform and negotiate meaning, so that learning moved on to a higher level. In this section, Kathy analyses her own experience as a researcher but also as a participant in this particular community of learners.

Caged darkness and free light

Browne uses tantalizing devices and images to signal there is more to *Zoo* than first meets the eye: black and white endpapers, a hamster in a cage, a snail breaking the boundary of a picture frame are only a few of them. The extent to which young readers recognize or heed this signal is, however, another matter. Do they know, for example, that objects can mean something other than themselves? Do they bring an open mind to what they see? Are they inclined to take risks and play with ideas? Are they willing to take time to look and look again, unearthing fragments of meaning and piecing them together? Finally, do they think that all this looking and thinking is worth the effort?

These questions (and many more) were preoccupying me as I was trying to make sense of the interviews I had conducted with pupils aged 5 to 11 on their understanding of *Zoo*. Some pupils stood out for their critical reading of image, their open-mindedness and their ability to 'tolerate ambiguity' while searching for meaning (Doonan 1993: 11), whereas others were clustered further along the continuum, taking image more at face value and unwilling to linger. There were, of course, pupils in between whose perception and interpretation fluctuated with each image as did their inclination to pore over details and play with ideas. As well as being interviewed, these same pupils had the opportunity to revisit the book in a group discussion, but this time there was no interview schedule and researchers were free to choose their focus. The interviews had given me a sense of where I would place pupils on the continuum from critical to literal, but this sense would be shaken in the group discussions when I would experience pupils thinking and talking in a very different way. This was especially true for those who had veered towards the literal with little recognition of pictorial metaphor and analogy, and who then went on in the group discussions to display a willingness to pore over image and work hard at excavating its symbolic meaning.

The transformation was particularly striking in the discussion I led with six 11-year-olds, four of whom had been interviewed individually and two others, Belinda and Scott, who had joined us at the end of the day. And this is where I return to the black and white endpapers, the hamster in a cage, and the snail, those rather enigmatic images at the beginning of *Zoo* that had proved confusing. The pupils' interpretation of the endpapers in interview, for example, were as an extension of the cover where a pattern of black and white wavy lines form the background to a picture of the family visiting the zoo. They each explained the artist's intentions in this way:

Lisa For like a zebra effect
Daniel Because he likes zebras, he likes to get the colour in somehow
Fabio To make it an idea of an animal skin. . . a zebra

Only Stavroulla passed, saying she had no idea why Anthony Browne should have done this.

Daniel was one of the interviewed pupils who had looked at the first few pages of *Zoo* and interpreted the notion of artist's intentions as entirely personal, probably based on his own experience of illustration. He responded to the hamster and the snail in a similar way to the endpapers:

> I think that he has got a pet hamster and he wanted to dedicate the book to the pet hamster.

> He probably likes snails and snails are so small . . . he wanted to put it in and so no one notices it but the people who read it, notice it. Well, he might like snails.

For Daniel, as well as many others, these images proved ineffective as early warning signals of the moral issue that lies at the heart of the book. For these to do their work, he would have to know that objects can represent something other than themselves, that colours can symbolize abstract ideas and emotions, and that the reading of image needs to be in the context of the whole book. It would be all too easy to judge Daniel's interpretation as weak and literal, but what follows demonstrates that he was only a whisker away from having profound insights into the meaning of the images and from being able to use metaphor as a powerful way of expressing his insights.

In response to a focused question about the endpapers later in the day during the group discussion, Lisa recognizes that 'they are totally different colours' but Daniel still persists with the zebra theme from the interviews: 'cos he probably really likes zebras'. Doonan (1993) reminds us that meanings do not come attached to this kind of enigmatic image and that some pupils will need help in selecting from a menu of possibilities and applying those that seem to fit that particular image within a particular context. My next question was framed to support the group in considering the endpapers in the context of the book as a whole and proved to be a pivotal question that causes the group to see in a different way:

Interviewer: What do you think Browne is trying to signal to the reader?
Belinda: Is it that he doesn't like animals in the zoo?

Daniel: It is probably like the black one represents the animals in the cages but the white one represents the animals free.

Interviewer: What are the colours doing to you that make you think in that way?

Daniel: Cos the black is like all trapped in a dungeon or something and the white is like far out in like the sky.

The moral dimension of animals in captivity has now been recognized and causes Daniel to respond in a much more reflective way, drawing on personal association to understand why Browne should have put a solid black page opposite a white one. I sense a buzz around the group as the thinking and talking changes gear and we are off – revisiting images and allowing our reading to be shaped by a powerful moral issue. We are all in a Vygotskian 'zone of proximal development', learning how to look at image, come up with interpretations and negotiate possible meanings. I am also struggling to ask the kind of questions and make the kind of comments that will move pupils on while still following their lead, a form of 'scaffolding' described by Bruner (1983).

Lisa had been the only pupil in interview who had recognized the caged hamster on the title page as symbolizing captivity: 'Because it's still an animal and it's in a cage and they should be free.' In the group discussion I ask why Anthony Browne had chosen to draw this picture when the book is about going to the zoo. Lisa responds by reiterating the association between the hamster and the animals in the zoo:

That's trapped as well? He's like supposed to be running around free rather than being kept in a cage.

There is further evidence of Daniel's realization that images can have metaphorical meanings as he reformulates his original idea of the book being dedicated to Browne's pet hamster to link Lisa's response to the artist's intention:

Because he probably thought that any cage that any animal is in is a trapped place, but when it's free it's better than being in, trapped.

There is no pressure on any member of the group to speak. Fabio has not yet chosen to enter the discussion, although he has been engaged in looking at the pictures. He had responded literally to many of the opening images in interview although he had interpreted the hamster as a signifier of going to see animals and their habitat at the zoo. His voice is now heard confirming Daniel's statement about the artist's intention and signalling that he too has recognized that image needs to be read in relation to the story in general:

Trying to give an idea of the animals which are caged.

Belinda hears this and extends the group's understanding of captivity by highlighting what could be happening right under their noses:

> It's like he was saying that it's not just the zoo where animals are trapped, it's at people's homes as well.

The link between human beings and animals is beginning to be recognized and will shape further reading.

The ideas are bouncing backwards and forwards. We move onto the image of the snail flying out of the picture ahead of gridlocked cars bound for the zoo. The ironic joke of a notoriously slow creature going faster than the traffic jam had not been spotted during the interviews with other groups of pupils. In her individual interview, Stavroulla had gone further than most in making a connection around slowness but had interpreted the intention as signalling that 'Not just snails are slow, people are as well'. She was a pupil who needed to be prompted to look and think again as she took few risks in exploring image and had so far chosen not to contribute to the group discussion. At this point in the group discussion I urge the children to try and get inside Anthony Browne's head and think why he might have planted this image; I urge them to read like an illustrator. Stavroulla takes up the challenge and a dialogue follows which demonstrates her struggle to read the image in the light of past experience and present context:

> Stavroulla: Because it's in a traffic jam and it's slow and snails are slow . . . and when it's going off the page it means the cars are going . . . because cars are going to go.
> Interviewer: But you're saying that a snail is slow?
> Stavroulla: And the cars are in a traffic jam so they're not going to go.
> Interviewer: So who's going faster?
> All: The snail.

I wonder if Stavroulla is drawing on her experience of computer games and interactive books which use similar devices to signal that players/readers should click here to move to a higher level or turn the page. Despite her lead, the visual joke is still not recognized by the group and here I refer to Styles and Arizpe's (2001) reminder that this would depend on sophisticated metacognitive awareness and 'familiarity with metaphorical linguistic terms and their application, such as "going at a snail's pace" or "the traffic was crawling along"'. I am about to admit defeat and move on when Scott's thinking loops back to the previous image of the caged hamster which the group eventually read as a metaphor for captivity. He now offers an interpretation consistent with this thinking and I see an opportunity to look at the snail in a wider context:

> Scott: It [the snail] might have been like Daniel said, it was kind of free-dom . . . sort of like freedom.
>
> Interviewer: He's there to represent freedom? Who's not free in this picture?
>
> Lisa: The family and well the other drivers as well. They're all trapped, aren't they?
>
> Interviewer: What are their cages?
>
> Stavroulla: Their cars.

Fabio enters the discussion again. Like Stavroulla, he has needed more time to hear thinking and language modelled, before he feels safe enough to take a risk and speak out. Here, he brings together a collage of ideas that have already been floated in the group and formulates them in his own words:

> I think the same as Daniel cos like the snail's getting away like, cos usually the animals are caged. Now all the cars and all the people are caged and . . . the snail's got freedom now.

Although the connection between the snail and the caged animals is question-able, there is little doubt that he understands that freedom and captivity are central themes in the book. He has established himself as an equal member of this community of inquiry, a community which is also 'interpretive', to use Stanley Fish's (1980) term in a pedagogical situation. Fish considers an 'interpretive community' as one which uses a group of strategies – identifying and analysing metaphor, irony, humour, for example – to understand text. As the children and the researcher in this particular group communicate and share their meaning making strategies, they are able to continue their collect-ive recreation of the text.

The snail is pivotal in shaping subsequent readings. Once it has been recognized as an icon of freedom, there is an expectation that Browne would have included similar icons throughout the book. Scott finds the butterfly outside the tiger's enclosure and notices it is the same colour as the tiger:

> They're like the same colour and he's trying to say like they're the same animals. One's stuck in the cage and one's out free.

He then goes on to draw our attention to a reflection in the water in front of the polar bear enclosure which Daniel thinks could be that of a swan 'flying free in the air'. We return to this image as we contemplate the final page showing the zoo buildings silhouetted against a moonlit sky with two beautiful wild geese flying away towards the horizon. It is Scott again who notices the birds and announces:

> Ah, they've gone free . . . they're free but how come?

I can be heard musing on the tape:

> They're free, aren't they? Ah. I'm trying to think, they're not swans, they're wild geese. I'm just thinking back to the polar bears. Is this a reflection of wild geese in the water, because swans can only fly a few beats. They can actually get up there, but they're too heavy, aren't they. But wild geese fly long distances.

The balance of power has been levelled and I am no longer the guide, but equally immersed in poring over pictures and making meaning. This is intoxicating and we are all experiencing the pleasure that derives from 'active contemplation' (Doonan 1993: 47).

So intent are we in testing our theory about icons of freedom that we become excited about a shape that looks remarkably like a fish in the water of the penguin enclosure. As we lean closer to inspect the image, I suddenly realize that the printed surface has been torn off to reveal the white paper underneath. We all dissolve into laughter and reluctantly take leave of the book and each other.

Three months after the initial research, I conducted a follow-up interview with Daniel to find out whether the experience of the group discussion had continued to impact on his personal construction of meaning. What was striking in this interview was not only his understanding of the symbolic meanings in the pictures, but also his ability to articulate abstract ideas more clearly, concisely and confidently. This is how he responds to the endpapers in relation to the book as a whole:

> Black represents the darkness in the cages and the white represents the free light. Animals should be free like the humans and not in dark cages.

Even more telling is his own pictorial response in which he uses image to represent the themes within the book and demonstrate his understanding of symbolism (Figure 6.1). Without a chance to draw in response to *Zoo* or to have a lengthy group discussion where the book was revisited, I would never have guessed the profundity of Daniel's understanding. Daniel was not an exception in this regard. If space permitted, evidence could be provided about the understanding of image other children reached through their interaction. This is a telling lesson for the classroom.

Figure 6.1 Daniel's drawing in response to *Zoo*

Conclusion

Kathy began her account by asking a series of questions about pupils' appreciation of image. Given the dramatic shifts in thinking and talking that occurred in the one hour session she describes, we would now add another set of questions to be answered by those who are responsible for shaping pupils' reading and viewing histories. They are as follows:

- Do pupils have access to the kind of complex texts that both excite and challenge them and do they have time and opportunity to explore them?
- Do pupils experience being part of a community of inquiry in which they are encouraged to take risks and play with ideas in the process of constructing meaning?

- Do pupils hear speculative thought and language modelled as a tool for dealing with ambiguity?
- Do pupils have opportunities to revisit texts to refine meanings, reconstruct their original thoughts and discover the text anew?

Setting up the conditions for such powerful classroom interactions about visual literacy between pupils and teachers, and among pupils talking together, requires the combination of rigorous yet flexible planning, careful listening and imaginative response on the part of the teacher, as well as outstanding visual texts for subject matter. In addition, there are challenges posed for teachers in acquiring the expertise to understand the complex language of the visual. It can be a steep learning curve for those of us whose own education privileged the verbal over the visual. However, it was evident from our study that both children and teachers could develop the skills needed to talk about picturebooks through group interaction if they found it personally, aesthetically and intellectually rewarding, as well as socially enjoyable. Through penetrating questions the teacher can provide a frame of reference within which children can relate their own experience to text and image and this in turn works to foster the development of language and thought (Vygotsky 1986). This development can be taken even further by focusing the discussion on the actual process of making meaning, on how 'meta-knowledge' is collaboratively constructed by members of a group (a description of this development can be found in the chapter on picturebooks and metaliteracy in Arizpe and Styles 2003).

In *Dialogic Inquiry*, Wells (1999) gives examples of how teachers become involved in 'communities of inquiry'. We also discovered that when trainee teachers conducted their own research, formulated questions and critically examined their data, they not only learned about picturebooks, but also discovered the language of the visual and how to use it with children. In the end, researchers, future educators and pupils formed 'overlapping communities of inquiry . . . in which everyone is able to learn and, at the same time, to assist others to learn' (Wells 1999: 265). Our initial view was that pupils' individual responses would depend on experience and disposition, but given the responsiveness of the diverse groups of pupils in our study, we now believe that creating the conditions described above can mediate individual experience and disposition and make it possible for us all to learn 'from the company we keep'.

7 An interactive pedagogy for bilingual children

Charmian Kenner

'Would you like to do more Gujarati at school?'
'Yes, write things in Gujarati, draw things and write the words, and make things.'
> (Interview with Meera, aged 7, in a south London primary school)

In this statement, Meera expresses her hope and belief that her home language, Gujarati, could be integrated into the everyday activities of her primary school class. For bilingual children, interaction between a rich variety of linguistic and cultural experiences is an ever present feature of their lives. If schools can build on these interactions, the potential contribution to children's learning is huge. To do so requires a commitment to developing education for a multilingual and multicultural society, with the all round benefits which this will entail for children from both monolingual and bilingual backgrounds. Whilst the need for a national educational policy is clear, practitioners also have a key part to play. This chapter will discuss how teachers can enhance children's educational experiences by enabling linguistic and cultural interaction to take place within the classroom, and between school and community life.

As teachers know, the quality of their relationships with children is key, and depends on a recognition of the 'whole child' as a complex and multifunctional person with an already established history in their home and community. In the case of bilingual children, an important element is the recognition of their bilingual and bicultural knowledge, which is a fundamental part of their identities as learners. I shall first look at what kind of knowledge children might have, based on the findings of research with young bilingual learners in London, England.

The next step is to make links with children's knowledge in curriculum activities, and I shall discuss how this might be accomplished, drawing on the experience of an action research project which created a multilingual literacy environment in a nursery classroom. While my own experience is with young learners, a stage when it is particularly possible – and crucially important – to build links with children and families, a multilingual approach can be used with any age group and I shall suggest how this can be done.

Bilingual children's knowledge and capabilities

The majority of children in the world are bilingual. Growing up with more than one language and literacy is part of life in many countries which operate multilingually (Datta 2000), and also occurs through the increasingly common experience of families moving to a new country. From birth, children have the potential to become proficient users of any language met within their daily environment (Baker 2000). By opening our minds to these possibilities, we can discover what children have already learned in the world outside the classroom.

By the age of 3 or 4, when they begin to enter the school system, many young bilingual children will have encountered literacy materials in different languages at home, ranging from a newspaper being read by a grandparent in Turkish, to an airletter being written by a parent in Gujarati, to a Chinese calendar on the kitchen wall. As part of their continual curiosity about graphic symbols, children start to interpret the potential meanings of these texts. In some cases, they are able to combine their interpretations with ideas derived from direct instruction in their home literacy, because family members may have begun teaching them some initial reading and writing.

For example, 4-year-old Mohammed, growing up in south London, was being taught by his mother how to recognize the letters of the Arabic alphabet in preparation for joining Qur'anic classes at the age of 5 (Kenner 2000). Mohammed's older siblings already had their own copy of the Qur'an, and Mohammed would receive his when he had learned sufficient Arabic – a strong motive for literacy acquisition. When Mohammed's mother prepared a poster showing the Arabic alphabet for use in his nursery class at primary school, Mohammed proceeded to demonstrate his knowledge of the letters. As well as being able to name some of the letters for his nursery classmates, he worked by himself to produce his own version of his mother's poster in which each letter was accurately written. His mother was astonished to see Mohammed's work because she had so far only taught him to read: 'He's never written any Arabic before!' The detail of the letters was a considerable accomplishment for a 4-year-old, and showed Mohammed's desire to become a writer in Arabic.

In contrast, 3-year-old Meera (who attended the same nursery class) was being taught to write only in English by her mother because her parents thought it would be easier for her to learn one literacy first. However, Meera herself had other ideas. As well as speaking Gujarati at home, she had participated in literacy events involving Gujarati script, such as sitting next to her mother while letters were being written to her grandparents in India and writing her own 'letter', or observing her mother filling in crosswords in Gujarati newspapers. When she saw her mother writing in Gujarati for a multilingual display in the nursery, Meera climbed on a chair to do her own emergent writing underneath. She stated 'I want my Gujarati' and 'I write like my mum'. Meera's determination to find out more about Gujarati writing, fuelled by its significance in her home life, continued during the school year with a series of spontaneous versions of a poster made by her mother about Meera's favourite 'Bollywood' film video. Figure 7.1 shows one of these, with the film title and some of the characters' names written in English and Gujarati, and Meera's drawings of some of the key events.

Comments by Meera as she was making these posters in the nursery showed how, at the age of 4, she was able to think about different aspects of literacy and enhance her learning by comparisons between her two writing systems. Like Mohammed, she looked closely at the detail of letters, noting that her mother's version of the English 'a' looked different, rather like an inverted 'p' ('my mummy done a "p" – never mind'), and considering in what order she produced the different elements of a Gujarati letter (asking herself as she wrote it for the second time 'Did I do the line first? Yes I did'). Noticing that her mother had written three groups of letters representing the names of the

Figure 7.1 Meera's poster in Gujarati and English about the film 'Nashib', with names of the main characters and drawings of events

film heroes in Gujarati, but that only two groups of letters appeared in English underneath, she asked 'Why three?' She had realized that there should be a correspondence between equivalent items in the two languages, and indeed it turned out that Meera's mother had not been sure how to transliterate the third hero's name.

Some children, like Mohammed, begin to attend community language classes at the age of 5 or 6, while also learning to read and write in English at primary school. A recent research project (Kenner *et al.* forthcoming) showed that young children are very capable of dealing simultaneously with more than one language and script. Case studies of 6-year-olds attending Saturday school classes in Chinese, Arabic or Spanish produced striking evidence of their ideas about different writing systems. This knowledge was demonstrated when the children were engaged in 'peer teaching sessions', showing their primary school classmates how to write in their home literacy.

Selina, for example, who had been attending Chinese school since the age of 5, was already proficient at writing Chinese characters. A page from her first year exercise book (Figure 7.2) shows the process of building up a character through the correct stroke sequence, and then practising it for several columns. Each stroke needed to be executed precisely, to achieve a character which was both correct and aesthetically pleasing. Selina was proud of her writing, demonstrating characters of considerable complexity to her primary school peers. She also understood that the Chinese writing system operated very differently from English. Chinese does not have an alphabet; rather, most Chinese characters correspond to an English word. Selina's mother was teaching her about the meaning of different elements within a character, for example, the symbol for 'fire' appears in a number of associated characters such as 'lamp'. Selina would point out the symbols she found within characters, such as 'fire' in 'autumn'.

Tala, learning Arabic, emphasized that her 'pupils' in peer teaching sessions must start from the right-hand side of the page when doing Arabic writing, and she provided a helpful arrow to remind them. She also commented on grammatical features of Arabic such as male and female verb endings, writing an explanation to emphasize (in case her audience was unsure) that 'femail is a girl' and 'mail is a boy'.

Brian showed his primary school class the typical way of learning to write in Spanish, by forming syllables which combined a consonant with a vowel. Using the example of the letter 'm', and translating his Spanish teacher's explanation into English, he told his classmates 'the M on her own doesn't say anything, just "mmm" – you have to put it together . . . with "a" it makes "ma" '. He also showed his 'pupils' how to write and pronounce the Spanish letter 'ñ' (as in the word 'España'), saying 'It's a different N'.

We can see that these children – all of whom were also making steady progress in English – were deriving considerable benefit from the experience of

Figure 7.2 A page from Selina's first year exercise book: learning the stroke sequence to build up a character (in the right hand column) and practising the whole character

biliteracy. As a result of their participation in the research project, their knowledge became evident to their primary school teachers, just as Mohammed and Meera's understandings had become visible in the nursery class. Later in this chapter, I will discuss how the teachers' responses enabled children's bilingual knowledge to become more closely woven into their primary school learning. First, though, I shall take a closer look at the complexity of children's home and community learning.

Linguistic and cultural interactions in children's home lives

Children's spoken and literate experiences are an integral part of their cultural lives. Bilingual children are often conceived of as living in 'two cultures', each relatively separate from the other. However, this is not necessarily the case. For all the children described above, their everyday experiences in homes and communities involved an intertwining of learning in Arabic, Gujarati, Chinese or Spanish with learning in English. In terms of spoken language, they often switched back and forth from their home language into English with older siblings and sometimes with parents too. This is a typical characteristic of communicative interactions in ethnic minority communities living in an English dominant society (Li 1994). If children continue to have plenty of opportunities to use their home language as well as English, they can become proficient in both, and proficient code switchers too, as was the case with a number of children in the research studies.

In terms of literacy, children's homes also involved a variety of texts in their different languages. Mohammed, for example, was being taught to write in English by his sister as well as learning Arabic with his mother. He engaged in 'café' roleplays in which he took orders for pizza and burgers and delivered these items on an imaginary motorbike, and asked his mother to draw up a register for a 'school' roleplay in an old register book from primary school. Meera's family ran a small supermarket and she often helped in the shop, bringing the leaflets available there into her play as well as becoming knowledgeable about the purpose of National Lottery cards.

The families of Selina, Tala and Brian had cable and satellite TV, giving them access to a huge range of programmes using different spoken and written languages. In Selina's home, the children would switch channels from *Who Wants to be a Millionaire?* in English to a 'soap' series from Hong Kong. Tala and her siblings would be watching Arabic TV news at one moment, followed by the archetypal English children's programme *Blue Peter*. Selina's living-room walls displayed Chinese New Year banners alongside posters of her favourite English pop group, SClub7. Meanwhile, Brian and his brother read the BBC children's magazine *Learning is Fun* as well as the Spanish books for children which their mother had brought from Colombia.

The children observed in the research projects were accustomed to such multilingual and multicultural literacy environments. These were the home settings in which their language and literacy knowledge was nurtured and developed. In comparison, their primary school lives could be characterized as largely monolingual and monocultural, and therefore as having only a limited connection with children's home experience. Let us now consider how such connections might be made.

Developing multilingual learning environments in the classroom

An interactive pedagogy for bilingual children involves several elements. The first of these is a teacher who sees bilingualism as a *resource* rather than a problematic condition, and wishes to expand her knowledge about her pupils' home and community learning. It is not necessary to be an expert on what happens in children's homes – indeed, this is not even possible, given the huge variety of linguistic and cultural experiences which would be relevant to any multilingual group of pupils. What is important, and will be sensed by children and families, is a clearly stated support for bilingualism and an open-minded interest in how children are achieving this.

Support and interest are most strongly demonstrated by the second element of the pedagogy, which is a *direct engagement* with children's bilingual learning in the classroom. In the research project in Meera and Mohammed's nursery class, I worked collaboratively with the teacher to find out in what ways it was possible to create a multilingual literacy environment. We began by informally talking with parents about literacy materials and events in different languages which children enjoyed at home. In this way we found out that, for example, Mohammed liked listening to a tape of a children's song about the Arabic alphabet. We invited Mohammed to bring this tape into the nursery so that the whole nursery group could hear it, and asked his mother to make a poster showing the alphabet letters (with a transliteration in English) so that we could sing along with the tape.

The third step is to *integrate* bilingual material into curriculum activities. In the case of the Arabic tape and poster, these became part of the nursery's investigation of how graphic symbols relate to meaning – an essential building block for early literacy. As well as the English alphabet, we now had a new set of different looking symbols which related to a different set of sounds. The teacher talked about this with the whole class, and, whether bilingual or monolingual, the children were intrigued. Extra impetus was given to their understanding of the concept of sound–symbol relationships. Mohammed's own Arabic alphabet poster was displayed alongside an English poster, next to a cassette player into which children could place different tapes. Over the next few weeks, the children were observed to select the English alphabet song, or the Arabic one, and to dance to the music while pointing to various letters on the posters, showing that they were thinking about the possible connections. Children also made their own alphabet posters, using the English and Arabic posters as a resource. Again, this extended the range of their investigations into literacy.

The fourth element of the pedagogy is to give *institutional support* to children's home and community learning activities. In the nursery, this was happening directly through the important place being given to bilingual learning in the classroom. For Mohammed, it meant that he gained the opportunity to further explore and reflect on his home experiences of the Arabic alphabet. A few weeks after making his first poster, he decided to make a similar one, again based on his mother's example. He also wrote some of the Arabic alphabet letters as part of a text which included a drawing of 'a snake in the garden'. The interest of his teacher and classmates legitimized Mohammed's Arabic learning, which would otherwise have occurred at the margins of officially recognized education rather than in the mainstream, and this had a positive effect on his involvement at home; his mother reported that she heard him singing the Arabic alphabet song more often.

Over the school year, many bilingual texts were produced by children in the nursery, and, by engaging with material which interested them from home, the multilingual work proved motivating to several who otherwise seemed to be 'reluctant writers'. Billy's main enthusiasm for writing at home, according to his mother, was shown when he sat alongside her as she wrote letters to Thailand, talking about what she would say to the family and doing his own writing at the same time. When Billy's mother wrote an airletter in Thai in the nursery, this led him to write some symbols of which he said 'Mu-ang Thai' ('Thailand') and 'I write like my mum' (Figure 7.3). This was the gateway to a spate of texts produced by Billy at home, including both English and Thai symbols as well as drawings of people, and to an increase in his writing at nursery. When his mother brought a birthday card to Billy from his aunt in Thailand to show us, she placed it in the nursery book bag which was designed to carry his school reading books. Her action symbolized the links built between home and school literacy.

In the pedagogy just described, each element of the process interacts with the others, leading to the development of a 'virtuous circle' which recognizes, sustains and extends children's learning. When we engaged with Meera's home language in the nursery by asking her mother to join in a multilingual activity for parents, we discovered more about Meera's interest in home literacy events; while she did her emergent Gujarati below her mother's writing, Meera began to talk about films and TV. By asking her mother more about this, we discovered that Meera loved watching Indian films with her family. Thus the second step of the pedagogic process linked back to the first, expanding our knowledge about Meera's home experiences. The third step, integrating the film material into the curriculum, owed its success to the centrality of film watching in Meera's family life. When Meera brought her film video into the nursery, we showed one of her favourite extracts during the nursery's weekly 'video time'. Her mother's poster about the film, written rapidly at our request in the nursery one morning before she left to go to work, then provided Meera with a link between home and school which inspired her to create five related texts over the next three months, adding to her learning in both English and Gujarati.

(b)

(a)

Figure 7.3 a) Extract from airletter in Thai, written by Billy's mother in the nursery b) Symbols written by Billy later that morning: 'I write like my mum' and 'Mu-ang Thai' ('Thailand')

The third element of the pedagogy, integrating bilingual learning into curriculum activities, has a direct effect on the fourth, because it is the strongest form of support for bilingualism from an institution which ethnic minority families perceive as particularly powerful – the school. It also links back to the first and second elements, because as parents and children see that home literacy materials are being used as part of the curriculum, rather than as temporary decoration, they are motivated to bring more materials and to participate in writing events in the classroom. When Billy's mother and other parents were asked to write airletters in different languages in the nursery, as if they were writing to relatives at home, they agreed to participate in this roleplay activity because they knew that their texts would be used for the children's further learning.

Another way of taking the fourth step – giving institutional support to children's home learning activities – is to initiate direct contact with community language schools. During the research project with biliterate 6-year-olds, the children's primary school teachers began to see evidence of their community school learning. The teachers were keen to meet their pupils' Saturday school teachers to find out more about this other educational setting. At a specially organized seminar, the two groups met together, with the primary teachers expressly stating that they were coming in order to learn. As the community teachers explained how they went about their work each Saturday, the mainstream teachers realized that these were colleagues with professional knowledge, whose commitment to their pupils was total despite their low paid voluntary status.

The seminar had a profound effect on the primary teachers' understanding of bilingual learning, giving them a much fuller idea of how such learning was both possible and productive. When the biliterate children taught their whole primary school class as part of the research project, the teachers used this new information to support the activity. Ming's teacher decided to give him the opportunity to teach Chinese in one of the periods assigned daily to reading and writing work, the Literacy Hour, and drew on what she had learned from the seminar to make suggestions about the kind of issues he could talk about. These suggestions linked in with Ming's own ideas; he had spontaneously set about planning his lesson at home the night before, and arrived with a set of activities already on paper. The lesson lasted for an hour and a half, with Ming's classmates thoroughly engaged in the challenge of writing Chinese characters on their Literacy Hour whiteboards. As soon as he arrived home from school that afternoon, Ming phoned me (I had also been present at the session) to ask 'Charmian, when can I teach Chinese again – the whole class?' He had already evaluated his lesson and decided which characters would be most appropriate to teach next time; the experience of teaching in mainstream school had thus validated and added to his Saturday school learning.

Maintaining an interactive pedagogy

Once having begun to make links with bilingual pupils' educational experiences outside the mainstream classroom, teachers can conduct an ongoing dialogue with children and families which enriches learning. This dialogue can include remaining aware of children's current home and community interests, and celebrating Saturday school work, for example, by making a photo display of children who attend community language classes and noting their achievements. In Britain, children can now be encouraged to record their knowledge in the European Language Portfolio designed for use in schools (CILT 2002).

Where multilingual activities have been incorporated into the curriculum, teachers can direct parents' attention to the texts made by children and what has been learnt from them, and this discussion can take place with monolingual as well as bilingual parents. The learning may involve general issues about language, such as how alphabets work, or specific content, such as how to write particular Chinese characters. In either case, teachers do not need to know the languages involved in order to facilitate learning; in the nursery there were at least ten different languages, of which we only knew one. We were able to draw on the knowledge of children, their siblings and other family members.

This interactive pedagogy can also be pursued with children in the upper primary years and with young people in secondary school. They may have had the opportunity to further develop their biliteracy knowledge at community language school, or they may have come directly from another country where they have been educated in a different language. As well as demonstrating their knowledge in activities which raise language awareness for the whole class, pupils can make use of their other literacies to write subject-based material. A project in a London secondary school involved producing web pages in English and Bengali (Anderson 2001) with a potential worldwide audience; this experience enabled the pupils to extend their range of writing in both languages. In this kind of work, texts brought from home can again be a point of reference; newspapers in different languages, for example, provide a resource for a vast number of culturally related topics.

Expanding multilingual pedagogies

Multilingual work in schools can flourish more widely if there is institutional support. At the level of the individual school, this is aided by a whole-school language policy which states that home languages are an integral part of learning. This, in turn, is given weight if national policies take a similar view. Taking

England as an example, it seems that the tide which has been running against multilingualism in education since the 1980s may be beginning to turn. Although bilingual children's knowledge has been little recognized in educational initiatives of recent years – the national curriculum of 1989 was set up on an entirely monolingual and monocultural basis – there are signs of change at a national policy level which can potentially support work in home languages in schools.

When the National Literacy Strategy began in 1998, the documentation contained the following statement:

> EAL [English as an Additional Language] learners who already know the sound system of another language and the principles of phonology and spelling can bring that awareness to bear when learning to read and write in English . . . Managed carefully, talking about literacy in languages other than English can help EAL pupils to identify points of similarity and difference between languages at word, sentence and text level.
>
> (DfEE 1998a: 107)

This suggestion appeared at the end of the Strategy document, and was not elaborated upon further. However, it provided an opening for teachers to conduct this kind of work, which would benefit not only children learning English as an additional language, but the whole class. A curriculum guidance document for early years produced in 2000 went further in requiring practitioners to plan 'opportunities for children to become aware of languages and writing systems other than English' (QCA 2000: 44), and stated that 'children's experience of different scripts at home should be acknowledged and built on when learning about the conventions of English' (QCA 2000: 47). More recently, National Literacy Strategy training materials produced for supporting children learning EAL have been revised (DfES 2002a) and now contain a module on 'Use of first languages in the Literacy Hour', supported by a comprehensive explanation (Bourne 2002) of principles and practice. Billy's experience in the south London nursery, discussed above, is used as an example in this document.

Other research on multilingual activities in classrooms in England includes exploring a West African story in the Literacy Hour to look at text construction in different languages (Gravelle 2000), using word processing to manipulate different scripts (Edwards 1998), dual-language book-making (Sneddon 1993) and drawing on children's home language knowledge to enrich vocabulary learning (McWilliam 1998). This research has also been quoted in national policy documents and acts as a rich resource for teacher training.

Multilingual work has been given extra impetus in England by the National Languages Strategy (DfES 2002b), which promises an expansion in primary school language learning. Researchers and educators with a multi-lingual vision are pressing to include a variety of languages in such pro-grammes, enabling children to build on their bilingual capabilities. Step by step, we therefore hope to expand the possibilities for bilingual learning in the curriculum.

Conclusion

Both in England and elsewhere, as increasing numbers of children live multi-lingual lives, teachers need to engage with this variety of experience and explore its potential to enhance learning. A multilingual pedagogy engages children positively by integrating their home and community knowledge into mainstream classroom work. The impact on children's self-esteem is consider-able and supports further learning both inside and outside school. Classrooms become sites where, as 7-year-old Meera envisaged, children can 'write things . . . draw things and write the words, and make things' in more than one language. Teachers become the active facilitators of this linguistic and cultural creativity.

PART 5
The Play of Ideas

In the previous section we have seen teachers working collaboratively to construct and contest meanings as they engage with picture books. We have also seen teachers and children working to integrate the worlds of home and school. In this section Teresa Grainger and Sandra Smidt explore similar themes, but in the enactive contexts of drama and play. Grainger discusses how children can learn to adopt multiple perspectives and to tolerate uncertainty and ambiguity as she teases out what is going on in a drama lesson in which teacher and children collaborate to create and inhabit a fictional world. In so doing, the children learn to see the world they have made in different ways. This is engagement of a kind that enlarges the imagination, increasing the capacity to understand how others feel, perceive and think, thus enriching their writing not by the addition of adjectives and adverbs, but by sharpening its focus and strengthening its dynamic. But drama as Grainger presents it also involves reflection, as the children evaluate what the hot seat can and can't tell them about a character, discuss the moral issues involved and consider what they are learning. This critical detachment comes not in response to an external demand, but as an urgent necessity, a means to help them understand the world they have created.

Although there is much nervousness among teachers about engaging in drama with children, its value is generally accepted by educationalists and recognized by parents. The same cannot be said of play. While it is still valued by recognized authorities on the education of young children, its place in official curricula, at least in the English speaking world, is increasingly marginal. And, as Smidt points out, many parents see play as making little or no contribution to their children's education.

Through a series of carefully drawn vignettes, Smidt demonstrates the complexity and productivity of play and the kind of human support that enables it to flourish. She moves towards a definition of play that has greater power than the implicit definition that shapes what goes on in most schools. She makes a plea for teachers to take children more seriously, observe them more closely, be more hospitable to their experiences and to communicate more effectively to both children and their parents what it is that the children are learning as they play.

Smidt sees that we have much to learn from the nurseries of Reggio Emilia. They show us ways not only of respecting and providing for children's play, but also of making the education of young children more significant and more inclusive. There is much 'border crossing' between the school and the community in which it is embedded. For Smidt play is productive because it is where the young child is in charge. Invoking Allan Luke, she argues that literacy learning needs to be more like this and, like the nurseries of Reggio Emilia, more open to the world if children are to cope with the range of literate cultures they may encounter in their lives and have some say in redesigning them. Education for literacy is a political enterprise.

8 Exploring the unknown: ambiguity, interaction and meaning making in classroom drama

Teresa Grainger

Introduction

In the current climate of accountability and prescribed curricula there appears to be little space for ambiguity and uncertainty. In literacy, accuracy in written construction and referential responses to text foreground much practice. Security and certainty are offered to teachers in the form of clear curriculum objectives, commonly used pedagogies (for example, shared and guided writing), and explicit assessment criteria (DfEE 1998a, 1999a). Such boundaries have created valuable shared frameworks within which the profession is expected to operate. Arguably, however, they have also limited teachers' and children's experience of ambiguity, their appreciation of multiple perspectives and alternative ways of seeing and doing.

Learning to live with ambiguity is both part of the process of working collaboratively and the process of making art (Nicholson 2000: 121). Teaching is an art form, not an exact science, and needs to remain open to the unknown, not limited by structures and strictures that prompt professionals to ask 'are we allowed?' Learning to tolerate ambiguity and uncertainty are critical life skills in a world in which technological innovations are driving rapid economic and social change. The ability to adapt to conditions of enduring unpredictability and contestability deserves the attention of educationalists. In the classroom, we should support children in handling the challenge of change and let them experience the unpredictable, preparing them for a world that cannot be anticipated; a world in which uncertainty is the norm. Their adaptability and flexibility will depend in part on their ability to appreciate multiple viewpoints, to value difference and to respond reflexively to the experience of living. These abilities are all elemental features of classroom drama.

As reader response theory suggests, all texts are open to interrogation and varied interpretations (Rosenblatt 1978), so through the exploration of literature, in storytelling and in drama, learners can develop and transform their perspectives, and learn to value those of others. Improvisational drama is a particularly rich medium for actively exploring the 'gaps in texts' (Iser 1978) in a manner which acknowledges ambiguity and leaves questions unanswered. As Moyles (1994) argues, one of the most significant attributes of play is the 'opportunity it affords for learning to live with not knowing'. In open-ended and interactive contexts in the imaginary world of drama, learners may safely experience the tension and confusion triggered by the unknown.

In this chapter I shall argue that drama, as the art form of social encounters, lives and breathes uncertainty, ambiguity and tension, and that through the adoption of different role perspectives, multiple meanings can be made. I shall explore how, through the acts of engagement and reflection, and through working alongside their teacher in role, children can come to tolerate uncertainty, trust the medium and make sense of their world. Young people need to experience the unknown in safe and supported contexts, taking risks and raising questions in order to learn to live comfortably with open-endedness and ambiguity.

Ambiguity in action

The uncertainty inherent in much drama often challenges teachers and children alike as the complex improvised experience unfolds. The risk taking required to teach drama has no doubt contributed to the primary profession's reluctance to embrace its potential, for teachers and student teachers are somewhat wary of this medium, with its connotations of theatre and performance (Wright 1999). Some professionals lack the confidence to engage fully and adopt a role and initially may prefer to employ drama conventions in the Literacy Hour, as part of shared reading or a precursor to writing for example. In this context, the teacher can safely become part of a short role play or a small group freeze frame, and extend their tolerance of uncertainty and experience of such open-ended conventions. Gradually, teachers can come to trust the art form, taking small risks and realizing that teacher in role work is not only possible, but also energizing and satisfying. Widening their experience of this tool for learning, teachers can learn to live with the relative unpredictability of drama's spontaneity and complexity. This may be challenging, but the motivating power of drama has the capacity to enrich both children and teachers' creative potential.

In classroom drama sessions which extend well beyond a brief foray in the Literacy Hour, the class will create and inhabit fictional worlds with their teacher, adopting and sustaining various role perspectives, and investigating, questioning and reflecting upon possible meanings together. The openness that characterizes such drama, contrasts markedly with much of the current directive teaching culture, and imaginatively involves the teacher, working both inside and outside the drama. In essence, the teacher weaves the artistic experience together through employing a variety of drama conventions and building a work in the process. The skills of instruction and management are somewhat displaced in this context, by the need to negotiate and renegotiate the direction and content of the experience. While a lesson plan with learning intentions will exist, teachers in drama need to feel at ease with releasing themselves from this, in order to respond to the needs and interests of the children and to let the drama venture into unknown, but imagined territory. Teachers may deliberately choose to leave doors open in the world of drama, to ascertain areas of interest or desire and may find themselves 'raising possibilities rather than confirming probabilities' (Taylor 1995) making the situation more complex in the process. Their focus will be on the quality of the learning, ensuring that through the collaborative interaction the children are able to construct and reflect upon meaning for themselves (Booth 1989). The following example, based on a missing girl scenario, gives an illustration of the open-ended framework and the kinds of learning involved. Together, the class explored a situation that invited speculation, questioning and varied interpretations of the imagined experience with all its ambiguities and contradictions.

A mixed age class of Years 3 and 4 children (aged 7–9 years) returned from assembly to a drama lesson with a known visiting teacher. On this occasion the teacher was in role as a police officer, urgently seeking to establish information about a fictional member of their class, Lucy, who not been seen since the end of school the day before. A handful of children responded immediately, imaginatively claiming to have seen her last night, to live next door to her, to have heard her mother shouting at her and to have observed her looking tearful recently. Further knowledge about Lucy was collected and her school books and a note were found, which simply stated *'I'm fed up with her, FED UP!'* In hinting at previous events and relationships and in foreshadowing possible future ones, the note and the evident absence of the fictional classmate operated as an effective pretext, as O'Neill (1995) describes such framing scenes in process drama. Roles were implied and ideas were generated by the process which began to operate as an 'animating current' in the drama, since in presenting the children with the problem in role, the teacher had sown the seeds of action (Taylor 1995). However, one group of children were unable to engage and suspend disbelief, and when the police officer left, despite the presence of their drama icon and experience of three prior sessions with the visiting teacher, they spoke to the learning support assistant to check on the reality of the situation. One child voiced the view that if it wasn't real, it was pointless, and was concerned with the ambiguity of intent – did the police officer mean what he said or was this pretend (Sutton-Smith 1997)? Inexperienced in drama and used to succeeding in the conventional demands of schooling and scribalism, this small group were clearly unsettled by the idea that this was a 'living fiction', an imaginary problem or 'puzzlement' of which they were a part (Chambers 1993).

Gradually, however, following a discussion about the nature of drama and imaginary worlds, these children's control of the mental process of metaxis developed (Boahl 1979; Bolton 1984). The group began to hold the real and the 'as if' situations in their minds simultaneously. Further uncertainty of a related nature emerged later in the drama, when questions were raised about Lucy's relationship with her teacher and the class watched the headteacher (the visiting teacher in role), interviewing Lucy's fictional teacher, Miss Arnold (this was their own teacher, Linda, in role). She voiced a degree of disinterest in the child's disappearance, reflected a somewhat distant relationship with Lucy and protested she could not know all her class well. The children discussed their views of this fictional teacher and some voiced concerns: 'I think she's hiding something,' 'She should know Lucy better', 'She doesn't really care', 'She's more concerned with her own life', 'I'm disappointed in her', 'It's not right, her attitude I mean'. It was clear from their awkward glances, somewhat embarrassed postures and evident discomfort in declaring their views, that although the children knew their teacher was in role, some were again experiencing the transparency of the seam between the fictional context and their own reality. This was discussed, and Jack perceptively observed, 'It didn't seem quite right, I mean I know Linda's not Miss Arnold, but it felt difficult – you know'. A sense of disorientation was evident, as the class sought to connect a working knowledge of their own teacher, with the more distant and disquieting nature of the teacher she portrayed. In taking up an identical role, albeit with alternative behaviour patterns, the illusion of their teacher's transformation was only partial. She was operating as a visibly 'social actor' yet was also observed as herself (Neelands 2000). These young learners, new to the world of drama, needed the reassurance and discussions provided by the reflection on the action, to enable them to handle their feelings, to voice their views and to interpret the text they were creating. As Heathcote (1980) has observed, reflection is a central component of drama, it enables learners to pause and consider the text they're creating, reading beneath it and against it in order to understand it more fully.

The power of the pretext and the mysterious disappearance of the girl prompted a strong desire for resolution on the part of the class: for closure and her safe return. However, drama is not restricted by linear plots, and through flashbacks and interior monologues, possible reasons for her disappearance were examined. The theme of bullying emerged and this too was explored, leading to subtle and more complex insights into Lucy's feelings and motives and her teacher's and parents' relative lack of awareness of the situation. In depicting where she was found, safe but tired and hungry, several groups showed a real sense of relief, both emotional and physical. The challenge of inhabiting the fictional world, while examining its myriad of possible realities and interpretations, had been cognitively, morally and emotionally demanding for the class. In reflecting on the drama afterwards, several commented they'd expected just to play about or act, but realized now, drama was demanding: 'I had to think fast', 'At times it was confusing – I had to work things out, that surprised me', 'It was great fun but hard work, I'm still not sure who's to blame', 'It wasn't all clear – we had to make our own minds up – that was hard', 'We don't even know how she sorted it', 'It's not ended really has it?'

In living through drama time, the class had experienced the uncertainty of the reality/fantasy divide, the predicament of the main character, the complexity and multiple perspectives of other characters (family, friends, teacher), and the unknown nature of the unfolding action, which at times was experienced as real. Arguably, active participants in any experiential learning encounter are working with ambiguity, particularly in the field of the arts (Craft 2000), however, in drama this is more marked, as the learners are both physically and psychically engaged in the dramatic action. As Claxton (2000: 18) argues, good learners are resilient and 'capable of tolerating the emotional discomfort of operating under uncertainty'. Drawn in by the imaginative predicament, the children experienced a genuine sense of tension, through their engagement in role as they responded to different interpretations of the main characters and explored the issues around her disappearance. There were additional uncertainties here too, due to the children's inexperience and therefore lack of trust in the medium of drama, and the particular power of the pretext, the girl's disappearance, which reflected a reality too often seen on the news. It was clear that the class were connecting Lucy's disappearance to real life and to their own concerns.

The additional lived experience of the drama was leant upon in the writing which followed, in which it was noticeable that most of the class used the opportunity to effect closure on the incident, to solve Lucy's problem. In the various letters, reports and diary entries produced, resolutions were described which both extended the known narrative and sought to conclude the drama. For example, one child, in role as Lucy, explained how the bullying had ceased now her teacher had intervened; another observed how she had talked to her nan who'd helped her get over it. A different child, in role as Miss Arnold the teacher, resolved to get to know Lucy better and to 'take more responsibility for my class'. Such work in role often provides a clearer than usual sense of perspective and voice, giving increased passion, power and sensitivity to children's prose (Barrs and Cork 2001; Grainger 2001, 2002).

Many of the children also chose to examine the moral consequences of the drama in their writing in role, almost as if they were talking to themselves, noting, for example, they'd never run away again, or they'd learnt to talk to someone first about their problems. In role as Lucy's mum, one boy observed in a letter to a sister, 'I must find more time to talk to her, it's really difficult being a mother'. The moral lessons voiced here had not been discussed overtly and are evidence of knowledge generated rather than transmitted (Winston 1998). These moral resonances mostly sought to close the narrative, to reduce the ambiguity experienced and to suggest a fresh start. Undoubtedly the children's views were also influenced by their knowledge of 'happy ever after' stories and an optimistic view of conflict resolution, but taken alongside other evidence from the session they reinforce the argument that uncertainty can be both challenging and artistically enriching.

Adopting multiple role perspectives

By acknowledging the rights of voices to be heard, questioned, challenged and evaluated, drama facilitates a more equitable distribution of power and influence than is often found in the primary classroom. This in turn, creates a climate in which children feel able to take more responsibility for their own learning and to influence the narrative that evolves from their own interpretation and through the adoption of multiple role perspectives. Perspectival learning is the essence of learning through drama, for the imaginary worlds that are created are metaphors to link personal experiences with the unknown or outer, social world (Henry 2000). Through the adoption of different viewpoints and the examination of alternative positions, drama opens up new ways of looking at the world which reflect the complexity of living and honour its diversity. With the teacher in role as well, the usual pedagogic power relations of the classroom are frequently altered, particularly if a less powerful role is adopted by the adult providing more space for the children to take the initiative and to take risks. Sternberg (1997) has argued that schools for the most part discourage risk taking, but in the safe world of improvisational drama, this is facilitated, especially when confident and knowledgeable teachers trust both themselves and the medium of drama.

In a drama exploring the nature of oppression, based upon Michael Morpurgo's *Blodin the Beast*, some Year 3/4 children (aged 7–8 years) decided to persuade Shanga, their revered and infirm shaman and leader, to go with them and submit to the Beast's rule. However, their teacher, in role as Shanga, blocked their requests, referring to his frailty and desire to finish his life's work, the weaving of a carpet. Gradually, a few of the villagers became impatient with him and Ashley exclaimed, 'Leave him, it's his choice to say here, I will lead you now'. This split the class, half of whom continued to urge Shanga to come with them, and offered their help to finish the carpet. 'I will never submit to Blodin,' their teacher in role replied. 'I cannot go with you, you must go on in life without me'. Irritated and determined, Ashley again asserted his role, 'If you want to accept death, we cannot stop you, but you can no longer be our leader. I will lead you now. Come' and he walked away from the old man followed by most of the class.

With a new leader taking up the fictional mantle, the class had the option of revisiting Morpurgo's text and exploring his narrative choices or construct-ing the unfolding drama with Ashley leading the village. In examining the consequences of their actions, both for individuals and for the community as a whole, a variety of insights were made and other roles were adopted. These included the role of the young man, Hosea, his parents and friends, a shaman from a neighbouring village and Shanga as a spirit after his demise. As Greene (1995: 128) observes, 'to recognise that there are multiple perspectives and multiple vantage points is to recognise that no accounting, disciplinary or otherwise, can ever be finished or complete. There is always more'. The various views the children voiced and heard clearly added to the complexity of the experience. At one point, symbolically, good met evil, and Shanga met Blodin the Beast, the youngsters taking up roles as one or the other. Those in role as the old man voiced particularly powerful views, which drew on the children's earlier encounters with him and reflected a sense of role identification and connections to other narratives: 'You deceive yourself Blodin, you believe you are powerful, but it's not true'; 'You think I am weak, physically I am maybe . . .'; 'You can never take my spirit'; 'You can kill me, but you cannot destroy true hope'; 'I will be no one's slave'; 'I am the way'; 'Someone has gone before me, someone who will defeat you and save the world.'

The final group sculptures, erected in the land of peace and plenty to commemorate Blodin's reign of terror and the lessons learnt, challenged the young people to represent the themes of their drama. The abstract sculptures which they made with their bodies, depicted the following themes:

- believe in yourself;
- hope;
- sacrifice;
- humans must make their own choices;
- do what your heart tells you;
- believe in your soul.

In selecting imagined materials to construct these sculptures, the children variously chose wire, wood, stone and curved steel, which also spoke volumes about the learning journeys taken and the myriad meanings, thoughtfully and aesthetically explored by the class through the session. Drama's many ways of learning and rich semiotic system, had provided the class with the chance to work together creatively, using sound, music, movement, space and speech to convey ideas. Drama uses a whole range of communication skills, provides access to a wide range of learning styles, and draws upon the multiple intelli-gences of the learners (Gardner 1993). It is evident that improvisational drama also has the potential to contribute to emotional intelligence (Goleman 1995). acts as a reminder that teaching and learning are cognitive, emotional and ethical acts (Krechevsky and Stork 2000), and can help learners stand in the shoes of others, see the world from their perspective and make meaning through a variety of artistic languages. In this process they are living with difference and experiencing alternative ways of being and knowing.

Exploring engagement and reflection

The constant oscillation between engagement and reflection is another significant feature of drama which contributes to the capacity to tolerate change and challenge. Children become actively involved in drama and often express themselves with enthusiasm and energy, which reflects the role the body plays in the generation of ideas (Johnson 1987). This physical and emotional engagement is balanced with reflective opportunities, which serve to focus the children's thinking and foster connections to the real world. Through making and reflecting upon the imaginary world, children can come to understand themselves and the real world they inhabit. This transformation of understanding is central to drama and is effected through the dialogic interplay between the 'here and now' and their own lived reality. The imaginative engagement of drama offers learners 'the opportunity to explore and realize a range of values and identities and experiment with alternate versions of reality' (O'Neill 1995). In contrast, focused reflection upon the action enables these versions and interpretations to be considered from a distance.

Despite the significance attached to reflection in education (for example Bruner 1986; Corden 2000), it is perhaps most often profiled in the plenary of lessons or at the end of units of work. In drama however, various forms of reflection permeate the entire experiential process. An example may help to illuminate the constant interplay between engagement and detachment. In a Year 6 class (aged 10–11 years), a drama based upon *The After Dark Princess* by Annie Dalton was created. The children, corporately in role as the anxious mother, Mrs Quail, were hot seating young Alice Fadzakerley, a potential babysitter. Building upon their knowledge of the actual text, and the insights generated in previous freeze frames, their questions were both demanding and searching. They probed Alice's past, her friends and family and scrutinized her values, beliefs and behaviour through perceptive and sustained enquiry. In role as Alice, their teacher became an almost 'holier than thou' teenager, whose commitment to her charges, workaholic nature and assured manner made her seem 'simply too good to be true', as Nathan perceptively observed. It was clear from the lively, but pressing nature of their questions that the class had begun to suspend disbelief and engage fully. Following the interview, the children, working in pairs, role played a conversation that Mrs Quail might have had with a friend about Alice. Then they pooled their collective knowledge of her character, and listed the known facts and opinions deduced and inferred from meeting her. In this detached discussion, while suspending their engagement in the drama, connections and comparisons were made with real life babysitters and the class began to understand Alice's cryptic phrase that 'there's more to me than meets the eye'. It was clear, however, that although the author's chapter had offered both a text and a possible subtext, the meta-text had been found through the experience of the drama itself, as well as through their reflection upon it (Bond 1995).

The children examined not only what they had learnt about the ordinary yet somehow mysterious Alice, but also *how* they had learnt it. They evaluated the hot seat as a tool for finding out about a character and decided that in order to find out more about her, they needed to meet Alice in other situations, particularly when she was in the company of her young charges. In this process, the children maintained a distance from the fiction and began to develop a meta-language to describe and evaluate their drama. Booth (1996) argues 'this type of emotional/cognitive experiencing, followed by reflective distancing, is the hallmark of drama'. Through this process, learners are challenged both to engage in imagined experience as if it were real, and to consider the experience, its meaning and construction.

However, collaborative discussions about the content or process of drama only represent one form of reflection. Talk, drawing, shared and independent writing can all help children reflect upon the insights gained during the imaginative experience. Such reflective activities can support them in summarizing and synthesizing the views, positions, themes and morals being explored. Making connections is also integral to this work, whether these are personal parallels, contrasts or metaphoric connections to characters, situations, emotions or themes. Children operate at these moments as 'onlookers' making analogies (Harding 1977) and are involved as both the 'teller and the told' (Meek 1988), interpreting the narrative from within and reflecting upon it as recipients of the text of their own creation. The third phase of drama sessions, following 'first encounters' and 'conflicts and tensions', is sometimes referred to as 'resolutions', when the drama is drawn together (Grainger and Cremin 2001). This also offers the children time to digest the dramatic experience and revisit their learning; in this phase, the class work to reach a possible conclusion, however transient or uncertain, and consider their own learning.

Conclusion

Drama involves creation, speculation, and reflection and prompts questions to be asked and connections to be made. In contrast to more traditional pedagogic practices, which encompass a more demarcated sense of right and wrong, drama operates in a 'no penalty zone' (Heathcote 1980) and provides considerable scope to explore language, interpretation and meaning. Recently the weight of objectives and pressure of assessment in the primary curriculum, has meant that the ability to reproduce 'desired' outcomes appears to have been more highly valued than the skill to create an 'original' product or take part in an imaginative experience. For example, in England 'construction and correctedness' have been profiled at the expense of compositional content in the national assessment of writing (D'Arcy 1999). Yet many educators and even policymakers continue to profile the need for creative development (for example DfEE 1999b; Prentice 2000; Robinson 2001; QCA 2002). Creativity and imagination are not additional elements in drama, but are central to the symbolic and communicative nature of the activity, encouraging empathy and insight (Cremin 2003). They also contribute to the uncertainty and ambiguity that characterize classroom drama. The open ethos and shared culture of improvisational drama fosters a tolerance of uncertainty and ambiguity, encourages the use of the multiple visual, verbal and physical languages of drama, and promotes meaning making through engagement, reflection and the active examination of others' perspectives.

Tension, uncertainty and ambiguity trigger the 'electricity' of drama, and demand the children's involvement, prompting them to respond to the situation in which they find themselves without knowing where it will take them. The fictional predicament forms the dynamo of drama and encourages the personal commitment and affective involvement, which enable children to learn from living and feeling in drama time. During the drama, the teacher searches for conventions that will unsettle the status quo and oblige the children to struggle with contradictions, challenges and others' views.

Through drama, as children move in and out of the felt experience and live interactively in an environment of possibility, they co-author new and living fictions and transform their understanding. Such drama practice or 'praxis', is generated by a desire to reflect and act upon the world (Taylor 2000) and to learn to accept the unpredictability of living. In drama, children explore the unknown, adopt multiple viewpoints, make meanings and connections and learn individually and collectively to tolerate uncertainty.

Acknowledgement

I would like to thank Linda Homewood and her class from Aylesford County Primary School, Kent, for their imaginative contribution to some of the dramas described here.

9 Six fingers with feeling: play, literacy and politics

Sandra Smidt

In this chapter I want to argue that teaching – particularly the teaching of young children and of literacy – is an intensely political act. If you hold the view that I do that the purpose of education is not to 'produce' learners who successfully pass tests or achieve good grades, but that it is about developing people who not only can read but do read and not only 'read' their world but interpret and challenge it, you will be sympathetic to this argument.

The argument arises out of my growing unease about how poorly we educators do in terms of explaining to students, parents and policymakers what it is about 'play' that makes it such an important learning mode for young learners, and from my observations of how demoralized and lacking in creativity many teachers are in the current educational climate.

Over the summer I began to redefine my long held beliefs about learning and, more particularly, about play, in light of a growing body of challenging evidence. Along with many other early years practitioners and experts I have held firm to the belief that young children learn best through play. What I have understood by this is that when young children can choose what they want to do they remain in control of what they are doing. Since they have chosen what to do they are interested in what is happening. What they are doing is both relevant and meaningful to them. If things don't go to plan they can change their agenda without permission or consequences. They cannot then fail. For many the distinguishing feature of play is that it is used by children as an integrating mechanism; through play children bring together all that they know and integrate new experiences into existing frames.

We say that play is self-chosen and indeed that is its defining feature. When teachers in schools invite children to 'go and play in the home corner' what the children do in there may or may not be defined as play since the children have been directed to do something. The choices children make are important and something that many adults do not pay enough attention to. It is clear that children often choose to do things like watch television, fight with other children, scribble on the walls. If we are primarily concerned with play as a mode of learning we have to think more carefully about what our role is in helping children know how to make choices. We know that for many adults play is still what children do when they have finished the real business of schools – work. For other adults self-chosen play is often held as sacrosanct and adults are excessively cautious of intervening. I would argue that there is an educational imperative for adults to play a more clearly defined role in helping children widen their knowledge and experience base so that they have wider things to choose to explore. We do this with literacy without any difficulty: why not with play?

Children who are not introduced to new experiences or ideas or concepts – things they may not have experienced before – but are left to choose for themselves, may be denied access to some of what gives meaning to life: books and stories; poems and songs; music and art; and other people's ideas. We need to think about what happens when children hear a story, listen to an explanation, look at a picture. Perhaps the question we need to ask is this: is the child being passive during this experience or is something going on inside the child's head that allows the experience to be stimulating, meaningful and often challenging? Some would argue that children take what is important to them from hearing a story, listening to an explanation or looking at a picture, for example, and then – through play, through representation – come to a deeper understanding of whatever aspect they have chosen to focus on. Widening children's exposure to stories, music, objects, places and experiences gives children more things to choose from when they come to making sense of the world they inhabit. And making sense of this world of theirs is the prime 'work' of early childhood.

Ben, aged 5, is being introduced to very formal aspects of literacy in his reception class. He takes from this experience what he needs to explore further and does this through a self-chosen activity of writing lists. One of his lists looked like this:

> sthaFGR
> TUCe
> UmeRC
> veenam
> itaL
> FRDS

He had integrated two things that interest him at the moment: his growing awareness of countries (through having been on holiday to Turkey, having been born in South Africa and having been on an anti-war demonstration) and his growing interest in writing things down that other people can read.

Early years experts talk of starting from what the child already knows and, through first hand experience in what Margaret Donaldson calls 'meaningful contexts', helping the child take the new steps in learning and development. Donaldson's emphasis on the importance of young children, in particular, having access to things set in a meaningful context arose as a way of helping children move from the concrete to more abstract and symbolic systems. Children handling concrete objects are laying the foundations for more conceptual work later. These are important points. They suggest the importance of knowing what the child already knows, taking us into the difficult terrain of discovering what 'cultural capital' each child carries. And they remind us that education is a serious business and that what children learn matters. In a political sense it is clear that those urging that young children learn primarily through play are trying to move the focus away from children doing what they have been told to do and from children doing routine and seemingly objective (and often meaningless) tasks.

Two small scenarios to illustrate some points:

> Some young girls playing in a park. Two of them are cousins, another two sisters, but the two pairs have never met before. They range in age from 4 to 7. No one is asking or telling them to do anything. In fact, no adult is taking much notice of them. But they are engaged in a complex sequence of activities, taking place all around the play area. They clearly adopt different roles, engage in complex dialogues, negotiate rules, communicate with one another and inhabit a world they have created. They have created this world out of their own experiences – some shared, some individual. Their play goes on for several hours and when it is time to go home tears are shed by the youngest. All four are exhausted. Have they learned anything? Do we know what they have learned and can we be sure that it matters?

> Ben, aged nearly 5, is playing with a set of building blocks. He has been ignored and mocked by his sister and cousins and is feeling extremely angry and hurt. An adult, Jon, lures him out of his room with the building blocks and sits beside him on the carpet, taking real note of what he is doing. Gradually, as Ben's anger subsides, he starts to give a running commentary about what he is doing. 'If I roll this one down the slope then it will hit that one and push the others over'. He tries and it works. He beams. Jon, alongside him adds a suggestion of his own. He is not telling Ben what to do but is a genuine 'play partner' – an equal in this process of trying things out and seeing what happens. The play goes on for at least an hour. At the end of it Ben is exhausted. We could ask the same questions about this incident as we did about the last.

Are there common threads in these incidents where children are clearly doing what anyone would describe as play?

Let us add to this another scenario, this time relating to adult 'play'.

> I have never used pastels before, but am drawn to them through seeing what others on the painting course are doing. I like the colours and am drawn to the fact that you can rub and scrub and blend them, making a terrible mess as you do so. I sit on the floor of my room and decide to draw what I can see – the window and wall of the house opposite through the window in my room. It is early in the morning and I 'play' with the materials – making marks, going over them with white to eliminate them, rubbing them with my finger, with a cloth, with a bit of sponge. I add water. When I look at my watch two hours have passed and on the page in front of me is a very strange but powerful 'picture'. Have I learned anything and if so what? Is it of value?

The common threads between these three scenarios are that in each of them the participants – children and adult – are so deeply engrossed in what they are doing that time passes almost unnoticed and the intellectual energy expended leaves the participants exhausted. No one could say that these are examples of anything other than play. In each the participants have chosen what to do and are following their own interests, or, in the case of the little girls, negotiated interests. This implies that what they are doing is meaningful and relevant to all the learners involved. Certainly what we need to add to any definition of play is that it is often deeply engrossing and involving; that it requires an enormous expenditure of intellectual energy and that is relates to things that are of interest to the learner. Critically we need to state and reiterate that play is an intellectual exercise.

Hannah sits on her bed, reading a book. Other children play around her and it is noisy in her room. She sits quietly, totally involved in what she is doing and quite oblivious to the games going on around her. She is totally engrossed and intellectually challenged. She has chosen what to do and is deeply engrossed in it. But is this play? Can we know what she is doing in her head as she reads?

Like most of you reading this chapter I would guess, I fit clearly (if not totally happily) into the mould of western educationalist, desperate to hold onto something of value under the onslaught of recent trends in education: 'Let's test children at 11, at 7, at 4. Let's test them every year. Let's make sure each child receives a Literacy Hour every day with aspects of word-, sentence- and text-level work. Let's make sure that children can answer questions rapidly. Let pace be a critical factor in our teaching.' So, holding fast to certain western notions relating to choice, child-centredness and some sort of 'freedom', I have shied away from what was staring me in the face. Millions of children throughout the world learn effectively and efficiently in cultures and communities where our notions of play are not held.

Barbara Rogoff (1990) details how children in many communities, learn through what she calls 'guided participation'. Where children and young people have a real role to play in the lives of communities, they do not play in any sense we might recognize, but pay close attention to what the skilled people are doing. This observation of what is happening is not a passive process but an active process and Rogoff suggests that children who become skilled observers also become skilled participants and that sometimes, as in New Guinea (Sorenson 1979), skilled participants go on to be skilled observers. Rogoff adds that in most cases the observation is not silent, but involves talk. The talk may often be in the form of the learners receiving directions, rather than being engaged in conversations, but since they are likely to occur in the context of the participation, they are available for observation and analysis.

Here is 3-year-old Pritha, watching her mother make chapattis. Pritha watches the movements of her mother's hands, takes notice of the tools being used, listens to the talk between her mother and aunt. Her mother gives her a lump of dough and a rolling pin and Pritha, constantly looking at what the adults are doing, moulds her piece of dough, throws it on the counter, uses the rolling pin, shapes it. It goes under the grill along with all the others and at breakfast everyone comments on how clever Pritha is. An analysis of this incident would suggest that the child was involved in using real materials for a real task in a meaningful cultural context. Was this play? Can we say what Pritha was learning through this activity? Can we suggest that she might have learned 'more' or 'more effectively' with a lump of coloured plasticine and no model to follow? These are questions that are difficult to answer.

Play is clearly something of enormous significance for children themselves. My concerns are not about the importance of play either in the personal and emotional lives of children or as a prime learning mode, but about how well teachers themselves understand key features of play. Teachers and educators really need to be quite clear about what happens intellectually when play is offered as a learning mode in the classroom. They need to be able to support children's learning in ways that allow children themselves to be aware of what they are doing and they need to make sure that they have lucid explanations which are accessible to parents. Liz Brooker's (2002) book clearly expressed many of these concerns. In her study looking at two groups of children and their families during the children's first year of formal schooling, she finds some painful and disturbing things. Of course Brooker looked at a tiny sample, in a very particular context, but nonetheless her analysis of the difficulties faced by many parents and children in dealing with a so-called open access school and a play-based curriculum filled me with foreboding. The definitions of play offered and the explanations of its importance did not persuade many of the parents, who found themselves alienated from the open access policy of the school. Many of the children, particularly those in the group defined as 'Asian', already disadvantaged, were becoming more and more disadvantaged through being in a system which made no sense to them and which did not know how to value and respect what they and their families brought with them. The difficulties of families revealing their cultural capital and of schools knowing what to validate and celebrate are profound and serious.

I am not arguing (and neither, I am sure, is Brooker) for a formal curriculum in the reception class. I continue to believe that our children start formal school far too young. But I am arguing that since this is the situation facing teachers who are offering a curriculum based on play, they must really understand what it is that they must do in order to ensure that all children, and not just those with cultural or social capital, are learning. Teachers need to step beyond the classroom to find out what it is that children really do know, what cultural capital they own, so that they can build on this. Schools need to consider the structures they have in place so that no parent or group is alienated. These are, by definition, political tasks.

Han Suyin is 5 years old. He has been in a reception class for a term. His school operates a limited version of the Literacy Hour from the very first term of formal schooling. Han sits, with 29 other children, for 45 minutes each morning, learning the names of letters, learning to chant the alphabet, to recognize words and to join in with repeated phrases in stories in Big Books. Han is happy. His parents told him that he would learn to read and write at school and they are happy when he comes home and tells them which letter he has learned and shows them how he can write his own name and recognize some words. He does not take a book home. All his school reading is done in the classroom. His parents are proud of him. He is proud of himself. His parents run a takeaway restaurant and they want his life to be better than theirs has been. They believe this will happen through education.

Han is allowed to play when he has finished his work. He prefers work to play. When it is work he knows what to do. When it is play he is unsure. He likes playing in the playground or in the park at the weekends, but in the classroom he is less confident. He is learning to decode and clearly not through play. Whether he will go on to be a reader is another question.

Han's cousin, Mei Li, goes to a school close by and is also in the reception class. In this school there are three reception classes in a large, almost open plan area. The school operates the High Scope approach which means that each morning the rooms are set up with exciting, challenging and visually attractive things to do and the children are invited to consider what they would like to do and record this on a card. Later in the day they 'review' what they have done. Sometimes groups of children are chosen to go and 'work' with an adult.

Mei Li is happy at school, she loves choosing what to do and chooses different things according to how she feels. She has friends and is confident and happy. She takes home a picture/storybook in a bag three times a week but no one reads this with her at home. Mei Li's parents are worried that she is not doing 'as well' as Han Suyin. She doesn't write her name clearly and doesn't recognize any words. When her parents ask her what she did at school she often just shrugs. They have not been into school to discuss her progress yet. They don't want to be seen as 'difficult' or 'pushy'. The school sent home a letter explaining about High Scope and everyone is friendly there. Mei Li's parents were happy when she was in the nursery class and played a lot, but now that she is in 'big' school they expect to see some evidence that she is learning to read and write.

Han Suyin's parents were happy with what was happening for him in school. It conformed to their own experiences and expectations. They expected that at school he would sit quietly and learn to read and write and that is what they see that he is doing. When I was a child I grew up in a middle class family where it was taken for granted that I would learn to read and write. The values of my home were academic. I saw my parents reading and writing. There were books and newspapers in my home. It never entered into anyone's consciousness that I might not learn to read. I lived in a culture where academic success was expected and valued: a community of aspiring academics.

When I went to paint in France I found myself in a totally new culture: a community of painters and drawers. Within this new community there was the expectation that anyone could paint and draw and those around me were all painting and drawing. As a child, becoming a reader was without struggle, but as an adult, becoming a 'drawer' was something quite different. I came to the enterprise with a whole history of having 'failed'. As a child I had been told that I could not draw and this myth I carried with me throughout my life. Any courses I had been on or attempts I had made merely confirmed this view. I entered my new little community with my baggage of failure and overcoming this was, for me, an intense struggle and a powerfully moving experience. If Mei Li's parents are not persuaded that she is learning, their anxieties will be conveyed to her. She may find herself entering Year 1 with the label and baggage of failure.

Our definition of 'play' (in the sense of being a mode of learning) now includes these features: self-chosen; risk-free; totally engrossing; interesting and meaningful to the learner; intellectually demanding; set in a community of other 'players' with a shared understanding; more transparent to the player than to the adults; and an integrating mechanism. In considering play as a mode of learning we also have to consider what it is that the teacher will do, the pedagogy that will best support such learning. Much recent evidence on the effectiveness of early learning programmes have found that the adult–child interactions are the key factors.

In the example of the little girls in the park, no adult was involved. It is almost certain that the girls were learning, but what they were learning is difficult to say. This, in no way, undermines the value of what they were learning. It just means that we are unable to analyse it. Ben's learning (in the block play example), because of his 'performance' and 'commentary', was easier to interpret. He was learning that he could predict what might happen, try out his plan and evaluate what happened. He was learning that some predictions were correct and others not. Because of the adult involvement he was learning that what he was doing was interesting to someone else. He was learning that if he got it wrong it did not matter and he could try something different. I would suggest that in this incident, as in many other play situations, the role of the adult was crucial. Here Jon, alongside him, was tuned into what he was trying to do and respectful of it. He did not try to subvert Ben's agenda in order to 'teach' him something on Jon's agenda.

And this seems to me a key feature of successful teaching, particularly where learners are learning through the kind of play we are talking about. When I was the 'poor' drawer in France the other students, who were more skilled, more experienced and more confident, clearly could see no value in what I was doing. They were helpful and often patronizing, suggesting that I use a thinner brush or more water or draw from a different angle. Because what I produced did not look like their pictures – recognizable, conventional, acceptable – they accepted my definition of my work as inadequate. But Francis – the teacher – looked more deeply at what I was trying to do and commented on what I was doing well. Making explicit what I was doing is something good teachers seem to do intuitively and new teachers struggle to achieve. 'Better six fingers with feeling than five without' retorted Francis, when I produced a drawing, with his help. 'What you are learning is that you can draw and you can't draw; that you can paint and you can't paint'. And this statement could be made about any learner who is taking risks. The teacher, tuned in to what the learner is trying to do, can focus on both what the learner has achieved – what they can do – and also on what the learner has yet to achieve. In our education culture, so devoted to meeting learning objectives, we break learning down into small items and lose sight of the whole. I liked the fact that I understood that I could do things within the greater context of not yet being able to do others. This helped me identify small successes towards a distant, but no longer unattainable, goal.

What the above incident highlights is the importance of ensuring that the learner is aware of what has or is being learned. Brooker's children were mainly unsure of what, if anything, they had learned. The same is true of many of the children I encounter who say things like, 'I just played'. One of the most important things that teachers must do is be explicit to children about what they are learning. And this means that teachers have to pay close attention to what children are doing when they play and know how to analyse this so that they can say just what it is that has been learned. This is a highly skilled task but one that many early years practitioners do well. What they do less well is share their analysis with the child or parent.

What I am arguing for is a tighter definition of what we mean by play underpinned by a much more detailed understanding by all those involved with children of why it is significant. Anything that allows children to encounter new experiences and revisit familiar experiences in a questioning and exploratory fashion should count as play. Anything that invites children to find ways (any ways) of representing and re-representing what they are seeing or feeling or thinking should be regarded as play. Anything that helps children not just accept what they see, hear and explore, but to ask questions and be helped to find answers should count as play. The words 'fun' and 'pleasurable' should have no place in any definition of play since they demean and trivialize it. Play, since it is intensely involving and cognitively exhausting, is much more serious than these words imply. Perhaps, what we need is a new word.

Teachers working with young children, have a series of difficult tasks ahead. They can no longer merely write a set of 'learning objectives' related to the early learning goals and anticipate that the children will be learning in any meaningful sense. They have to pay extremely close attention to the children in their care and work out what interests and engages them. Lilian Katz continues to remind us all that what children learn is important. Should we continue to bombard young children with a set of trite activities relating to making prints with leaves or patterns out of types of pasta or should we ensure that we envelop young children in the real things from their culture and ours – the shared culture we are building in classrooms. The nurseries in a region of Italy, Reggio Emilia, are very good at this. The cultures they address are less diverse than those many of us face. The nurseries consider what might interest the children and allow them both to build on what they already know and take them into new worlds, offering them a myriad opportunities to represent and represent again, differently perhaps, what they see, think and feel. Central to their philosophy is an aspect of play we haven't considered. The Swiss architect, Noschis, talks about the importance of children having opportunities to encounter real craftsmen, workers and adults in their work places and beyond. For him play should not 'isolate children from the neighbourhood but be a privileged space for playing what is observed in the neighbourhood' (Noschis 1992: 7). This is attended to in the nurseries by ensuring that each one has a piazza (central meeting space which is found in every Italian town, city and village). Here the children can spill out to meet adults and other children and to integrate aspects of what they have seen, heard and experienced in the piazzas of their beyond-school cultures. It is easier for those working in a smallish fairly monocultural city like Reggio to know what experiences will be familiar to many children, and hence to bring them into the classroom culture, than it is for teachers in large cities with diverse cultures. Nonetheless, the principle remains. If we talk about 'building on children's experience' we have to know what this experience might be.

Many early years teachers in the Anglo-American model seek to come up with a Reggio Emilia curriculum or model of education. Those working in Reggio know that they offer no model, method or recipe and that what they offer cannot be copied because it is based on context, culture and values. The story of how the Reggio system came about is an Italian story, set in the very particular historical, economic and political contexts prevailing at the time. We cannot copy Reggio Emilia, but we can learn from it. Peter Moss (2001) argues that we can learn many important things from Reggio and perhaps the most important is what he refers to as 'border-crossing'. Because the work in the Reggio schools is constantly documented and researched, involving people from many disciplines and backgrounds, what has happened is that early childhood has been linked to a wider intellectual culture and tradition, to a range of different perspectives and theories. Moss argues that in the Anglo-American early childhood systems, developmental psychology has been and remains the dominant way of looking at young children. One of the other significant features of the Reggio experience has been the ongoing involvement of workers and trades unionists in the lives of the centres. This fact makes early childhood a central feature of the whole community and situates children as citizens of their own neighbourhoods.

Moss argues, critically, that our cultures – those of the UK and the US, in particular, are dominated by a particular philosophy which includes a view that children are required to 'be given' objective and value-free knowledge in a world where universal solutions are possible. Moss says 'the dominant intellectual paradigm of Anglo-American early childhood work is based on a rationality which renders power, choice and responsibility invisible.' It is salutary to reflect that a system which encourages children to question arose out of the legacy of fascism. What is worth exploring here and in the paragraphs to come is what Moss refers to as 'emancipatory learning' – emancipatory in the sense of empowering learners to develop critical thought.

We have known since the Jesuits that the early years of life are crucial in terms of learning and development. Hence they hold in them possibilities for influencing future generations. In the early years children are beginning the journey which will either lead them to be docile conformists or challenging thinkers. I recently met a young woman who told me that she had been 'born into a politically apathetic generation'. I reacted with horror at the thought that political apathy could be conceived of as being almost genetic. Paolo Freire, the great Brazilian thinker and writer, developed a model of emancipatory literacy where he envisioned a dialectical relationship between people and the world they live in on the one hand, and between language and the possibility for changing that world, on the other. This view does not see literacy merely as a technical skill to be acquired but as the essential foundation for cultural action to transform the immediate world. So literacy is perceived as a political project where people take responsibility to read, to understand and to change their own experience, but also to restructure and redefine their relationship with a wider society. So literacy is about changing one's immediate and one's wider social world. For Freire human beings – teachers and learners – are the engines of analysing their own experience with regard to political, social and cultural capital. For him literacy and power are intimately linked. Giroux, in his introduction to *Literacy: Reading the Word and the World* (1987) says 'To be able to name one's experience is part of what is meant to 'read' the world and to begin to understand the political nature of the limits *and* possibilities that make up the larger society.' It is interesting, in light of what we are saying about the context within which the Reggio centres arose, that Italy was the birthplace of the political theorist Gramsci who, in his analysis of society, held that language itself was instrumental in stilling the voices of the oppressed and in legitimizing oppressive relationships and regimes.

And what about play? Play – by its very nature – allows control to pass from the adult to the learner. The child, drawing on all that has been experienced, selects what to pay attention to and explore. In a small way the child is able to exercise power and take responsibility. In classes where the how is more important than the what, the journey more valuable than the destination, good educators value what it is that children choose to do and then seek to understand and extend it. In this way the curriculum becomes what the children choose to do and the learning a dialectical relationship, empowering both the learner and the educator.

Allan Luke (1998) in discussing the ongoing 'reading debate' argues that we should not be asking the question 'What is the best way to teach reading and writing?' In his analysis all literacy programmes work to some extent. He adopts a more political analysis, suggesting that what we need to ask is how we can help students deal with the range of literate cultures they may encounter in their lives and how we would have them design and redesign those cultures and their texts. Luke may be talking more about older learners but his arguments can certainly be applied to younger learners when he starts discussing pedagogy. He goes on to argue that what is needed now is a different framing of the question of the role of the educator. He believes that we can no longer try and compensate for society but must equip our students with the tools they need to alter their own material circumstances. The links here with Freire are clear. This empowerment of people – particularly those who have been systematically disenfranchised – means helping them become truly literate and that implies that we must regard literacy competence as a kind of cultural capital. Bourdieu (1977) defined cultural capital as something within the learner but validated and legitimized by the educational system. In our societies children who come from homes where bedtime stories are part of ordinary life carry within them this cultural capital – some experience that is recognized and valued by teachers and schools. Luke argues that this cultural capital can only empower the learner when it works in combination with economic and social capital.

From this it becomes clear that the role of the educator is a far more political one than many educators would care to accept. In our society – as in Australia and the US – teachers are being systematically de-skilled by being offered a series of recipes. Teachers in England, as in other developed countries, are required to perform tasks without having any control of or say in their construction, their conceptualization or their evaluation. Teachers are functionaries. Luke says it very clearly: 'In effect, this means the stripping of thinking, autonomous action and creativity out of teaching, and their replacement by standardised sequences, patterns and materials'. What effect this will have on teachers is frightening. Teachers are being alienated from their pupils and the communities in which they teach. Often those teaching the youngest children are forced to deny their hard fought understanding of how young children learn best in order to fulfil the 'pedagogical' functions determined for them by those furthest from the world of play and learning. The local conditions, the cultural norms and the idiosyncrasies of lives in classrooms are being destroyed as teachers are called on to respond to the increasingly centralized processes imposed on them.

We may have much to learn from what is happening in South Africa. There, after a history of oppression, the new government has come up with a new national curriculum, underpinned by a strong political awareness: echoes of Reggio and the legacy of fascism. In the curriculum the purposes of language include personal, communicative, educational and aesthetic purposes. But they also include cultural (to understand and appreciate cultures, languages and the heritages they carry), critical (understand and challenge the relationship between language, power and identity, understand the dynamic nature of culture and resist persuasion) and political (assert or challenge power, persuade others about other viewpoints and develop and sustain identities). What a long way we have yet to travel!

PART 6
New Texts and Textual Dimensions

The complex transformative nature of literacy is a running thread through this book and is particularly highlighted in this section by Eve Bearne who examines the multimodal nature of text, and by Angela Packwood and Trinka Messenheimer who present a multidimensional mode of writing.

Initially, Bearne challenges the profession to recognize that as the fabric of literacy alters, newly integrated theories are needed which take account of the many dimensions of text (the visual, the physical, the oral and the written) as well as the situations in which they are made. Bearne contributes to such a reformulation and argues that teachers and policymakers need to begin by recognizing multimodal texts in their own right, and becoming acquainted with an appropriate descriptive vocabulary which can be used to discuss, debate and examine such texts. She seeks to shift the focus away from genre theory towards a more open and flexible way of encapsulating texts and their production, and uses an example from the classroom to demonstrate the way in which children play with the possibilities of texts they know. Young people's capacity to move with ease across apparent textual boundaries has been well documented by Mackey (2002). But Bearne goes further in shaping a new language to describe multimodal texts and in demanding that national curricula and assessment structures 'catch up with young readers and text makers' who live and work in a multimodal world. To achieve this would transform both pedagogy and practice and would work towards a more contemporary 'literacy of fusion' (Millard 2003), towards critical literacy in the twenty-first century.

Angela Packwood and Trinka Messenheimer are also aware of the pressures and consequences of the accountability culture in England and the US. They perceive that teachers have developed coping strategies involving routines and tasks determined by the assessment frame and children have come to see writing mainly as an instrument for learning, not as a tool for personal knowledge construction. Such learners may become competent writers, but are also likely to become disengaged, disinterested writers with little sense of their own agency or autonomy. This has certainly been borne out by recent research into children's perceptions of writing in the primary phase (Grainger *et al.* 2002, 2003). Through analysing autobiographies and interviews by published writers, Packwood and Messenheimer show that authors see writing as a recursive and reflective activity over which they have choice and control and which they use primarily for epistemic purposes. Packwood and Messenheimer offer a more dynamic model of writing than the one currently used in schools, and argue that children need to develop knowledge about themselves as writers, about the writing process, and about writing, in order to make informed choices. Ways to achieve this are outlined and the profession is challenged to travel beyond the constraints of the present, back into a future in which children can develop as autonomous, engaged and reflective writers.

In examining the fabric of literacy and the purpose of creating, Bearne and Packwood and Messenheimer acknowledge the influence of high stakes assessment. They move beyond this, however, contributing to the debate about an alternative future in which in school literacy builds more explicitly upon children's knowledge and experience of text, and the institutions of assessment recognize both the purpose and nature of the enterprise.

10 Playing with possibilities: children's multidimensional texts[1]

Eve Bearne

While some educational theorists are quite comfortable with the use of the word 'literacy' to describe new forms of communication, I am not. This is partly because a ready use of the word can operate against radically rethinking what new forms of texts are doing for children, learning and communication. Partly also because in a pedantic way I want to assert that the dimensions of text include much more than 'words' and that using the term 'literacy' continues to privilege words over other forms of communication, particularly the pictorial, diagrammatic, photographic, gestural and moving image. The world of communication is not standing still. A profound change is happening because of the newly pervasive and more dominant presence of image made possible by technological advances. Of course, image and word (both in writing and speech) have co-existed for some time (Kress 1997; Lanham 2001) but the relationships between the different modes of communication are in process of being remade. This raises serious questions about the nature of learning and even more insistent questions about teaching. In this chapter I want to argue that for the potential of pupils' literacy knowledge and experience to be energized in the classroom, teachers themselves need to know how such texts work and to recognize and value the contribution of multimodal texts to children's reading and writing.

Children now have available to them many forms of text which include sound, voices, intonation, stance, gesture, movement, as well as print and image. These texts have changed the ways in which young readers expect to read, the ways they think and the ways they construct meaning. Necessarily then, children bring to their reading and writing a wide and varied array of resources and experience through which they interpret any unfamiliar texts that they meet. However, it isn't just a matter of investing texts with the voices, sounds and gestures, which are part of children's reading (and viewing) experience, but that their reception of text assumes different organization – one which is spatially cohesive and which uses a different kind of orchestration of the elements which make up any act of reading. In their writing, too, children reflect the multimodality of their reading, depicting sound as part of the pictorial element of text construction, making their meanings clear through written word, image and sound (in dialogue and as depicted in images), and in font size and shape, layout and decoration of their writing. They play with the possibilities of the texts they know.

The text experience of young learners about new combinations of modes of representation prompts a reappraisal of older theories of representation, of communication, of writing and reading (Bearne and Kress 2001: 93). This is even more necessary and compelling because of the effects of the major shifts in forms of text which are now part of our world. I use the word 'world' deliberately, not just in a lazy way of assuming that there is no other place but western Europe, but as a deliberate signal that communications are now increasingly worldwide. That is not to suggest that access to communications is equal across the world or across cultures, but, rather, to signal that new ways of thinking about literacy must be wide and culturally sensitive and attuned.

If common frames of reference for communication are now being reshaped, then it follows that we are in the process of re-theorizing communication and literacy, of seeing language, literacy – and the way we think – differently. As a contribution to the process of seeing literacy in a new way, I want to explore some ideas about texts. I want to consider how a theory – and so a descriptive vocabulary – might be developed to take account of the several dimensions of texts, including the movement, the sound and the dynamic, implicit in print texts – both visual and verbal. I am more concerned here with the production of texts, although, of course, text production is the 'other face' of text reception. Put another way, I want to sketch a theory which can combine understanding of representational *modes* (what the culture provides as a means of making meaning: speech, writing, image, gesture, music . . .) with the existing and emerging *media* of dissemination (what the culture makes available as a means of distributing these meanings as messages): book, magazine, computer screen, video, film, radio. Further, I want to exemplify the ways that shifts in media require thinking about all representational modes as part of a whole system of meaning. To do this means examining the *affordances* (what is made possible and facilitated/made difficult or inhibited) of the different modes and media. The pivot of this theory is related to the *logics* of texts – the text cohesion which makes for coherence.

However, I don't want to examine texts as isolated from the situations in which they are made. Any adequate pedagogic theory has to take into account theories of individual development; issues of classroom culture and the nature of knowledge; and social, cultural ideological and political discourses which surround schools, classrooms and learners. This is a demanding agenda and in focusing on children's texts and their production I assume a theory which takes account of situated literacy and communicative practices (Barton 1994; Marsh 2001). Theorizing about practices rather than simply about the products of literacy also acts as a reminder that such theories need to include the unobservables – the values, attitudes, emotions, social and cultural relationship networks – which surround literacy events (Street 1993). An analysis which takes into account both the visible and invisible elements of literacy events allows descriptions of how groups of people – as well as, but perhaps distinct from, individuals – in a variety of social settings are regulated by and regulate literacy practices. Situated literacy means looking at the detail of text production but sets such an analysis within the wider political frame. In sketching an integrated theory of multidimensional text, my starting points are: children's production of texts, how these can be analysed and the implications for teaching.

Transforming experience through text production

A close focus on texts, then, does not necessarily mean taking a narrow view. Texts are shaped by historically developed cultural and social practices and have to be seen as such. No text is innocent of influence. Even if they subvert known forms, writers work within some notion of genre – the patterned forms of writing which have been developed in our society to carry particular kinds of messages. However, drawing on patterned expectations about forms of writing does not imply straightforward replication. Texts themselves, as well as their writers, have the potential to act on the world, being part of newly developing cultural and social practices. Writers make selections or choices about what to tell, how and to whom, and in doing so, categorize experience: a cognitive operation which sets mental frameworks for later, more complex forms of categorizing, selecting and generalizing of experience or facts. But it doesn't stop with organizing and synthesizing ideas. Text production is a dynamic process of interaction which transforms ideas, experiences and text knowledge, creating a new text with the maker's own particular mark on it. While this is not a straightforward matter of reproducing existing forms, the individual is inevitably influenced by the social and cultural settings of family, home, educational arrangements, governmental views of what counts as valid or valuable literacy and the texts and forms which are part of the culture.

Transforming understanding and experience by making a text in its turn extends experience. In developing their awareness of and their capabilities using different genres for writing, children not only learn how to organize writing but also extend their experience of different ways of thinking about texts. For teachers, coming to understand genre as a way of organizing thought as well as describing texts, is essential if children are genuinely to be able to use writing to form and communicate their thoughts. Both teachers and children need to pay attention to just how texts have been put together, how they can be reorganized, if necessary, to do the job better. And further, they need to be able to talk about it together. In the past few years there has been a move towards using linguistic terminology explicitly in teaching reading and writing. This can be extended to describe, analyse and evaluate new and newly emerging forms of text. Children deserve to be given greater scope in their text making by explicit discussion of variations in the structures, purposes and effects of multimodal as well as written texts.

A starting point would be teachers transforming and extending their own knowledge and experience of multimodal texts. However, it is not enough to expect individual teachers to extend their expertise; this would have to be supported by inclusion of multimodality in institutional arrangements for assessment. One move towards this is to include multimodal text *production*, as well as reading pictorial and media texts, explicitly in national curricula.[2] In the UK this would also mean a more encompassing vision of text production within the National Literacy Strategy. However, it is important to stress that settings or situations are also theoretical constructs. Human beings are constantly remaking their social worlds which are, as Gee points out, 'actively created, sustained, negotiated, resisted, and transformed moment-by-moment' (Gee 2000: 190). Classroom literacy itself is a continually shifting construct. Readers, texts and institutions change and so should ways of helping children get hold of the kinds of literacies that are given high prestige. The classroom is the site where young text makers actively transform their experience of all the spoken, cultural, visual, multimodal and print texts they meet. The process of transformation is often activated at the intersection between the horizontal and vertical discourses of children's home and school knowledge of texts (Bernstein 1996). It is important to be aware of the range of possible text types which children draw on from the situations of both home and school. This is likely to help in developing ways of describing text production which can include knowledge from both the horizontal and vertical domains without dishonouring the text makers, their knowledge or their cultural experience.

Genre – the continuing debate

Criticisms of genre theory argue that children's learning consists not of putting together different 'skills' (Martin and Rothery 1986) but of a gradual refinement and reworking of experiences which are visited and revisited throughout their schooling (for example Bearne and Farrow 1991; Barrs 1992; Lee 1997; Wyse and Jones 2001). Indeed, as far as writing is concerned, it is questionable, and open to argument, whether any adult writer can ever claim to have got to grips with all the 'skills' necessary for writing in a wide range of genres. Since writing changes with time, even mature writers continue to learn and develop their expertise. Also, according to this view, writing is seen not so much as expressing ideas and exploring meaning but mainly as constructing texts. Luke and Freebody describe the constraints operating within even the most apparently apolitical approaches to genre teaching:

> instructional approaches that focus principally on the description of linguistic technologies of texts and the cognitive architectures for the construction and processing of text run the risk of mirroring or reproducing these sociocultural restrictions and constraints rather than elucidating and transforming them.
>
> (Luke and Freebody 1997: 4)

It is wise to heed these warnings. Perhaps it is time to shift attention from genre theory towards a more flexible way of describing texts and the ways in which they are made, treated and given value.

This is where, for me, the word 'grammar' comes in handy. The grammar of any utterance, any representation, any text, describes the patterns which make it comprehensible to members of the culture in which it is produced and received. Where syntax describes sentence grammar, text grammars similarly represent expectations that certain texts will be structured according to developed conventions. Text cohesion is a critical component of how texts are put together and hold together. The potential to generate an infinite number of meanings – in whole texts and sentences – without repetition seems to me the essence of 'regulated improvisation' (Bourdieu 1977). Indeed, without straying into the detail of Wittgenstein's private language argument, it seems to me that it is communicative structuring which makes improvisation possible.

Different types of text have varying patterns of cohesion which contribute to the overall shape or architecture of the text. Narrative or report depend on chronological cohesion; texts which are represented visually or diagrammatically depend on spatial cohesion. In films, cohesion depends on repeated visual motifs, perspective, close-up on characters' faces or exchanged glances, choices of setting, colour, intensity of light, the organization of time sequences, the use of musical or sound patterns to underpin the affective elements of the text . . . as well as the text cohesion of dialogue, the connectives, conjunctions, pronoun references, deixis, substitution, ellipsis, lexical patterns. In picture books, lines, vectors, the direction of characters' eye gaze and spatial organization act as visual connectives and conjunctions; repeated visual motifs echo the text cohesion in narrative verbal text created by lexical repetition or ties; gesture and stance, sustained and changed through framing, as well as depicted action, give narrative cohesion.

It may be more fruitful, then, to look at the features which help distinguish between different kinds of text in terms of the range of components of text grammar rather than through the now increasingly contested notion of genre. Text grammars, the patterned expectations of texts, make it possible for members of communities to share meanings. Easily accessible mass media increases the potential scope for sharing meanings across and within communities. If text makers want to shape content and meaning for communication with the vast range of possible communities of meaning, then they need experience of the ways texts are structured and organized. They also need to examine the variations and subversions which are possible. Shaping meaning gives coherence to a text: the writer's ideas follow a logic intended to convey something to someone – often described as 'purpose' and 'audience'. This, in turn, means choosing structural, organizational and language features which are linked to the purpose and audience for the text. While holding in mind a principle of uncertainty, there has to be some kind of rule of thumb for distinguishing between different types of communications, particularly if there has to be some principled teaching about text organization.

In *The World on Paper*, David Olson argues that print technology and the growth of communications via a 'paper world' contributed to the development of particular kinds of pictorial representation. These have led to new ways of thinking and the development of a 'common frame of reference' for communication – 'the theoretical model into which local knowledge was inserted and organised' (Olson 1996: 232). In an increasingly multimodal world these common frames of reference are being reshaped through digital technology, resulting in a revolution as significant as the print revolution. If Olson is right, we are in the process of retheorizing communication and cognition, of seeing 'our language, our world and our minds in a new way' (1996: 233). Shirley Brice-Heath explains that new types of visual symbolic text require a different conceptual approach from reading in a linear way. It is not just that reading is a different kind of act, because of new forms and formats but that it demands a way of thinking which depends on different kinds of conceptual categorization:

> The line between word and image is getting harder to draw; the visual through colour, line and form enables understanding of metaphor – our ability to map interactions, experiences and cognitive operations across concepts to form images.
>
> (Brice Heath 2000: 124)

This emphasizes the dynamic interplay between received images and imagining, highlighting the complexity of the relationship of outer and inner experience. Different ways of representing knowledge and experience bring different features of the world literally into view and so change ways of thinking about the world. Globalization is more than a matter of socioeconomic awareness, it is the way we think now. Shifts from the possibilities for literacy practices offered by the page (literal and visual) to the several dimensions of the televisual multimedia world mean that children are being introduced to different ways of structuring thought. Not only are there now many more kinds of text to refer to than in the past, as children make meaning of new experiences, events and practices, they also think differently from adults' developed frames of reference.

Children are already ahead of adults in this new conceptual world of text. As they interact with texts, or make their own, it becomes immediately clear that they have already become part of the paradigm shift about how texts work to make meaning. Adults may struggle with the conceptual differences of the 'textnological' revolution, but children are already there, reading and producing texts in many dimensions and investing them with meaning drawn from their own wide repertoire of cultural experience. If new technologies promote different ways of thinking, developments in technology mean that there are now more ways to communicate meaning, and these depend on spatial cohesion as well as chronological structure. This means that children produce texts in a different way, assuming the integration of image and word and supplying sound, elements of gesture and movement as they compose their own meanings.

Developing a new language

Different ways of representing the world bring a different perspective and so change ways of thinking about the world, creating new possibilities for ways of representing the world. In turn, new representations trigger changes in language to describe them and prompt reconsideration of definitions of reading, writing, depicting, literacy, literature and texts. While it can be argued that all texts are multimodal (Goodman and Graddol 1996; Unsworth 2001), it is quite easy to recognize the different modes of television or a video game: printed words, sound, image and action. The affordances of texts, their modes and media of representation, depend on cohesive devices of time and space. The combined modes or dimensions of written word, image, sound and gesture give texture, colour and substance to meaning. I want to use one specific element of grammar – cohesion – as a starting point for sketching out the possibilities of an integrated theory of multimodal, or multidimensional texts. The cohesive patterning of any text leads to coherence, giving it meaning as well as shape. I want to call the relationships between the different elements of the text held together by cohesive patterning 'textuality' and to use this complex interweaving of elements of meaning as part of an integrative theory of text production. In their multimodal texts children make their meanings clear through written word, image, sound in dialogue and as depicted in images and these are bound together by spatial arrangements, the relationships between the verbal and visual text and typographical details which capture sound and movement.

Clinton's book, *Alien Race*, is a fine example of textuality. It was written as part of an extended writing project with no whole class input on content at all. For this narrative, Clinton draws on his experience of texts he has met mostly outside the classroom. The opening page builds tension immediately, introducing unfamiliarity into a familiar setting (Figure 10.1). By the use of dialogue, implied sound effects, a typographically emphatic statement and a visual image, the reader is immediately led to understand something of what this book is about. Clinton builds anticipation through a build up of verbal, aural and visual elements on this single (black and white) page.

The cohesion is created by the juxtapositions of text and image and, importantly, through the use of white space. Chapter 1 (Figure 10.2) continues the use of typographical features, depicted movement and dialogue; once again the voices sound in the (western European) reader's ear as we recognize the

One day in the future:

"Hey Mum! I'm goin to the park with
 J.J. and Mike."
"Yes love see you later."
"What shall we do then?"
"I don't know."
"Play some soccer."
"Be quiet Mike."
"Ray what's that sound?"
"I don't know, do I?"

IT HAS BEGUN

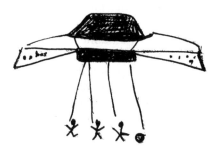

Figure 10.1   The opening page of Clinton's book, *Alien Race*

intonation which accompanies 'Wo!' and 'Yep', familiar from film, television and informal talk.

Throughout the book Clinton uses the pictorial element of his text to indicate movement, but also size and extent. The written text on page 7 (Figure 10.3) is laconic:

> 'Man, this is Evil.'
> 'I agree with ya.'
> 'Yep me too.'

but accompanied by a suggestive image of fire trails from rockets cut off from the verbal text but moving upwards towards the block of text. However, as part of his cohesive patterning, Clinton includes a significant white space between the words, almost like an intake of breath before an impact. As many

Chapter One

"Well it don't look very nice."
"What shall we do?"

"I KNOW!"

"Where shall we run to?"
"Just keep running and shut up."
So they ran and ran but then Mike tripped
and fell so they all dived for the ground.
"Wo! A very lucky escape."
"Yep a very lucky escape."

Figure 10.2 Chapter 1 of Clinton's book

published authors of picture books, Clinton leaves the reader to read into the gaps. The double page spread of pages 8 and 9 (Figure 10.4) shows a telling use of space to create an impression of the power of the alien force.

At the bottom right of the spread Clinton uses visual signals of movement to drive the narrative forward and urge the reader to turn the page. In filmic fashion, the action, extent and power of the battle is signalled by visual images whereas the human and emotional element is carried by dialogue, as shown by the double page spread on pages 10 and 11 (Figure 10.5). Here, Clinton has captured the multidimensional quality of film in an apparently two dimensional text.

The kinds of multimodal text Clinton has made is familiar in homes and classrooms, seen often in televisual, comic, graphic novel or video form. These text experiences are represented more and more frequently and there are now

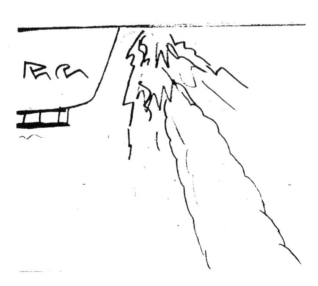

Figure 10.3   Cinton's 7th page

A super extra terrestrial group of combat ships.

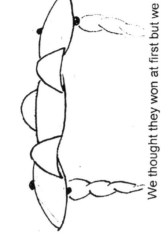

We thought they won at first but we didn't give so we let them eat this......

Then it was their turn.

Figure 10.4 Clinton's double page spread (8th and 9th pages)

One of our future fighters from
USSA airforce.....

Chapter Three

"I'm sure glad about that new fighter

of ours."

"Ray."

"What?"

"Your mum and dad have just been killed

by one of the aliens."

"Oh no!" (cry)

"You alright Ray?"

"Sort of...."

Well after that everyone was angry.

The aliens had killed over half the

population of America.

So we went for

em!

LIKE ARROWS

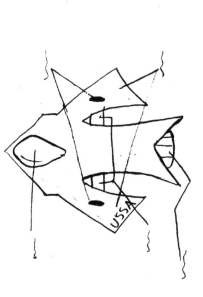

The Fireball ship..........

Figure 10.5 Clinton's double page spread (10th and 11th pages)

far more instances of depicted sound and movement in young people's texts than even ten years ago. Newspaper, magazine and designed information book reading brings knowledge of designed text which uses spatial rather than chronological cohesion. However, for examinations and assessments rather than personal expression, texts are expected to be written rather than designed.

At about the same time as Clinton wrote his multimodal story, he also designed and made an information book about dinosaurs. Figure 10.6 shows part of his layout design where he uses his text knowledge. In most assessment tests of writing composition, pupils have to show the ability to write imaginative, interesting and thoughtful texts which are appropriate to task, reader and purpose. They must show evidence that they can select and adapt form and content according to purpose, viewpoint and reader, and convey ideas and themes in appropriate styles. Young writers have to show that they can organize and present whole texts effectively, sequencing and structuring information, ideas and events, and construct paragraphs and use cohesion within and between paragraphs. They have to be able to select and use structural devices for the organization of texts; order and group ideas and material within sections of their texts to elaborate meaning; and maintain cohesion in texts of increasing variety and complexity. All of these aspects of composition can be seen in multimodal as well as in written texts. In his narrative and informational texts, Clinton certainly demonstrates his ability in these strands. However, while it is encouraging to see that assessment frameworks are capable of describing multimodal as well as purely written texts, there are some areas which still need consideration.

One essential move will be to recognize multimodal texts as texts in their own right, not as 'imperfect' written texts. While some young writers find it relatively easy to slip into representing sound, image and movement in words, others end up writing only the words of what in their heads is a multimodal text. Their writing may seem to lack organization and cohesion while it is in fact only a partial representation of the full story carried in the mind's eye and ear. To a reader steeped in narrative written text this can seem staccato and disorganized, without the explicit connectives which are the hallmarks of coherent written texts. When asked to write, children may supply the words, but sometimes it is clear that the pictorial and moving elements of their inner narratives are not being represented on the page. They are thinking in a twenty-first century way but – sometimes desperately – attempting to respond to the teacher's twentieth century request for writing-dominated forms of narrative. If teachers are to help children distinguish between written and multimodal text making and the occasions when it is useful to present ideas in a particular way, they will need to be given assurance that they can include multimodal texts as part of their explicit teaching for assessment purposes. Such a 'transformative pedagogy' recommended by Millard (2003) will need a

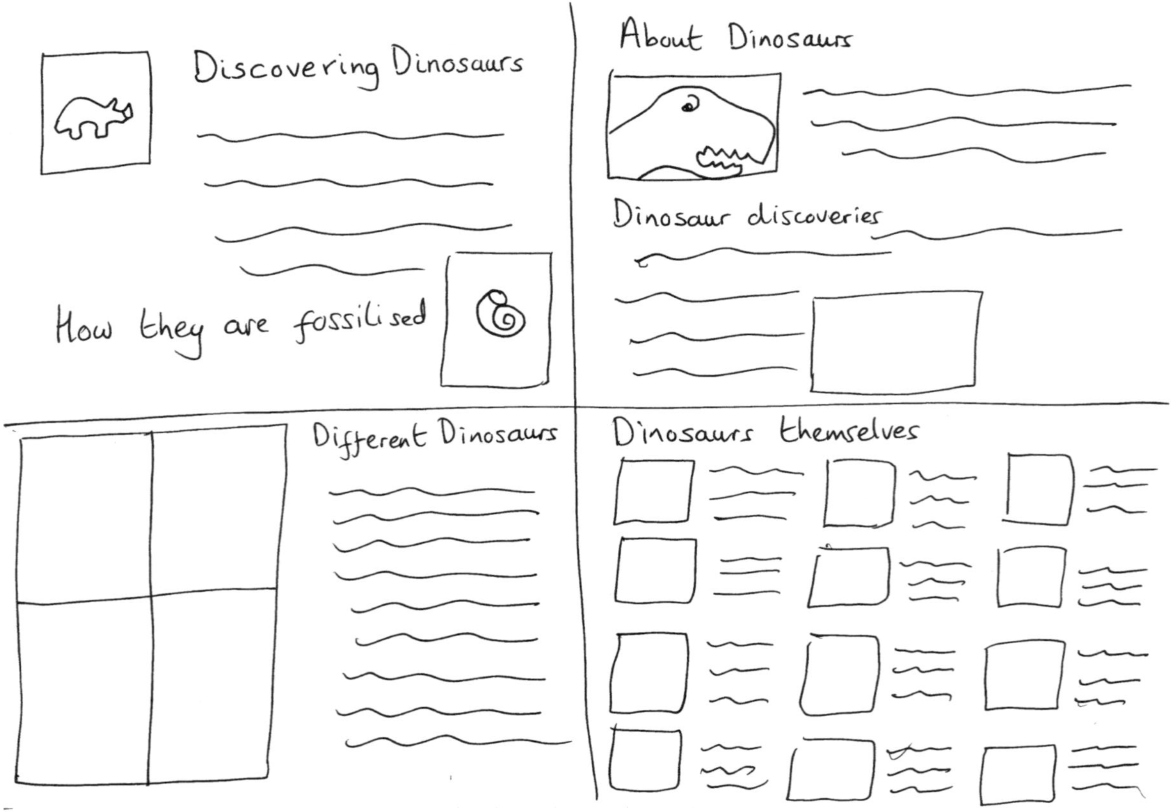

Figure 10.6 Clinton's design for four pages of an information book

commonly agreed descriptive vocabulary for written and multimodal texts for such assurances to have weight. A common frame of reference will depend on increasing awareness – and discussion – of text structure and this will depend on national curricula catching up with young readers and text makers as well as their teachers, who work daily in a multimodal world.

It will also be imperative not only to recognize the text knowledge brought into the classroom from children's experience outside school, but to make it possible for such knowledge to interact with new text knowledge introduced in the formal setting of the classroom. A theory of text (making and reading) should help make explicit the text cohesive differences between a purely written telling and a multidimensional one and expose the social, cultural and situational expectations surrounding different types of text. It should offer insights into children's production of texts as they draw on their experiences of what they read and see, what they know and what they show. Since the technological revolution has prompted new thinking about how texts can work, there has to be an accommodation to 'textnology' and its cultural significance. A theory which has text, its patterns and dimensions, their affordances and cohesive structures as central features should offer a means of integrating views of different ways of reading and representing, different ways of thinking and the experiences brought to texts by young people with an increasing range of text experience. This in turn has implications for an understanding of the interactions between school approaches to text making and children's cultural experience. The pedagogic implications are clear: if young people's knowledge and experience of text are genuinely to be valued and built on, then teachers, and the institutions of assessment, need to develop a more precise, inclusive and multidimensional way of talking about texts.

Note

1   This chapter is an expansion of some ideas I explore in Bearne (2003).
2   At the time of writing, the Qualifications and Curriculum Authority (QCA) is providing a research grant for members of the United Kingdom Reading (Literacy) Association to undertake a description of the features of multimodal texts at Key Stages 1 and 2.

11 Back to the future: developing children as writers

Angela Packwood and Trinka Messenheimer

> Power is about being able to craft a piece of writing so effectively that its purpose is achieved . . . Such power doesn't come from nowhere. It comes from practicing writing for real reasons. It comes from having read powerful writing. It comes from having been taught, and I mean taught, the basic skills of spelling and punctuation in the context of real writing events. Those who write well have more power and therefore have more control over their lives.
>
> (Fox 1993: 20–1)

Over approximately the last decade governments around the world have been undertaking substantial and far reaching programmes of educational reform with the stated aim of driving up standards (Levin and Riffel 1997; Hargreaves *et al.* 1998; Levin 1998; Denmaine 1999). In response to this pressure teachers have had to implement a constantly changing curriculum for the most part externally imposed. Curriculum content has been codified to ensure consistency of practice. One result of this is an erosion of the degree of control that teachers and learners are able to exercise over the selection, organization and pacing of educational knowledge (Sainsbury 1998; Burgess-Macey 1999). In turn this has strengthened the boundary between what may or may not be transmitted as educational knowledge and between curriculum knowledge and learner's knowledge (Bernstein 1971). Consequently teachers' expectations of children as writers are increasingly framed by educational knowledge determined by external agencies.

We have now entered the era of accountability and standards and government's attempts to regulate, standardize and test writing are in danger of creating an overly constrained conception of the writing process. With the drive to 'measure' writing as solely a product, the tests are not process orientated, rather they are a 'snapshot' of a predetermined writing exercise through which children's writing ability is ranked. This has generated a new genre of writing – 'writing for tests' – that schools practice in order to teach the process. In many classrooms the writing focus is solely on this test practice while in other classrooms valuable time is being taken away from process writing to accommodate the test demands.

There is therefore a conflict between the emphasis on writing as a measurable product and teacher's belief in the importance of process which results in dilemmas for teachers as they have to mediate the sometimes contradictory demands of externally imposed initiatives and their own personal and professional beliefs. In order to resolve these dilemmas, teachers develop what Hargreaves (1978) has described as 'coping strategies'. When the coping strategies are successful they can become embedded in the routine of teaching and learning at both classroom and school level (Hargreaves 1978). The adoption of successful coping strategies is not unproblematic if, for any reason, the strategies are inappropriate. We would argue that the imposition of standards and accountability, whether through the mechanism of tests or prescribed teaching structures and content, may not necessarily produce the change in either pedagogy or achievement that they are intended to produce. Instead teachers may develop a range of inappropriate coping strategies ranging from compliance through accommodation to resistance, any of which may undermine, either consciously or unconsciously, the desired change. In the case of writing, the coping strategy has tended to be to determine writing tasks and routines according to what is to be assessed. The predominant focus is on achieving independence and proficiency in the technical features of the writing task, and in the ability accurately to record curriculum knowledge, not in developing children as autonomous writers who have power and control over their writing.

The result of this is that writing is in danger of being defined in an increasingly narrow way. If writing is seen as being merely instrumental, the purpose of which is to demonstrate technical competence and knowledge retention, then teaching writing in a skill-based way will produce competent, though *disengaged*, writers. Writing will be defined as a technical ability operating through the application of the secretarial skills of writing, grammar, syntax, spelling and punctuation on words, sentences, paragraphs and texts. Competency is assessed as the product of the accurate application of the technical skills within the textual context, requiring little or no engagement with the process from the writer.

In contrast, if writing is defined as a vehicle for learning about oneself and the world, as well as being a way of sharing and critically evaluating knowledge, beliefs, attitudes, culture, traditions and so on, it demands that the writer be *engaged affectively* with the process. These engaged writers need to operate within the expert model and to use writing in an epistemic way (Bereiter 1980). That is, to use writing as a reflective, metacognitive tool.

The importance of using writing as part of an active process of reflecting upon thinking derives from the conceptual shift occurring in the 1980s, when educationalists such as Donald Graves (1983) began to look at the process of writing from a constructivist viewpoint. The notion of authorship, ownership and control were foregrounded in approaches to writing such as the writer's workshop. These strategies supported children in developing as writers who had control and choice over the writing they engaged in and were able to use writing to make sense of the world (Murray 1982; Graves 1983; Calkins 1984; Corden 2002).

The current standards-driven agendas in education have reversed what seemed to be a paradigm shift in the teaching of writing. Reform based on the adoption of standards puts pressure on an increasingly narrow pedagogical focus. The links between teaching and testing become tightly prescribed by external demands and agencies. Children's achievement is conceptualized as a functional level of proficiency in basic skill areas, particularly literacy and numeracy. The pressures teachers find themselves under because of this narrowed focus and increased accountability have resulted in, among other things, the use of restricted teaching strategies (Messenheimer and Packwood 2002a). This has an impact on the way children perceive writing.

The small scale survey of children as writers in the UK and US undertaken by Packwood and Messenheimer (2002) has shown that in the UK children judge being a 'good' writer primarily by the neatness of their handwriting rather than by content or appropriateness. In both countries the pupils in our survey saw writing as primarily an instrument for learning. Few perceived that they used writing to communicate at school, although clearly they saw this as a real purpose for writing at home. The overriding pressure in England to practice and present neat handwriting was illustrated by pupils identifying this as both a genre and a purpose for writing at school.

For both groups of pupils the main audience for their writing at school was the teacher. This is consistent with the pupils' notion of the purpose of writing at school being other-directed (in other words, 'because the teacher tells you to'). Writing is a tool for gleaning information in content areas. Most pupils at school do not see themselves as an audience for their writing, presumably because they are not writing for their own purposes. They see the main purpose of writing as being to demonstrate to teachers what has been learned. There is little notion of themselves as writers in control of the process, rather writing is a performance, the content, audience and purpose of which has been determined externally rather than internally. A focus on a limited definition of writing has been recognized as being problematic, resulting in more time being spent on practising writing, than developing children as writers (Ofsted 2000). In addition, the strategy has not narrowed the gap between the achievement of boys and girls. In fact, the gap is wider (Ofsted 2002).

Bereiter and Scardamalia (1987) identified two models of writing based on the types of knowledge needed. The first is the task execution model, which is linear in operation, it is the one they categorize as being novice. Here writers are using declarative and procedural knowledge to construct texts. Declarative knowledge is an understanding of the structure and purposes of elements of the writing process. Procedural knowledge is an understanding of how to combine those elements of the writing process. For the novice writing is a technical ability operating through the application of the secretarial skills of writing, grammar, syntax, spelling and punctuation on words, sentences, paragraphs and texts. At this level success is a product of the accurate application of the technical skills, requiring little or no engagement with the process from the writer. The knowledge is applied almost formulaically in response to a teacher-directed task. The writer has been taught that the rules for writing narrative are different from those for exposition and is able to write in either genre when told to do so. However, they may not have sufficient understanding to be able to decide for themselves when and how to use either genre. The writer has knowledge but not control, and that knowledge has been transmitted by the teacher.

The second model is of writing as a process akin to problem solving. It is one adopted by expert writers who are able to use conditional knowledge which is an understanding of how, and when, declarative and procedural knowledge of the writing process can, and should, be combined in order to achieve particular purposes (Bereiter and Scardamalia 1987; Collins and Collins 1997). In this model declarative and procedural knowledge are transformed by the learner. The writer has both knowledge of, and control over the process. In order to develop this degree of control children need multiple and varied opportunities to develop knowledge not just about the process but about themselves as writers, about the writing process and about the demands of particular writing tasks including how to consciously transgress textual structures. In this model, the expert writer is able to consider alternative ways of handling writing tasks and to make informed choices about the writing process. The level of awareness of the writing process itself is what determines the model of writing being operationalized. Developing as an expert, engaged writer requires extended periods of concentration and engagement in which writers need to draw on all their motivational, cognitive, affective and linguistic resources. They must believe that their writing is of value (Codling and Gambrell 1997).

What we would argue is that these two models should be seen as composite parts of a larger model, presented below. If the models of writing held by published authors are investigated it can be seen that writing is a recursive process in which revision, planning and transcription occur in varying orders and recur at various times in the writing process (Winokur 1986; Murray 1990; Barton 1994; Packwood and Messenheimer 2002). Writing is more a synthesis of recursive practices, skills and abilities, some of them cognitive, some affective and some linguistic that operate simultaneously. We have conceptualized this meta-knowledge as epistemic after the work of Bereiter (1980)

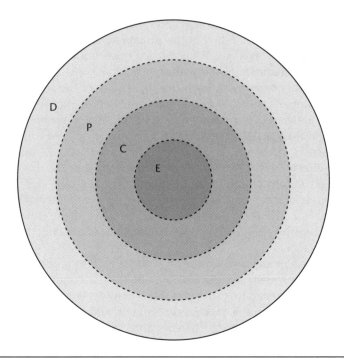

Declarative knowledge (D) An understanding of and competence in: handwriting, spelling, selection of vocabulary, use of vocabulary, punctuation and grammar.

Procedural knowledge (P) Applying the above in appropriate compositional forms – writing down what comes to mind – applying technical competence to a flow of ideas.

Conditional knowledge (C) An understanding of how and when technical and operational knowledge of the writing process can, and should, be combined in order to achieve particular purposes in different registers.

Epistemic (E) The ability to use writing as a tool for a reflective search for personal meaning – as a way of constructing knowledge through a variety of discourses and in a range of identities.

Figure 11.1   Epistemic model of writing

(see Figures 11.1 and 11.2). This is a dynamic not static model of writing. The intersecting lines are permeable as writing is a recursive process and children will move between elements of the model depending on the purpose for which writing is being used. It is not intended to be perceived as a hierarchical model, it is developmental. It is our contention that, at present children's writing experiences are designed to practise declarative and procedural knowledge. When conditional knowledge is applied it tends to be in a disengaged way because of the child's lack of control over the purpose for which they are writing.

Type of knowledge	Role of writer
Declarative knowledge An understanding of, and competence in: • handwriting; • spelling; • selection and use of vocabulary; • punctuation; • grammar.	Novice Disengaged
Procedural knowledge Applying the above in appropriate compositional forms – writing down what comes to mind – applying technical competence to a flow of ideas	
Conditional knowledge An understanding of how, and when, technical and operational knowledge of the writing process can, and should, be combined in order to achieve particular purposes in different registers	Expert Disengaged
Epistemic knowledge The ability to use writing as a tool for a reflective search for personal meaning – as a way of constructing knowledge through a variety of discourses and in a range of identities	Autonomous writer Engaged

Figure 11.2   A knowledge-based model of writing

The model identifies the types of knowledge required by the child to develop as an autonomous, engaged writer who has power and control over their epistemic writing. While the most able children may operate with the expert knowledge of writing, most children will be operating as novice writers, in a disengaged way. We would argue that, with the pressure to achieve a narrowly defined competence as a writer, there is little or no opportunity for children to become engaged writers and develop beyond this point to make writing an integral part of their meta-cognitive strategies. Nor are the restricted pedagogic strategies that teachers develop in order to cope with the demands made on them supportive of such development.

One of the advantages – and joys – of exploring the process of writing is that writers have an urge to explore the process through the medium itself, therefore there are numerous sources of writers on writing, ranging from autobiography (Dillard 1989) through reflection (Lamott 1995) to 'how to' books (Goldberg 1986). In order to explore the process from the perspective of those who practice the craft, rather than from that of those who teach it, we read over 500 texts and interviews by published writers about the process of writing. Also included were a set of 26 author autobiographies: a series written for children about writing. We did not restrict ourselves to those writers who might be considered 'literary'. We also looked at popular writers – Stephen King (2000) and R.L. Stine (1997) and poets such as Annie Lamott (1995), as well as teachers who are also writers, for example, Mem Fox (1993). In order to develop a model we extracted quotations from the writers about how they write, when they write, why they write, how they revise and edit, what they do when they are blocked, what supports their writing, what inhibits their writing. An illustration of the type of quotation we worked with is the following by Lloyd Alexander:

> First, read as much as humanly possible. Read everything – fiction, nonfiction, history, biography, poetry, science, everything possible. You can't read everything that's been written, but you can try. Second, write as much as you possibly can. Write stories or poems. Keep a journal, keep a diary. Write notes to yourself, or whatever comes into your mind. It doesn't matter what it is. Don't even worry whether it's any good or not. If it's bad, throw it away. Nobody will ever know. It's a matter of practice, writing, the same way that a pianist practices the scales, or a ballet dancer who constantly exercises. Simply do it continually. It really does help. It's a matter of getting fluency, of not being scared of blank paper. It starts a good habit pattern. Writing every day, even if you have to throw out what you've written, is marvellous practice. It builds up the kind of discipline you need to keep on working no matter what else happens.
>
> (Alexander 2001: 4–5)

The quotations were then analysed to produce a model of the writing process held by published writers. This model was one of a recursive, reflective engaged activity over which they exercised control and choice and which they used primarily for epistemic purposes. An external audience for their work was almost secondary. Their primary audience was themselves and often they were using the writing to work out solutions to problems or deal with issues that concerned them. The writing process was one of making meaning for themselves first and for an audience second.

Within that model we looked at what experiences the writers had identified as contributing to their meta-cognitive understanding of the way in which writing operated at an epistemic level, that is, to their ability to use writing as a tool for a reflective search for personal meaning. Although all writers acknowledged the need for an understanding of declarative knowledge, for them it was very much a first stage in the process of engaging with writing. Their main emphasis was on the way in which constantly writing, revising and editing their own work and engaging with the work of others – reading as a writer produced their deep understanding of the process. ← link of reading + writing!

What emerged from the data was a clear indication that for writers the key source of their meta-cognitive knowledge about the writing process was drawn from their engagement with texts, whether those were their own works in progress or the reading of other people's work. Progression was grounded very firmly in what they had done before. All the published writers talked about using what they had journaled, jotted, logged or diarized as being a source of ideas and inspiration. If they were engaged in writing a book then re-reading what they had written the day before was the starting point for what came next.

The results were then used to identify ways in which teachers could incorporate the findings into their teaching, in order to support children in the process of moving beyond disengaged competence to an engagement with the epistemic level of writing. This gave us the following three questions which we answered from the writers' model of writing.

1   How can the writer's experiences support the reflective meta-cognitive knowledge necessary for epistemic writing?

Those who write only when required to do so, and in response to another's agenda will not transform the declarative, procedural and conditional knowledge to develop the potential to use writing as an epistemic tool. Therefore children need to:

- discover for themselves what's missing from their own texts;
- internalize the writing processes illustrated in others' writing;
- understand that there is a complex, evolving interaction between what is written and the process of writing it;
- develop a wide knowledge of discourse structures;
- keep a reader's writing journal in which to respond to texts;
- read as much as possible and as many different types of texts as possible;
- read texts in their entirety;
- choose texts to read;
- have texts read to them (in their entirety);
- read texts they don't like;
- re-read their own work as a 'springboard' for further writing;
- verbalize the writing process.

2   How can writers engage with texts in order to acquire reflective meta-cognitive knowledge?

Assessment driven reading/writing connections (that is, reading texts or part of texts only to explicitly deconstruct the writing process as a means to teaching elements of the process) do not promote reflective meta-cognitive strategies. As identified by published writers and in research (see for example Barrs 2000; Barrs and Cork 2001) one of the key elements of developing as an autonomous, engaged epistemic writer is the ability to read like a writer.

Therefore children need to:

Very – social constructivist

- pay careful attention to detail;
- keep a writer's notebook, log, journal, diary;
- write and re-write, draft and re-draft, revise and edit for a real purpose;
- understand that re-writing is an integral part of the creative/compositional element of the writing process, not just a secretarial activity;
- write every day;
- not have every piece of writing marked;
- write for themselves;
- write in different places, at different times.

Many of the experiences identified above, which would move children on to the expert writer model and beyond it to the epistemic level, are missing from models of teaching writing. Those which do occur, such as verbalizing the writing process, or drafting and editing are too often narrowly defined and applied (Dadds 1999; Fox 2000; DfES 2002c). Children need time, space, support and the power to make decisions for themselves in order to become autonomous, engaged, epistemic writers.

3   What is the interrelationship between children as reading writers and teachers as writing facilitators in the epistemic writing process?

To conceptualize writing as a dynamic, multidimensional process means that the task for the teacher becomes one of supporting children to go beyond the declarative and procedural dimensions of writing to the conditional and epistemic dimensions – where choices are made and writing is used as a powerful personal tool.

Therefore teachers of writing need to:
- be practising writers;
- allow/encourage children to 'think aloud' the writing process;
- allow children to read texts in their entirety and to respond to them as writers;
- write jointly with children;
- model writing;
- allow children to construct the meaning of a text over time;
- encourage children to see reading, like a writer, as a deeply active process;
- allow children to articulate their relationship to a text (reactions, expectations, meanings);
- help children develop a reflective meta-language through which to talk about texts and themselves as writers;
- allow children to explore alternative discourses and identities

through encounters with a wide variety of texts, including electronic texts;
- respond to children's writing as a 'real' audience (giving a genuine reader's response rather than a teacher's response);
- support children in generating their own knowledge about a particular topic and then selecting from this to meet the purpose of the writing.

For writers to be engaged, the nature and purpose of writing in schools has to be defined in a way that foregrounds the process, including emotional involvement, not merely the skill base necessary for technical competence based on word-, sentence- and text-level deconstruction. Teachers have to feel secure and confident enough to move beyond the perceived constraints that change has imposed on their classroom practice. Part of this confidence comes from knowing how children learn to write and knowledge about writing itself. This moves beyond the technicist definition of subject knowledge to be found in prescribed teacher training curricula and requires that teachers understand the complex relationship between reader and writer as identified in the model above (Messenheimer and Packwood 2002b).

Under pressure teachers work with a linear model of the writing process where planning leads to transcription which is followed by revision (Flower and Hayes 1981). This linear model describes the way in which the product – the text – develops. It does not describe the inner process of developing as an epistemic writer as identified by the authors we analysed. Some teachers believe that because they 'teach' writing and children 'learn' to write, one must be as a result of the other, whereas developmental research suggests that children learn a great deal about writing without being explicitly taught it (Hayes and Flower 1980; Emig 1983; Hume 1983; Bereiter and Scardamalia 1987). The role of the teacher, therefore, has to be not only to teach explicitly the declarative, procedural and conditional knowledge necessary to the writing process, but also to ensure that there are ample opportunities for children to learn the 'hidden curriculum' that our analysis of writers on writing revealed; for example, that good writers steal – ideas, vocabulary, settings, styles – which they then make their own.

Therefore, in order to support the development of children as autonomous, engaged epistemic writers, teachers need to be able to move beyond the instrumental demand of skills-based assessment, to resolve the dilemmas they face by drawing on their professional knowledge and expertise as teachers of literacy, making explicit how their strategies support the development of children as writers. They need to be able to resist the move to drive up standards by teaching children to be expert test takers. This is particularly important when it comes to developing children's sense of themselves as writers, to using writing as an epistemic tool in a reflective search for personal meaning.

PART 7
The Social Construction of Literacy

Throughout this book we have seen children learning not through solo encounters with text, but with the aid of others, both those more proficient and those who also have much to learn. Peter Geekie and Gordon Wells give us forceful accounts of such learning that are both sharply particular and also powerfully theorized. For both Geekie and Wells, meaning and intention are crucially important elements in cognition: child learners do not process information like computers, but develop understanding as intentional human beings. Both see learning at its most productive as an essentially social process.

We see this in fine detail in Geekie's presentation of 5-year-old Amy learning to write. Over a school year we see Amy's relationship with the task of writing a 'story' change as she moves from dependence on her teacher to independence, in terms of choice of topic, selection of words, use of a range of strategies to enable her to set the words down on paper and evaluation of her text's comprehensibility. After eight months in Rhonda's class, unprompted, Amy is using for herself the strategies Rhonda began to model for her and her classmates in the first days at school. Amy's communicative intentions provide the shaping dynamic for this complex process.

As they write a story on dinosaurs together in one of the three classrooms discussed by Wells, the communicative intentions of a group of 8-year-old Portuguese speakers also shape their learning. But for them the process of learning to write is even more complex than it is for Amy, as they are writing in English, a language new to them, so vocabulary choices and grammatical markers pose particular problems. Through collaboration with one another these difficulties are largely overcome as the children strive together to produce a story that is satisfying to them as well as comprehensible to others.

For both Geekie and Wells literacy learning is in large part a matter of increasing awareness of process. Towards the end of the school year, Amy carefully talks her way through the various means of recalling how words are written that Rhonda has helped her to learn. Wells shows us a class of 6- and 7-year-olds learning to discuss the thematic patterning of texts by grouping

Post-it notes the children have written at home with their parents, expressing their responses to a picturebook. As they shift the comments around, the children are learning to see ideas in new juxtapositions, moving towards a meta-language about the texts they are working with and the processes they are using to construct or construe them. They are also learning to integrate understanding developed at home with what goes on at school.

Both writers end by listing what they see to be the key principles underlying the richly successful practice they have shared with us. Just as their teachers have helped the children at the centre of these accounts to develop an awareness of what they should do to operate successfully, so both writers help the readers of these accounts towards a greater awareness of what we must do to enrich our own teaching.

12 Social and cultural influences on literacy

Peter Geekie

For too long research into literacy development has been dominated by models of cognition that have no place for the intentions and emotions of authors and readers, and which offer explanations in terms of information processing rather than meaning making. And it seems strange that, while information processing psychology has been under attack from within the discipline of psychology for a very long time, it has exerted an extraordinary influence over pedagogical practices in reading.

Information processing theories in psychology grew out of the cognitive revolution of the late 1950s. In the first instance this revolution aimed to replace behaviourism with a new psychology that had meaning as its central concept, but it was not long before the emphasis started to shift from the construction of meaning to the processing of information (Bruner 1990: 4). The computer became the metaphor for the mind. The fact that this conception of cognitive activity was not well equipped to deal with what Bruner (1996 5) has called 'the messy, ambiguous, and context-sensitive processes of meaning-making' seemed to be of no interest to the proponents of the new psychology.

This was only one of the problems that the new cognitive science was seen to have. Harré, for example, has commented that

> in both behaviourism and computational cognitive science human beings, explicitly or implicitly, are taken to be passive, mere spectators of processes over which they have no control. Processes of seeming higher-order control are just processes among other processes.
>
> (Harré 1995: 144)

The passive, information processing child implied by these theories is seen in the teaching practices derived from them. Children learn to read because they are taught, we are told, and what they must be taught is phonological awareness and word decoding skills.

The surprising thing is that more humane conceptions of children as learners have not made a greater impact on research into the nature of literacy development. In 1987 Bruner and Haste spoke of a 'quiet revolution' that was taking place in developmental psychology. The basis for this revolution, they said, was not just that psychologists had begun to think of children as social beings who learnt through interaction with others

> but because we have come once more to appreciate that through such social life, the child acquires a framework for interpreting experience, and learns how to negotiate meaning in a manner congruent with the requirements of the culture. Making sense is a social process; it is an activity situated within a cultural and historical context.
>
> (Bruner and Haste 1987: 1)

This conception of learning is more in keeping with the nature of literacy itself. Negotiating meaning and making sense are basic to all literate behaviour. And writers and readers produce and interpret written language texts in accordance with the frameworks for action provided by their culture.

Neither can *what* is learnt be separated from the *act* of learning. The relationship between literacy and the mental processes is symbiotic. The sign system of language provides new cognitive tools and so changes the way the mind operates. And texts provide readers with new ways of thinking about the world and their place in it. Unless the social, collaborative and cultural nature of literacy learning is recognized, it is difficult to see how we can progress beyond tired disputes about whether learning to be literate necessarily involves the explicit and structured teaching of decoding skills, and whether automatic responses to print must be developed before meaning enters at all.

In this chapter an effort is made to examine literacy development as a 'joint, mediated, meaning-making activity' (Cole and Engestrom 1993: 22). The discussion draws on data collected in a class of 5-year-olds in their first year of school in Australia. Six children were watched during a full school year as they learned to write, and video data was collected as they wrote simple texts under the guidance of their teacher in their own classrooms in conditions as natural as circumstances permitted. The episodes in this chapter are drawn from that body of data and focus on one of the children, Amy. Her teacher is Rhonda. In attempting to understand why Amy learns so quickly we might also develop a better understanding of the fundamentals of effective literacy instruction.

Getting started

Gordon Wells (1986) has said that, in learning to speak, children have to work out the way language is organized for themselves. But it is not a solitary enterprise. They need the collaborative help of interested conversational partners who, in aiming to achieve understanding of the topics that are raised and of the activities they are engaged in together, provide clear and relevant evidence of how language works and feedback that enables children to evaluate the appropriateness of their current hypotheses.

(Wells 1986: 51)

Similarly, in Rhonda Fisher's classroom, the children gradually worked out how *written* language is organized. But not by themselves. The interested conversational partner in this case was Rhonda, and the conversation accompanied collaborative attempts to construct written texts. Joint text construction, for example, was one of the regular activities of this classroom, beginning in the first week of school. Rhonda referred to these texts as 'chalkboard stories'.

The construction of the 'chalkboard story' followed a standard form.

1   The intended text was clearly stated.
2   Each word was identified and written in turn. Rhonda usually invited the children to participate in the act of identification by asking a question like, 'What's the first/next word in my story?'
3   As each word was written Rhonda involved the children in finding ways to write it. Usually this meant either searching for the word in the classroom (instigated by a question like, 'Where can we find/where have we seen X?'); or by engaging in a phonemic segmentation of the word, with the children suggesting a letter (or letters) to match each 'sound' as it was identified.
4   The text was regularly re-read to maintain it as the focus of attention and to help in identifying each successive word.

This was not 'story writing' as that term is generally understood. It was a school-based activity operationally defined through Rhonda's conduct of her 'chalkboard story' sessions, and it provided the basis for what was done during the individual writing sessions that followed.

Episode one is taken from a 'chalkboard story' session recorded in the third week of school. There had been several previous joint text constructions but it is evident that the children are still far from being competent in this situation.

Episode one	
Rhonda:	. . . that's my story for today * Friday is my favourite day because tomorrow we have a holiday * listen again [She repeats it]
Rhonda:	so the first word in my story is 'Friday' [A number of children call out letter names]
Rhonda:	just a minute * what I want you to do is think about 'Friday' and think about if I've ever written 'Friday' in our room * or if you've ever seen the word 'Friday' [Above the chalkboard is a permanent display of the days of the week. In addition, on the chalkboard, Rhonda has written 'Today is Friday'.] [As Rhonda speaks, many of the children direct their attention to the sentence on the chalkboard. Rhonda notes their response.]
Rhonda:	and now I want you to spell the word 'Friday' * what do I write first? [Some of the children call out 'F' and Rhonda writes it on the chalkboard]
Rhonda:	what comes next? [Rhonda writes the word as the children name each letter in turn]
Rhonda:	[she speaks as she finishes writing 'Friday'] now I want the word 'is' [She makes the initial sound twice] [Some children call out 'E' and others follow their example] [Rhonda turns and writes 'e' on the chalkboard after 'Friday'. Then she turns to the group again]
Rhonda:	ssss [Some of the children call out 'S!'] [Rhonda writes 's' on the chalkboard]
Rhonda:	right * let's read what we've got

Guided participation

To a casual observer early in the school year, joint story constructions like the one from which this episode was extracted might have seemed chaotic. The children responded enthusiastically and loudly, but their responses were often approximate at best. This does not matter. Although the children as yet know almost nothing about 'story writing', Rhonda is inviting their participation, and sustaining it by whatever means are necessary, because learning to be 'story writers' in this classroom is largely a product of what Barbara Rogoff (1990) calls 'guided participation'. And as time goes by there is a 'transformation of participation'. At first, without the adult's support, the novice writers would find participation difficult, but they gradually assume greater responsibility for the completion of the task until the adult is little more than an onlooker.

Rogoff has also examined the nature of effective instruction. In a series of studies she found that the most effective tutors were those who involved the children in 'shared and guided decision making' and engaged in 'strategic thinking aloud' about the task at hand. Rhonda behaves like the effective tutors in Rogoff's studies by inviting the children to participate in joint problem solving (the problem of finding 'Friday') under her skilful guidance. She knows how to get it done, but she wants the children to think their way through the problem with her.

Learning about the mental processes

Middleton and Edwards (1990: 28) have suggested that

> The awareness of having and using a 'memory', and the awareness of its properties, may well arise as a matter of difficulty – as a matter of *not* being able to remember something, of being suddenly reminded, of having something on the tip of your tongue and of trying to square an offered version of events with what another speaker says.

In this episode, although Rhonda has written the word on the chalkboard not more than 20 minutes earlier, the children do not remember having seen 'Friday' before, so Rhonda makes the *process* of remembering explicit. 'I want you to *think* about 'Friday', she says. And what they are to think about is whether she has ever written 'Friday' in their room (it is in the sentence 'Today is Friday' on the chalkboard) or whether they have seen it in the room (when she was writing the sentence with them Rhonda referred to the display of days of the week above the chalkboard). She is referring to recently shared experiences that she quite reasonably expects the children to remember. And they do. Most of them respond by looking at the sentence on the chalkboard.

Rhonda is not only making the children aware of remembering as an activity. She is showing them what remembering means, given this problem (how to write 'Friday') in the context of this specifically defined activity (writing a 'story'). Instead of being an individual and unconscious reflex, remembering becomes something that can be consciously controlled in cooperation with other people. Learning about remembering in this sense is an important part of learning to be a writer in this classroom.

Analyzing the spoken word

David Olson (1996: 85–90) has challenged the widely held belief that writing is the transcription of speech. Instead, he says, writing provides a conceptual model of speech, and learning to read is learning the model that the alphabet provides. So when Rhonda engages in the phonemic segmentation of words during these sessions (as she does when she writes 'es' in the 'chalkboard story') she is showing the children that speech can be treated *as if* it is made up of a series of discrete sounds. Olson goes on to say that

> those who assume that reading is decoding assume, erroneously, that the phonology is available to consciousness; those who assume that reading is meaning detection assume, erroneously, that sound-symbol mapping is either irrelevant or impossible.

(Olson 1996: 85)

Rhonda does not avoid dealing with sound-symbol mapping, but she uses the alphabetic model only as a way of thinking about the relationship between speech and writing. It is not an accurate model (for example, the sounds of spoken language are not discrete, like beads on a string), but it gives children a way of starting their exploration of this aspect of written language.

Starting to write

Just as young children test their hypotheses about spoken language through the feedback they receive during conversations with interested and competent adults, so must novice writers have opportunities to test their hypotheses about written language by writing and receiving feedback as they write. That is why the individual writing sessions in Rhonda's classroom were crucial to the children's growth as readers and writers.

The following episode was recorded about the same time as Episode one, but it is taken from an individual writing session. Amy is trying to write 'went'. So far she has written only the 'W'.

Episode two	
	[Rhonda looks at Damien and gestures towards him as she speaks]
Rhonda:	you had 'went' in your story yesterday * can you remember how to spell 'went'?
	[Damien turns towards Rhonda]
Rhonda:	have a look and see how you spell 'went'
	[Damien opens his story folder]
	[Rhonda turns to Amy and points at Damien]
Rhonda:	well he's going to help you spell 'went'
	[She turns to Damien again]
Rhonda:	how did you spell 'went'?
	[Damien continues to look through his folder. He picks up one sheet and looks at it]

> [Amy looks over his shoulder. She points.]
> Amy: oh E
> Rhonda: (nods) yeah E
> [Amy looks at Damien's story again. Then she starts to write E]
> Rhonda: (to Damien) yeah * and then what?
> Damien: W-E-N-T
> [Amy finishes writing E]
> Damien: N-T
> [Amy does not look up]
> Amy: N-T
> [She writes the letters as she says them]

Using the collective consciousness of the class

Damien sits next to Amy. Yesterday the 'story' he wrote with Rhonda's assistance was, 'I went to Bristol Beach', and Amy took part in the protracted discussion that occurred about how to spell 'went'. In this episode, when Rhonda finds that Amy is uncertain about what to do next, she reminds Damien that he wrote 'went' during yesterday's writing session and tells him to look for it in his writing folder.

By involving Damien in the solution of the problem (how to spell 'went') Rhonda is showing Amy that, if other children can remember what you cannot, then asking them for help is an acceptable problem-solving strategy. In another session a little later in the year she tells the children, 'If you need help just ask each other.' It is an explicit statement of what later becomes an assumed principle of behaviour in this classroom.

Using the teacher's consciousness

The children in this episode are only 5 years old and are limited in their capacity to attend and remember strategically. They are also novice writers. If they are to be able to participate in this activity at all, Rhonda has to act as a 'vicarious consciousness' for them. She has to use *her* capacity to remember and attend and plan on their behalf when they cannot do it for themselves.

In this episode, however, Rhonda has not simply done the cognitive work for the children. She has enabled them to use their *existing* mental capacities, and in doing so she has shown them what attending and remembering can mean during this type of activity.

This enabling effect is especially notable in what Amy does. At the beginning of the episode Amy seems not even to understand the immediate purpose of the activity, but when Rhonda draws her attention to Damien, she watches closely as he searches through his writing folder. When he finds the needed text and holds it up, she scans it without further prompting and fixes her attention, not just on the relevant word, but on the precise information in that word that she needs (the letter 'E'). It seems that, despite earlier indications to the contrary, Amy

1   was aware of what her purpose was all the time (to find the next letter in the word 'went');
2   had not forgotten the discussion about how to spell 'went' on the previous day, and did remember the content of the 'story';
3   was capable of exercising her memory and attention in successfully searching for and locating the next letter in 'went'.

What seemed to be incompetence was really a production deficiency.

Common knowledge

These children are operating in a zone of proximal development. They can do with assistance what they could not do independently. But the capacity to profit from the assistance given in this episode is dependent on the fact that there is shared experience (writing 'went' on the previous day) to which the children can be referred. Being able to attend and remember is of little use if there is nothing relevant to remember, and nothing pertinent upon which joint attention can be established.

Developing control

Learning to control the higher mental processes

Episode three was recorded five months after school began. Amy's 'story' for the day is 'My birthday is in October. I will be six'.

Episode three	
Amy:	in/
Rhonda:	[nods]
Amy:	October
	[Amy makes eye contact]
Amy:	uh * I
Rhonda:	where can we find October?
	[Amy immediately looks at the display of months of the year above the chalkboard]
	[Rhonda follows her gaze]
Amy:	ummm
	[She points at the right end of the display]

Amy:	O?
	[She turns and makes eye contact]
Rhonda:	[nods twice]
Amy:	I can I can write this story for myself
	[Amy starts to write 'October'. She copies the word a letter at a time]

Amy has already written, 'My birthday is in', identifying each word in turn, and spelling them correctly without assistance. But in this episode, although she identifies 'October' as the next word, she cannot remember how to spell it. It is, once again, one of those moments when the socially constituted nature of remembering becomes visible.

During joint story constructions, and on other occasions as well, Rhonda has frequently asked questions like, 'Where can we find "October"?' (It is part of a display of months of the year above the chalkboard), and 'Where did we see "yesterday"?' (It is on the chart headed 'Words We Know'). When Rhonda asks her question in this episode Amy immediately looks above the chalkboard.

In Episode two Rhonda explicitly reminded Damien that he had previously written 'went', and directed him to look for it. But five months later this exchange between Rhonda and Amy is embedded in the now familiar discourse practices of the classroom, and refers to the frequently shared experience of searching for the names of the months of the year during writing sessions. Much more can be assumed now. Rhonda does not have to tell Amy to look for 'October'. A question framed in a familiar way is enough to invoke the relevant display as contextual and Amy's act of remembering is there for all to see.

Becoming conventional

As soon as a 'chalkboard story' had been completed, Rhonda would write a standard version immediately under it and the children would be asked to examine the two versions of the text to see how many words they had got 'right', and to compare their invented spellings with those that were conventionally correct. Rhonda would also extract words from her 'chalkboard stories' and discuss them with the class. One of the words she dealt with in this way (about a week before Episode four was recorded) was 'having'. She wrote it on the chalkboard and demonstrated how the final 'e' is dropped from 'have' (and similar words) when 'ing' is added.

Episode four is taken from an individual writing session seven months after school began.

Episode four

           [Charles has written 'haveing' in his 'story'. Rhonda notices]

Rhonda: [to Charles] and what do you do in 'having' when you add 'ing'?

Amy: you leave off the E [she points at the 'e' in Charles' word]

           [Rhonda makes eye contact with Amy]

Rhonda: [nods] mmm

           [Charles crosses out the 'e' in 'haveing']

Rhonda: you remember [to Charles]

Charles: oh yes [he crosses it out again more heavily]

Rhonda: [to the table at large] remember how if there's an E on the end of a word and you want to add 'ing' you drop the 'E'

           [About a minute later Amy leans across to attract Rhonda's attention]

Amy: I'm going to write coming and leave off the 'E'

Rhonda: Good

This episode is like Episode three, except that what is being invoked as contextual this time is not the prior experience of searching for words displayed in the classroom, but a prior discussion about conventional ways of writing words. The shift is from search and recognition, to principle and application.

The exchange gives some insight into the way that Amy is learning. Rhonda has provided evidence of how written language works in her discussions of words like 'having'. When she notices that what she *hoped* had been learnt had, in fact, been forgotten (Charles has written 'haveing') Rhonda reminds the children of what was previously said ('What do you do in "having" when you add "ing"?'). The children remember, and the 'e' in 'haveing' is crossed out.

Next, Rhonda does what teachers often do when something has been forgotten (Edwards and Mercer 1987: 82–6). She recapitulates the general principle ('If there's an "E" on the end of the word and you want to add "ing", you drop the "E".'). She behaves as if it is common knowledge when, clearly, it is not. The stated principle is invoked as part of the mental context shared by Rhonda and the children, and is potentially available for further action.

Almost immediately Amy recognizes that a word she is going to write is one to which the same principle applies, but before she writes the word she tells Rhonda what she is going to do ('I'm going to write "coming" and leave off the "e" '). She is showing Rhonda that she understands that what is true for 'having' is also true for 'coming'. Being able to state the principle shows that it is under her control. She is working out how written language is organized with Rhonda's assistance.

Becoming a writer

Exercising joint consciousness

This episode was recorded in mid-August, nearly eight months into the school year. Amy is writing about a visit to her house by twin girls in her class.

Episode five	
	[Amy re-reads the last part of her text and then hesitates. Then she turns towards Damien]
Amy:	how do you write 'yesterday'?
	[Damien points at the wall on the other side of the room]
Damien:	look behind you
	[Amy turns and looks]
Damien:	I'm spelling it [this means that he is currently writing himself]
	[Amy continues to look for the word. Damien looks at his text and reads from it. He looks up as he speaks]
Damien:	Y-E-S
Amy:	Y [she turns around and starts to write] oh I can do it
Damien:	Y-E-S
	[Amy looks up at Damien]
Amy:	I've found it
	[She writes 'yesterday', looking frequently at the chart]

Attending and remembering in this episode are, once again, observable social processes. When she cannot remember how to spell 'yesterday', Amy asks Damien to help her. He looks up and points, establishing which display Amy should attend to, and then provides the first three letters. This is sufficient to distinguish the word unambiguously from the others on the chart. Amy finds the word and copies it.

The children are now thinking together and exercising their mental functions cooperatively. Joint attention is managed efficiently through dialogue and the problem is solved collaboratively. A transformation of participation is taking place. Writing has become something the children do together while their teacher watches.

Mastering the activity structure

Episode six is taken from the same session and follows immediately after Episode five. Not long after this, what Amy did as she wrote was rarely audible or visible. In this episode the processes can still be seen and heard.

Episode six

Amy: yesterday * the [she writes 'the'] twins [she copies from where she has written it before]
       [Amy starts to re-read what she has written]

Amy: yesterday the twins **came** cuh [she writes 'c'] A [she writes 'a' and then looks up towards the front of the room where 'came' is on display]
       [Emma asks Damien how to spell 'come'. Damien spells the word for her and then says, 'I don't even have to look any more'. Amy writes 'me' to complete 'came']

Amy: to [she writes 'to'] **play** [she writes 'play'] **with** wuh [she writes 'w'] eh [she writes 'er'] thuh [she writes 'th', pauses for a moment and then adds 'e'] with **me** [she writes 'me'] with me **at** [she writes 'ta'] my [she writes 'my'] at my **house** * huh-ou [she writes 'h' and then looks up at the Sentence Maker and copies 'house']

Amy identifies each word in turn, using repetition and emphasis just as Rhonda did during joint text constructions. And she re-reads what she has written. Again this reflects Rhonda's practice during 'chalkboard story' sessions. In other words, Amy has appropriated Rhonda's strategies and ways of speaking to guide herself through the 'story writing' activity. What has happened is what Edwards and Mercer (1987: 161) have referred to as cognitive socialization. She has learnt the ways of thinking and behaving that make her recognizable as a writer *in this classroom*.

In writing her 'story' Amy also shows that she has learnt a variety of strategies to spell the words she needs.

1   She copies 'twins' from where she has written it earlier in her text.
2   She analyses 'with' into phonemes and matches each phoneme with an appropriate letter or letters. The resulting word is recognizable but not conventionally correct.
3   She listens to what other children are saying. When Damien spells 'come' for Emma she extracts just the information she needs to finish writing 'came': the last two letters.
4   She recalls commonly used words, apparently prompting recall by simply saying the word.
5   She locates 'house' in the Sentence Maker and copies it.

Remembering is involved in the writing of each word, and all of these acts of remembering have a history. They have their origins in the dialogues and discussions about writing that took place during 'chalkboard story' constructions, and as Rhonda helped children individually with their 'story writing'.

When a child has found and copied a specific word frequently enough he or she doesn't even have to look any more, just as Damien said. But recall of this nature is not automatic. It is voluntary. It is of the same nature as no longer having to use a recipe book to cook an egg custard. The recall is deliberate and structured and is based on a finite number of repetitions of a well defined process. After four custards we don't have to look any more.

Moving on

This episode is taken from the same session as Episode five and Episode six.

Episode seven

Amy:	Mrs Fisher [Rhonda makes eye contact] I've finished
Rhonda:	read it to me
Amy:	the twins * yesterday the twins came to play with me we played a catty game and we played a game but and but but I but I don't know but I don't know but I don't know * what that game was ** but it but it and it and it and
Rhonda:	Does it make sense?
Amy:	uh huh [meaning no]
Rhonda:	well you read over it and have a look and see if you can make it make sense
	[Rhonda turns her attention to Damien]

The dialogue in this episode still has written language as its topic, but the focus of discussion has changed. Although there are unconventional spellings in Amy's text Rhonda does not attempt to correct them. Instead she asks Amy to read her 'story' to her. It is other people's minds that are now being considered. Would a reader understand what has been written?

Amy discovers that she has left out a word. This is a simple problem that is easily fixed. But it is not a trivial matter. She is developing an awareness of potential readers whose difficulties of interpretation must be anticipated and allowed for.

Amy is also learning that written text is different from spoken text. It provides visible evidence of what has been said, and a basis for evaluating the adequacy of the expression of intention. She is being made aware of the fact that a writer is always confronted by the question of whether what has been written is a true representation of what was intended.

The text itself also deserves comment. It is no longer a bland basic statement ('My birthday is in October') which has been chosen at least partly because Amy already knows, or can find, the words she needs. Her story about the twins is a genuine and detailed account of a recent experience.

Bruner (1986) has said that intellectual growth is achieved by the process of 'objectifying in language or image what one has thought and then turning around and reconsidering it' (p. 129).

Amy is learning that it is possible to take something from the flow of life and objectify it in writing. What might have faded from memory has now been recorded. It can be re-read and reconsidered and revised. Amy's focus is shifting from the mastery of the 'story writing' activity to the use of writing as a way of making sense of experience.

Summing up

So what does Amy's progress as a writer tell us about learning to be literate? Here are some of the things that seem most important.

1   The program of literacy development in which Amy was involved required her to *write* from the earliest stages. This makes good sense. Writing is the productive aspect of written language. It provided opportunities for Amy to test her hypotheses about written language, and it gave Rhonda opportunities to provide immediate and responsive feedback.

2   Amy was clearly not an information processor developing automatic responses to the phonological aspects of print before she started to consider the meaning of what she was writing and reading. Meaning was involved at all times.

3   Without Rhonda's assistance Amy's progress would have been much slower. It was Rhonda who provided evidence of what 'writing a story' meant and what Amy needed to do to become a 'story writer'. It was Rhonda who made it possible for Amy to participate in 'story writing' from the earliest stages by doing for Amy the cognitive work she could not, at first, do for herself. Literacy development was a social and collaborative process.

4   Rhonda's chalkboard stories provided Amy with a simple framework for learning. What was being learnt was not so much 'writing' in a global sense, but 'writing a story'; a context bound activity which involved a standardized procedure for participation, and standardized ways of solving the problems of how to spell the needed words. This meant that writing became a task which fell within the competence of

the children despite the limitations imposed by their youth and inexperience.

5   Teachers need to begin thinking of mental processes like remembering, not as functions of the individual mind, but rather as processes that can be socially constructed. Whenever Amy failed to remember what had happened previously, or where to look for needed words, or what to do next, she was made aware of her mental processes and learnt how they could be used to solve her problems. Her mental processes were, in fact, constituted by the talk and action involved in collaborative 'story writing'.

6   In order to learn to write Amy had to develop voluntary control over her mental processes. At the same time learning to be literate led her into new ways of thinking (for example, using the written text as a way of objectifying reality). But it is not possible to separate the various strands of development. They are simultaneous and mutually dependent.

7   The development of voluntary control over mental processes like remembering is, of course, of little use if there is nothing to remember which is relevant to the task at hand. The growth of a body of common knowledge upon which learning to be literate can be built is crucial. A wide range of literacy activities needs to be thoughtfully organized by the teacher. But what matters most is that the teacher should engage in dialogue with the children about their writing *as they are doing it*, constructing an intersubjective context for understanding by referring explicitly to those things which are relevant to the completion of the task but which the children fail to recall spontaneously.

8   Learning to be literate also requires the development of an awareness of thinking as a mediated process. Amy had to learn that alphabet charts, word displays, books, posters, and 'stories' on display in the classroom could all be used to overcome the limitations of her natural mental processes. Similarly, she also had to be aware that the collective consciousness of the class was available to her. Other children could be called upon to exercise their mental capacities on her behalf.

9   The children should learn that the alphabet offers a helpful way of thinking about the relationship between spoken and written language, but that ultimately it is convention that determines how words are written, not rules governing sound–letter relationships.

10   Amy was asked to check what she had written; to consider whether it might be clear to a potential reader. This was the beginning of new ways of thinking; of confronting the 'latent ambiguity of language' and realizing that the meaning of something can be checked against written text as well as by reference to the world of experience. And she

began to write texts that objectified her experience and made it potentially available for scrutiny and revision. Without exaggerating what was achieved, it was clear that, in little more than six months, Amy was beginning to go beyond mastery of the activity structure to tentative explorations of the nature and possible uses of the written word.

Conclusion

Beginning to Read by Marilyn Jager Adams (1994a) is a detailed exposition of the information processing perspective on reading and reading instruction. In it Adams says that through writing children learn that reading is about thinking. They learn, for example, that 'text does not contain meaning but is meaningful only to the extent that it is understood by its reader'. But while this goes well beyond word recognition, she also tells us that

> the print on the page constitutes the basic perceptual data of reading. Rather than diverting efforts in search of meaning, the reader's letter- and word-wise processes supply the text based information on which comprehension depends.
>
> (Adams 1994b: 2)

In other words, the complex interpretive processes involved in skilled reading only become possible when the 'basic perceptual data' are being received and processed without conscious effort. So, according to this view of reading development, decoding strategies must be *taught* in a structured and systematic way to the beginning reader. Only as fluency develops will attention be shifted to the development of comprehension and interpretation.

In this chapter an attempt has been made to show that such a view of literacy development fails to explain what happens when children like Amy are observed in the process of becoming literate in their own classrooms. The episodes in which teacher and child work collaboratively on Amy's understanding of literacy, and on developing her competence as a writer, show that meaning can never be separated sensibly from literacy development at any time. They show that literacy and thought are closely related, and that the development of one is necessarily connected with the development of the other.

Learners like Amy are problem solvers and meaning makers rather than rule learners or information processors, and their teachers are people like Rhonda who, through talk and action, help children to construct the new ways of thinking that learning to be literate both requires and promotes. In classrooms like this, children become not just readers and writers, but also independent and confident learners who understand what literacy is and how it relates to their lives and the lives of others across time and space. These are the true basics of literacy. And Amy and Rhonda show that they are achievable in ordinary classes everywhere as long as the emphasis is on the learning child, and the social processes involved in thinking and learning, rather than the instructional method.

Note: key to data transcriptions

The way the extracts from the videotaped data are represented in the text is not intended to produce an analysis of linguistic data but to represent the talk as accurately as possible while simultaneously making it easy to read. The transcription code is as follows:
Normal use of question marks and exclamation marks is maintained.

* pause of one second or less.

Bold type   emphatic speech.

CAPITAL LETTERS indicate that the speaker is using letter names.

Y-E-S indicates that the speaker is spelling the word using letter names.

No capital letters (except for names) or full stops are used for direct speech but normal punctuation is used for comments or additional details.

When either teacher or child engages in phonemic segmentation of a word an attempt has been made to indicate the type of sound produced, but no attempt has been made to record phonemes accurately.

13 Action, talk and text: integrating literacy with other modes of making meaning

Gordon Wells

Around the world, and particularly in English speaking countries, there is currently a crisis with respect to the development of literacy. Far too many children are failing to achieve the centrally established, age related standards in reading and writing, and the proportion of adults judged to be 'functionally illiterate' also remains unacceptably high. Since the mastery of literacy is considered to be the schools' responsibility, not surprisingly it is argued that it is the inadequacy of schooled instruction that is responsible for this state of affairs. As a result, in many of the world's industrialized countries, new curricula and stricter accountability procedures are being introduced in attempts to overcome the perceived problem. In many cases, however, the policies that are being implemented, rather than remedying the problem, seem likely to further exacerbate it.

In a literate society everyone needs to read and write. For some it is essential for their occupation; for others it supports a variety of forms of entertainment; for all, reading and writing are necessary for the transactions of everyday life. In the teaching of literacy, on the other hand, far too little attention is paid to the real-life purposes that reading and writing serve. In line with the accountability criteria set by state and national policymakers, reading and writing tend to be treated in many schools today as ends in themselves rather than as the means for communicating and thinking. Unfortunately, children are given tasks to perform that focus on the 'mechanics' of literacy as a set of skills to be mastered quite independently of their immediate use for communicating and thinking about issues that are of intrinsic interest and importance to them.

In this context, it is important to recall Vygotsky's argument that 'teaching should be organized in such a way that reading and writing are necessary for something . . . Writing should be incorporated into a task that is relevant and necessary for life' (1978: 117–18). As he fully understood, without the motivation created by purposes of their own, children fail to develop the drive to learn to read and write and, as a result, they have considerable difficulty in mastering the knowledge, skills and dispositions that would enable them to read and write fluently and meaningfully. In this chapter I shall present some examples of ways in which teachers I am working with are trying to follow Vygotsky's injunction. But first I need to outline the underlying philosophy that guides our work.

Action, talk and text: the development of ways of meaning

In order to understand present behaviour, Vygotsky (1981) argued, it is necessary to study the history of that behaviour, both at the individual (onto-genetic) level and at the phylogenetic and cultural–historical levels of the development of human society. Following that advice, I decided many years ago to investigate the development of meaning making. My first investigations concerned the development of language in contemporary society, based on a longitudinal study of children's naturally occurring interactions at home and at school (Wells 1987). From that study it became clear that what drives children's language learning is their desire to participate in the activities of their families and communities and that what most facilitates their progress is the assistance they receive from their interlocutors in conversations in which the child's interests are taken up and extended.

Some years later, I began to explore the phylogenetic development of meaning making, greatly aided by the work of Donald (1991) whose research focused on the role of modes of representation in the development of 'the modern mind'. Space does not allow me to go into detail here but, in summary, his argument was that there have been three major developments in human ways of knowing, each made possible by the emergence of a new 'arte-fact'. Humans' most basic meanings result from 'acting into the world' (Freeman 1995). As with other species, not only do we gain information through feedback on our actions, but our actions also communicate about our intentions to our co-participants. What distinguishes humans from other spe-cies, on the other hand, is the use of symbolic representations to communicate and think about our actions and intentions. Even before the advent of speech, our earliest ancestors developed what Donald calls 'mimesis', the use of demonstrative action and gesture to pass on cultural knowledge from one generation to the next. When speech emerged, this served similar purposes in joint activity but with the much greater precision that language's 'meaning potential' (Halliday 1978) makes possible. In particular, with its basic tendency to categorize objects, actions and attributes through the use of nouns, verbs and adjectives – which refer to classes rather than particulars – speech greatly increased humans' ability to organize their experience through narrative and generalization.

Writing was the third major addition to the meaning making toolkit.

Invented some 4000 years ago, writing provided a way of giving relative permanence to meanings made in face to face interaction. It thus created an 'external memory' (Donald 1991) which, over the centuries, led to the gathering and organization of written information and, in the last two or three centuries, to the development and systematic testing of theory in almost all fields of human activity. But, as Olson points out, the use of writing has played another important function in the development of the modern mind: 'What literacy contributes to thought is that it turns the thoughts themselves into worthy objects of contemplation' (1996: 277). It thus provides a powerful tool for meta-cognition, whereby we become conscious of, and better able to control, our own knowledge and the means by which we achieve it.

In tracing this historical sequence, Donald makes one further important point: each new representational tool did not replace what already existed but added to and complemented the tools already available. So, just as thousands of years ago speech did not replace the mimetic mode of communication, neither has writing rendered speech obsolete, even in those domains where the written text is most widely used. Prior to writing, authors frequently discuss their intentions with colleagues and friends in order to develop and clarify their plans; during the actual drafting and redrafting of the text, they also seek readers' reactions and suggestions for revision. Readers, too, often discuss what they have read in order to compare their interpretations and responses, particularly if the text calls for some form of action (Heath1983); this is particularly common when the text contains diagrams, graphs or mathematical (or other) symbolic formulae. In other words, although the written text can stand alone relatively independent of any specific context of use, particular activities of writing and reading remain enmeshed in a nexus of action, talk and text.

Fascinating as this account of the historical development of our ways of knowing is, however, from an educational point of view it takes on even more significance when we recognize that it also captures the history of individual development. Of course, ontogeny does not recapitulate phylogeny as a simple repetition. Children born into contemporary technologically orientated, literate societies do not have to reinvent from scratch each of the major meaning making tools just described. However, they do have to appropriate them and make them their own, as they take part in the activities in which they are used. Furthermore, as has been convincingly shown, children's developmental trajectories retrace the sequence in which these tools entered into and shaped the development of the 'modern mind' (Nelson 1996).

Understood in this way, children's mastery of the social practices of reading and writing is to be seen as the addition of a further set of tools to their kit of meaning making resources complementing those that are already available but in no way replacing them. Furthermore, just as all the modes of meaning making are used together in most large scale undertakings in society at large, so the most effective way for children to master their use is by taking part in similar endeavours in the classroom, in which the texts that they read and write are integral to activities that are of personal and social significance within their classroom community.

In the sections that follow, I will try to give an idea of the many different ways in which this very general principle can guide the planning of curricular units so that children both exploit and come to understand the interdependence of action, talk and text in achieving goals in which they have a shared investment.

Understanding the world through stories

One of the first uses that was made of language in prehistory, so it is supposed, was the telling of stories, particularly stories (myths) that explained humans' relationship to the world in which they lived. Although not the first use made of writing, the recording of stories that had previously been passed on by word of mouth was, from very early on, a particularly important function served by written texts. It is not surprising, therefore, that in the early stages, children enjoy learning to read and write through the medium of stories, particularly when they have the chance to discuss the texts with their peers and to compare their interpretations and responses.

One of the implications of accepting a Vygotskian, social constructivist, theory of learning is the recognition that each individual interprets new information in the light of their existing knowledge, interests and current purpose. This applies to information obtained from reading just as much as to information gained more directly through participation in material activity. As Rosenblatt (1938) pointed out many years ago, a written text does not transmit the writer's meaning to the reader as if it were a pipe transporting water. Reading involves a transaction between the reader and the text, which results in the construction of a particular interpretation specific to this reader and to this occasion and is thus likely to be different to some degree from the interpretations constructed by other readers of the same text in other times and places. Rosenblatt goes on to distinguish two stances to a text: the 'efferent' and the 'aesthetic'. When responding from the efferent stance, readers are motivated by specific needs to acquire information; their concern is to understand what the text (or its author) is saying. On the other hand, when readers are responding in the aesthetic stance, it is their own response to the experience of the text that is primary.

Two important implications follow from this understanding of the reading process. First, there is no one correct, authorized interpretation of any text. Thus, since many alternative interpretations are possible, it is valuable for readers to compare their interpretations with those of others in order to see the text from many perspectives. However, and second, not all interpretations are equally justifiable; although readers bring their personal experience to their transactions with the text, they need to provide warrant for their interpretation by reference to the actual wording of the text. While the first of these implications is most important in relation to transactions with imaginative literature and the second in relation to presentations of generally accepted facts and theories, both are always relevant. Which is given precedence depends on the purpose for reading – on which of the two stances, aesthetic or efferent, is most appropriate for the task in hand.

Whatever the purpose for reading, however, there is great benefit in readers talking about the text in order to clarify their own interpretations and to compare them with those of others. On the one hand, they have the opportunity to hear and respond to the contributions of their peers and, on the other, in formulating their own response to the text in order to contribute to the discussion, they frequently arrive at a deeper understanding than they would have achieved if they had merely read the text on their own. As many readers have recognized: how does one know what one thinks about a text until one has tried to explain one's interpretation to others?

Seeds and webs

My first example of the discussion of a story comes from Mary Ann Van Tassell's class of 6- and 7-year-old children in Toronto. Since these children were still beginning readers, she encouraged them to take books home from the classroom library that they thought they would enjoy so that their parents could read them with them. In order to have a record of their responses, she asked the parents to write the children's reflective comments on Post-it notes and to stick each note on the appropriate page of the book. Then, when several children had read the same book, she planned to discuss the story with them and create a web of their thoughts about it, in which their notes were spatially related in terms of ideas that were connected in some way.

The following extract occurred after three children had read *A Friend for Mrs Katz*, a story about an old woman who lives alone and is befriended by Larnell, a boy who gives her a kitten for company. Each of the children had contributed a number of 'seeds' on Post-it notes and, in this extract, two of them are deciding with their teacher how to arrange them on a large sheet of paper to show the connections among them. (The third child is absent because he is sick.) So far, notes referring to cats have been arranged in one group and they have been considering a note that refers to the Jewish custom of putting stones on the graves of loved ones who have died. Karla has found two seeds that she thinks should go together.[1]

Karla: [pointing to a 'seed' and reading] It's because it says
It is good that Larnell and Mrs. Katz became friends.'
Teacher: '– that Larnell and Mrs. Katz became friends'
Karla: And this says
'That was nice what people do to see and say "Hi" to people that died'
Teacher: '– that was nice what people do to see and say "Hi" to the people that died'
Ashlynn: '– what people do to see and say "Hi" to the people that died'
Teacher: Yes. so what is it that's connected? – that connects them? What is it that connects them? [the two seeds just mentioned]
Karla: <That they're both like – they both say what**>
Teacher: How is this – you mean because this [pointing to the first seed] shows that they were friends?
Karla: [nods]
Teacher: And THIS is saying that they're friends? [pointing to the other]
Karla: [nods]
Ashlynn: Why don't we put this one before that one <altogether then>?
Teacher: Well are these all connected though? [referring to the seeds that Ashlynn indicates, which refer to Passover, friendship, and the graveyard]
Ashlynn: No
Teacher: They're not – this one [the seed of friendship] is connected to all of those Could we put it kind of in the middle and put these around it?
Ashlynn: Yes
Karla: Yeah

It must be unusual for 6-year-olds to be engaged, as they are here, in considering the relationship between the different themes of a story and providing justifications for their opinions. But what is particularly interesting about the procedure that the teacher has invented is that, by having the children's comments on different aspects of the story written on small Post-it notes, their ideas do indeed become objects that can be compared, and physically placed in different relationships to each other. As the teacher suggests:

> Throughout the conversation, both girls struggle to explain their reasons for connecting seeds. This is meta-cognitive talk. They are not used to making these thoughts explicit, and it is exactly this type of talk that moves the conversation beyond discussion of the literal into the more abstract themes of the story. At this point, both students needed help in making these connections explicit.
>
> (Van Tassell and Galbraith 1997)

As she also tells the children at another point, there is nothing final about the first way in which they decide to arrange their seeds, as they can always move them later, if necessary, when they see a better way of relating them. As they arrange the seeds in the web, therefore, the children are learning a very important feature of composing in writing – that ideas can be revised, as can the way in which they are put together in the text as a whole. And, although they are probably not fully aware of it, they are also learning that when ideas are arranged in different combinations, new meanings emerge from these alternative juxtapositions. As Karla added when they had completed the task, 'We never knew things could fit together like that.'

Following the use of the web in Van Tassell's class, her colleague, Barbara Galbraith, extended the idea of a web to investigate story elements, such as plot, key events and characterization, in the novels that her grade three students were reading. Here, too, the web served as a form of synoptic text, enabling the students to make connections at a meta-level that they were less able to see as they simply read through the story, page by page. And, once again, it was through talking together about the 'seeds' they had identified that they were able to build larger patterns of meaning.

Schools for dinosaurs

The next example involves a different kind of talk about a text under construction, which occurred in a classroom of 8-year-old students, many of whom were still mastering English as their second language. In this example, a group of five Portuguese-Canadian children were working together collaboratively to create a text to share with the rest of the class. The task the teacher had set was to base what they wrote on the research they had been doing on dinosaurs, and they embarked on the task with enthusiasm. In the following extract, we see them not only generating an amusing 'story', but also helping each other with all aspects of the writing process. The transcript below contains a small number of extracts from a conversation that remained focused on the task for about 40 minutes.

> Tanya: Think of the title. Dinosaur Time
> Tony: Back in the dinosaur time?
> [Children sit in silence thinking for a while]
> Tanya: Dinosaur school?
> Tony and Barb: [simultaneously] Yeah
> [Group agrees eagerly; several laugh]
> Barb: It will be fun then
> Tony: How do you spell dinosaur?
> [Several look round the classroom to find the word displayed]

Eric: Wait, You have to vote on that [the title]
    [All put their hands up]
Barb: Who's going to be the writer?
Tanya: Tony, who else?

Having fairly quickly decided to write about 'Dinosaur schools', they begin to negotiate the opening of their text. Immediately, a number of problems arise as Tony, the designated leader, scribes for the group.

Eric: You're doing it all in capital letters? [referring to title]
Tony: Of course!
Barb: Don't write it two spaces . . . just write –
Tony: Dinosaurs school [reads what he has written]
    Oh, period . . . now for the story
Eric: Put – you didn't put a dot right there
Tony: [laughs] I'll put three [he adds three periods after the title]

The exact location of dinosaur schools is discussed over the next several turns and the inside of volcanoes is decided to be a suitable location. Together they generate the first sentence and Tony begins to write.

Tony: Baby – [as he writes]
Many: Baby dinosaurs. dinosaurs [group members chime in]
Tanya: Hm. You put dinosaur. . DinoSAURS [emphasizing the plural form]
Tony: I can't do anything now [refers to erasing]
Eric: What did he do wrong? dinosaur school?
Tanya: Dinosaurs, he must put dinoSAURS [again emphasizing the plural]
    like thousands of them, more than one
Tony: So, so that's what the school is
Tanya: A school with one kid? [laughs]
Barb: Dinosaur school, school of one kid
Tanya: Baby dinosaurs must go to school inside a volcano [laughs]
    Once every five years, a fire alarm will go on as an eruption
Barb: Ya, that's funny [everyone laughs]

Tony continues to scribe what the group has composed while the others monitor and comment on what he is writing.

Tony: Baby dinosaurs schools are in – are in. volcanoes
Tanya: WERE in
Eric: Were in –
Tanya: They are not right now, are dinosaurs living right now?
    WERE [repeating as Tony writes]

> [Tony continues to write, vocalizing each word as he attempts to write it]
>
> Tony: – were in volcanoes, in a volcano
>
> Tanya: In volcano. S [emphasizing plural]
>
> Tony: V O K–V O K [invents spelling] . . . V O K–K A
>
> Eric: Tony, I think you've got it wrong . . . it's V O L – volcanoes
>
> Tony: [continuing to vocalize as he writes] Every five hundred years –
>
> Eric: I know***** [his utterance is unclear but seems to be raising an objection]
>
> Tony: Okay
>
> Tanya: Yeah, five years because they won't be alive in five hundred years
>
> Eric: Yes, they would
>
> Tanya: But they wouldn't be babies anymore
>
> Tony: [agreeing] Yeah
>
> Barb: They'll be five
>
> Eric: So they'll be in grade six**
>
> Tanya: They are in grade six . . . they'll be in school, they'll be teenagers, not babies anymore
>
> Tony: I made a mistake
>
> Barb: Who cares?
>
> Tanya: They'll – . . . they'll be in high school

These extracts, which involved only the first few lines of their final text, show very clearly the complexity of the challenge facing novice writers. First there is the search for what to write. Here the decision was somewhat assisted by the teacher's specification of the general topic and by the knowledge that the rest of the class was the intended audience. But even when the general idea has been decided on, as it was fairly early in this writing episode, writers have to generate specific detail and ensure that there is coherence in the emerging structure of meaning. Then there is the problem of 'wording' – the choice both of appropriate words and of their correct morphological structure for their role in the context of the sentence. Finally there are the conventions of spelling and punctuation to grapple with as the spoken version of the text is encoded in graphological form. Not surprisingly, managing all these levels simultaneously can seem an overwhelming task, particularly when the physical formation of the letters is still also very time consuming.

For this group of writers, all of whom were still mastering English as their second language, there were obvious benefits in undertaking this task collaboratively. Not only were they able to draw on the diverse range of relevant expertise that was distributed among the group, but together they were able to overcome the problems of short-term memory involved in retaining the intended meaning that had been composed while dealing with the difficulties of accurately representing it on the page. And, most important, their shared commitment to the task sustained their motivation to continue.

Here is the text that they had produced at the end of the 40 minute activity. Probably because of its witty inventiveness, the class judged it to be the best produced by any group.

DINOSAURS SCHOOL . . .

Baby DINOSAURS Schools were in VOCKANOS.
Every 5 Years The Fire Drial would Go On as an ERUPTION
THEY WriHT About People. THE Paper was 10 mters long. And
The Pencil is 5 mters long. There Close is poka Doted. And THERE
Poget is about THE Fugter. THE Librery is called Home read stone.
And The books or made of saled. Rock. THEY live in haya rock.
THERE Brians or as small as marbells. THERE LUnCH is Brontobrgers.
THERE TOYS ARE all With batreries, THERE HOUES is MADE OF
Pebulls.

(by Tony, Tanya, Barbara, Margaret and Eric)

This practice of writing collaboratively is also helpful for older students, particularly for second language learners or students with learning difficulties, who lack confidence in their ability to compose extended texts on their own. Not only does the social nature of the enterprise increase their interest in and enjoyment of the task, but where they might be reluctant to review and revise their text when writing individually, they are more willing to do so when their contributions are challenged by peers whose opinion they value. Of course, the ultimate aim is that they should take responsibility for the texts that they produce in solo mode, but for many students the support of collaborative peers is an excellent way of assisting them to reach this stage.

Becoming a community of readers

My final example of story sharing comes from Zoe Donoahue's class of 9- and 10-year-olds. Donoahue makes a practice of reading to her children every day as she believes that reading is essentially social in nature. Not only do readers transact with the writer's text, they also interact with each other about their interpretations and responses. One of her aims in reading aloud, therefore, is to create and foster a community of readers in her classroom.

Typically she serializes a novel, one chapter a day, and follows each chapter by a time for discussion of the story so far, how it might continue, and what aspects of the story individual children find particularly significant or memorable. One year, when she was reading *Mrs Frisby and the Rats of Nimh*, she decided to video-record these discussions in order to investigate just how children were taking up the opportunity to share their responses. To her dismay, she discovered from viewing the first two recordings that there was little true discussion. As teacher, she nominated each speaker and provided some kind of response to their contribution and then proceeded to nominate the next speaker. Thus, since the students addressed their remarks to her, she was acting as the pivot of the talk and, as a result, the ideas that individual students introduced were not being taken up by their peers and corroborated and extended or countered from an alternative perspective.

In order to make the talk more truly a discussion, Donoahue decided to change the 'ground rules' for their book talk. In future, she would nominate the first speaker and then any other students who had something they wanted to contribute to the topic could do so without being nominated, provided that they took turns and made explicit how their contributions related to those that had preceded. From the beginning, once they had understood the new format, the children had no difficulty in sustaining their discussion without the need for the teacher's control. And Donoahue, for her part, found herself much better able to appreciate the various points of view that were expressed and to focus her contributions on facilitating their collaborative meaning making.

Here is an extract from the discussion of a later chapter in *Mrs Frisby*, in which the children are speculating about how the rats – who had learned to read – would make their escape from their cages in the laboratory (Justin is one of the rats).

> Wil: I think that Justin was* their guard that they have \<now>.
> And that Justin – I think that gets out and***** and he gets out – well, and Jennifer doesn't.
> Dyl: You know that picture that they had \<of> a little air vent?
> Well, I think that the guy – the rat that got out, went through there.
> Ann: Well, I think that the steroids are going to other rats*** . . .
> Cal: They're trying to make you LOOK stronger
> T: Well, yes, they do help with strength, BUT, what was the thing they said the steroids would do for the rats?
> Ss: Hold them down.
> T: Hold them down . . . but there was something else, too.
> Ric: Increase their lifespan.
> T: Yes, increase their lifespan. Good listening, Ricky.
> Yeah, so, that's interesting. They're saying some different things than we might have thought about the steroids.
> Wil: I don't think it's steroids that increase their lifespan \<so much.>*
> If a person takes steroids – \<it doesn't increase their life>.
> Dyl: It'll SHRINK their lifespan . . . it does the exact opposite

Cal: And I think that Justin finds a way OUT and then all the others follow
      – like all the others get out and go out the same way
T: <All the other**>?
Cal: Yeah, in the 'A' group . . . then some of them don't WANT to go out
      because they had – like a different – you know how it said <they were
      going to get the guns and needles>.
      I think 'B' and Control Group don't want to get out.
T: Yes . . . I wanted to ask you last time, but we got busy with other things –
      Do you UNDERSTAND what the concept of the CONTROL group is in
      science? Does anybody know?
Dyl: They're the people who don't get anything – anything done
T: And why would you want to have a group who had nothing done to
      them?
Cal: <so you can see> the differences
T: Ok . . Does anyone want to explain another way?
      That's good Callie, but sometimes it helps to hear it another
      way.
T: Andre, can you explain that . . in your own words?
And: [coughing]* the* of the control group, just like stays, just at their
      same I.Q. And the other – two other groups – two in this case – get like
      – they test each other and they time them and all that, and they see
      the differences and then they can find out how much SMARTER they
      are and how much faster they learn
Pat: I think also that <our> group escapes but <they're> smarter and the
      people who don't escape are the rats of Nimh . . . how they're cap-
      tured by Nimh
And: And the rats of Nimh – and the rats of Nimh came back just a few
      chapters ago – with the wire and the radio –
Pat: No, no that was THEN, that was then
Andre: That was – no it wasn't
Pat: Yes it was
Jes: I think it was the rats that didn't get a chance – that DIDN'T get back,
      the** ones, and they brought wires for – that they came back a little
      while ago, right? And then they came back AGAIN with wires so that
      the smart rat could build the radio
Mat: Except they're not rats
Ss: Oh [expressing disbelief]
T: What do people think about what Jessie is saying? Anything to add –

From the chapters already read, which began the narrative part-way
through the sequence of events that made up the story, the children knew that
some of the rats escaped but they did not as yet know which rats or how.
Presumably it was the smarter ones, including Justin; but what had the steroid

treatment to do with the escape, if anything? Depending on the effects expected from the administration of steroids, this treatment could possibly be a key to the explanation of how one of the three groups managed to escape. At this point, however, there seemed to be as many opinions as speakers. It was in this context that the teacher made her first intervention, not to test the children but, by clarifying the likely effect of steroids, to help them to make a better informed prediction as to how the story would unfold. Arguably, this was also the purpose of her request for an explanation of the function of a control group.

As is so often the case, in choosing to engage students in a particular activity, the teacher had more than one goal in view. Without doubt, her first goal for these book talks was to provide an opportunity for the children to further explore both the story and their reactions to it. However, she also had goals relating to the nature of productive discussion and the ground rules that would be likely to promote it. Her third intervention, asking what people thought about Jessie's suggestion, was clearly related to this latter goal, reminding them not to be so eager to offer their own opinions that they gave inadequate thought to the opinions of others. This was borne out by her closing comment at the end of the discussion:

> T: That was a GREAT discussion. Lots of REALLY good comments. That's why we kept at it for so long because you were so focused on the discussion you were REALLY listening to one another

As she commented in the article from which the above extract is taken, these discussions not only deepened the children's appreciation of literature; they also depended on and contributed to the general classroom ethos of caring and collaboration.

> I have always found the shared experience of teacher read-aloud of novels a strong influence on the building of classroom community, and this was even more the case once control of the discussions was given over to the children. The expectation in our community was that children would initiate and sustain our discussions about the novels. Through joint participation in discussions, the children became skilled at this. As a mentor, I participated in the discussions by making comments and asking questions that allowed children to work and to learn within their zones of proximal development (Vygotsky 1978). My comments and questions provided scaffolding for the children, the apprentices, so that they could become full members of the community. Their growing ability to make relevant comments and build on each other's ideas, without the teacher being the sole authority, had a profound influence on the children's sense

of themselves as a cohesive group who enjoyed listening to stories and talking with and listening to one another.

(Donoahue 1997)

Literacy as a tool for knowledge building and understanding

Just as a literary text takes on more meaning when it is appreciated and explored within a community of peers (McMahon *et al.* 1997), so the reading and writing of informational texts can serve as a means of supporting a community's shared search for understanding about the material and social world in which they are growing up to take their place as informed and concerned citizens. Elsewhere (Wells 1999, 2002), I have spelled out in some detail the reasons for making understanding rather than knowledge the goal of learning. Briefly, my argument is that 'knowledge' is too easily converted into a commodity, to be transmitted, received and reproduced for show – what Freire (1970) referred to as the 'banking' conception of knowledge. Understanding, by contrast, always has implications for action and is only manifested when it is reconstructed for a particular purpose in a particular situation. Understanding, rather than the simple 'possession' of knowledge, is what guides effective and responsible action.

Much of the collaborative research carried out by my teacher colleagues in Developing Inquiring Communities in Education Project (DICEP) was concerned to create such classroom communities focused on understanding. Adopting an inquiry approach to the curriculum, children were involved in purposeful reading and writing at many junctures: to record observations; to find relevant information from reference books; latterly from the Internet to create multimedia representations of what they had come to understand in order to present it to audiences beyond their own classrooms; and, most importantly, to keep a log or journal of what they found out and their reflections on both process and product.

Space does not allow me to describe any examples in detail here, but the teachers' own accounts can be found on the group's webpage (see Donoahue 1997) and in their chapters in the group's recent book (Wells 2001). However, a flavour of the children's enthusiastic involvement in the theme-based projects in which they were involved can be gained from the following quotations from their writings.

The first two are speeches by the principals for Province West and the Wishga'a band in a hearing of the claim brought by the Wishga'a band for the return of their ancestral land. The class had researched the history of similar land claims in British Columbia and, as a culmination of this curriculum unit, they enacted a hearing of this (fictitious) case before judges of the Supreme Court of Canada (played by two other teachers). Working in groups, these

12-year-olds put much effort into preparing speeches in the registers appropriate for the roles they were playing.

Keith opened for Province West:

> Good afternoon, your honors. My group and I are representing the government of Province West. We feel strongly that the land that the Wishga'a are claiming to be theirs, although they FEEL it is theirs, truly isn't. During this presentation, we will talk about economic issues, human rights issues, and other land claims issues. I will now pass the stand on to the next speaker, who will talk about economic issues.

Concluding the presentation by the Wishga'a band, Frank had this to say:

> So in conclusion, I have to say that to me it is somewhat ridiculous that the government would even think that the land belongs to them. Our tradition has been broken, our bands have been separated, and our land has been taken . . . Having our own government is a necessity because many problems have been inflicted on us. We believe that if we govern ourselves, we could give help that we are not getting right now. We are prepared to sign a treaty saying that we wouldn't evacuate nonnatives from our land. We KNOW the land is ours and will ALWAYS be.

As these students realized, preparing for this role play not only helped them to understand the issues at stake but, more importantly, it changed their values by helping them to empathize with the plight of First Nations people and the points of view of those whose lives would be affected by the decision for or against their claims.

The second pair of quotations was written by a 7-year-old at different stages in an investigation of energy through the making and testing of elastic powered vehicles. At the end of a session in which the children had been observing how far their vehicles would travel under various conditions, Alexandra wrote the following entry:

> Today our group made sure we got acurat answers on how far our cars move. First we looked at Jansens car. After 2 minutes me and katie realizised that Jansons cars wheels were rubbing against the box thats called friction. Then the car wouldent go very far because there was to much friction.

The second is her reflection on the value of keeping a journal as part of the process of conducting an inquiry:

> When you write stuff . . . You can always remember it and then, when you share in groups you can write more stuff so. so whenever you share you learn more.

Like her peers, Alexandra had clearly begun to understand the key role of writing in coming to understand.

Apprenticeship into literacy

In earlier times, many young people learned the trade or craft by which they earned their living through an apprenticeship. Living and working in the workplace of a master craftsman, they learned the knowledgeable skills of the craft by helping the master and then, with his help, gradually taking over responsibility for more and more of the tasks until they had fully 'mastered' the craft themselves. In this context, the knowledge and skills specific to the craft were not learned in isolation but as resources required in the course of creating the crafted artefacts.

In today's more complex world, this way of passing on knowledge and skills from one generation to the next is no longer the norm. Instead, we have preparatory institutions which specialize in teaching and learning quite separate from the context of use. They are called schools and universities. In these institutions, the knowledge and skills that are taught often have no immediate purpose in the lives of the learners and so they are presented and perceived as ends in themselves; what is valued is being able to show that the knowledge has been 'acquired', not that it has been understood and can be put to use in 'real life' situations. Unfortunately, many students do not learn well in this 'encapsulated' setting, and even those who do succeed in acquiring what is taught frequently cannot later put their school knowledge to use in the world beyond school because it has never become part of their personal understanding of that larger world and of the activities by means of which it is sustained (Barnes 1976).

From a social constructivist perspective, however, the concept of apprenticeship still functions as a powerful metaphor of what Vygotsky (1978) described as learning through 'assisted performance in the zone of proximal development' (Tharp and Gallimore 1988). And, like Donoahue in the quotation above, many educators recognize that, even in school, the most effective learning occurs in a 'community of practice' (Lave and Wenger 1991) in which, through participating in joint, purposeful activities, members master the knowledgeable skills necessary to achieve the valued goals of the classroom community.

Literacy is such a resource of knowledgeable skills and, as we have seen in the preceding examples, the ability to read and write can be progressively mastered through using written texts as tools in the achievement of goals that are meaningful and of importance to the community. Expressing the same idea, Frank Smith (1983) described becoming literate as joining the literacy club and learning how to take part in club activities from more experienced members. Parents and other family members form the first literacy club and many children make considerable progress in their apprenticeship in literate activities before they go to school. Whatever their preschool experience, however, all children need their schooling to provide an extended apprenticeship into the larger community and its varied activities, in which literacy almost always functions as a valuable and necessary resource.

In adopting the metaphor of apprenticeship, however, we must not ignore the difference between mastering the use of material tools, which can frequently be learned through observation and guidance, and mastering the use of symbolic tools, whose skilled use is largely unobservable and can only be inferred from the finished product. It is for this reason that an apprenticeship into literacy must involve overt and explicit talk about texts and about the mental processes by which they are created and interpreted. A central activity in the literacy club is therefore conversation which weaves the connections among readers, writers and texts, the experiences that give them meaning, and the purposes they serve in the lives of the members.

Conclusion

In this chapter, my aim has been to show the complementary interrelationship between action, talk and text. In contemporary life, each of these modes of meaning making is completed and enhanced by the other two. Reading and writing texts may be the last of these three to be learned, but written texts only take on their full meaning in relation to the activities in which they play a part and to the talk that surrounds their composition and interpretation. At the same time, written texts add an important new dimension by enabling meaning to be given material permanence in the printed or written word so that it can be engaged with by people in other times and places. Re-engaging with written texts also allows writers and readers to rethink and revise both their texts and their ideas.

In helping children to become literate, therefore, and in encouraging them to exploit the power of literacy to achieve purposes of personal and social significance, five basic principles need to be borne in mind:

1   Reading and writing are not ends in themselves, rather, they are means of constructing and communicating meaning for purposes and in situations that benefit from the features of written text that depend upon its permanence as a material artifact.

2   Texts do not carry meaning in themselves, rather they require readers and writers to transact with the written text in order to match their intentions as writers or interpretations as readers with the cues to meaning that are encoded in the graphic display. At the same time, since readers and writers bring different experiences and purposes to this transaction, it is important to remember that the match that is made will differ from one individual to another.

3   Since meaning making is an inherently social activity carried out within a community that shares assumptions about values, ends and means, learning to both read and write, and using texts to act, to communicate and to learn depend on collaboration with other members of the community. Such collaboration occurs most naturally and easily through talk about the text.

4   It often helps to have an object in view – a purpose for reading and writing that involves the creation of some artefact for which the reading or writing of the text is a means. Such objects can include: a shared view of the text; an action that depends on the conclusions reached through engaging with the text; a model of what was at issue in the text; a written explanation of a phenomenon observed; or the outcome of solo deliberation. A teacher's choice of the 'right' object is a great spur to exploratory discussion, particularly when a number of competing ideas or strategies are raised.

5   Making meaning through reading and writing involves skills and knowledge that are specific to these activities. Furthermore, there is often a need deliberately to teach these knowledgeable skills. However, the teaching should, whenever possible, be related to the learner's current purpose and to their current abilities.

These principles may seem rather abstract to parents or teachers anxious to help their children to read and write effectively and with personal satisfaction. The ways to put them into practice, however, are almost self-evident. The first and most important concern must be, as Vygotsky advised, to ensure that reading and writing are undertaken for some purpose that is of significance to the learner. Enjoying a story or poem, finding out about a topic of interest, communicating important ideas and feelings to others, providing information that others will find interesting or helpful – all of these are worthwhile and satisfying reasons for reading and writing.

Furthermore, such occasions for reading and writing arise much more naturally, particularly in the classroom when adult and children see themselves as members of a community rather than as isolated, competing individuals. Where activities are undertaken jointly and collaboratively in order to achieve some valued outcome, there are many situations in which it is natural to read or write in order to contribute to the end in view (Wells

2002). And, since the text that is read or written is of importance to other members of the community as well, it is equally natural to talk about it – to discuss its significance to individual members or its effectiveness in communicating the intentions of its writer(s). Thus perhaps the most important requirement for a literate community to flourish is that there should be frequent and rewarding opportunities for its members to have conversations with each other about what they are doing, and why, and about how the texts they are engaging with are helping them to better understand themselves and their purposes.

Note

1   In this and all subsequent examples:

CAPS are used to indicate emphasis;
underlining to indicate overlapping speech;
< > to indicate uncertainty about transcription;
*   to indicate an unintelligible word-like segment;
-   to indicate an interruption;
and . to indicate a noticeable pause, with the number of full stops/periods corresponding to the duration of the pause in seconds.

References

Adams, M.J. (1994a) *Beginning to Read: Thinking and Learning about Print.* Cambridge, MA: The MIT Press.

Adams, M.J. (1994b) Modelling the connections between word recognition and reading, in R. Ruddell, M. Ruddell and H. Singer (eds) *Theoretical Models and Processes of Reading* (4th edn). Newark, DE: International Reading Association.

Alexander, L. (2001) Interview transcript, 8 August www.scholastic.com/teachers/authorsandbooks/authorstudies/authorhome.jhtml?authorID=1&collateralID=5315&displayName=Interview+Transcript.

Alexander, R.J. (2000) *Culture and Pedagogy: International Comparisons in Primary Education.* Oxford: Blackwell.

Alexander, R., Rose, J. and Woodhead, C. (1992) *Curriculum Practice and Classroom Organisation in Primary Schools: A Discussion Paper.* London: Department for Education and Science, HMSO.

Alexander, R.J., Wilcocks, J. and Nelson, N. (1996) Discourse, pedagogy and the National Curriculum: change and continuity in primary schools, *Research Papers in Education*, 11(1).

Anderson, J. (2001) Web publishing in non-Roman scripts: effects on the writing process, *Language and Education*, 15(4), 229–49.

Arizpe, E. and Styles, M. (2003) *Children Reading Pictures: Interpreting Visual Texts.* London: Routledge.

Askew, M., Brown, M., Rhodes, V., Wiliam, D. and Johnson, D. (1997a) *Effective Teachers of Numeracy.* London: TTA.

Askew, M., Brown, M., Rhodes, V., Wiliam, D. and Johnson, D. (1997b) The contribution of professional development to effectiveness in the teaching of numeracy, *Teacher Development*, 1(3): 335–56.

Aubrey, C. (1997) *Mathematics Teaching in the Early Years: An Investigation of Teachers' Subject Knowledge.* London: Falmer.

Averignou, M. and Ericson, J. (1997) A review of the concept of visual literacy, *British Journal of Educational Technology*, 28: 280–91.

Baker, C. (2000) *A Parents' and Teachers' Guide to Bilingualism.* Clevedon: Multilingual Matters.

Bakhtin, M. (1981) in M. Holquist (ed.) *The Dialogic Imagination: Four Essays.* Austin, TX: University of Texas Press.

Bakhtin, M.M. (1986) *Speech Genres and Other Late Essays.* Austin, TX: University of Texas Press.

Bal, M. (1985) *Narratology: Introduction to the Theory of Narrative*. Toronto: University of Toronto Press.

Ball, A. (2000) Teachers' developing philosophies in literacy and their use in urban schools: a Vygotskian perspective on internal activity and teacher change, in C.D. Lee and P. Smagorinsky (eds) *Vygotskian Perspectives on Literacy Research*. Cambridge: Cambridge University Press.

Barnes, D. (1976) *From Communication to Curriculum*. Harmondsworth: Penguin Books.

Barnes, D. and Todd, F. (1995) *Communication and Learning Revisited*. London: Heinemann.

Barrs, M. (1992) Genre theory: what's it all about? *Language Matters*, 1991–92(1): 9–16.

Barrs, M. (2000) The reader in the writer, *Reading Literacy and Language*, 34(2): 54–60.

Barrs, M. and Cork, V. (2001) *The Reader in the Writer*. London: CLPE.

Barton, D. (1994) *Literacy: An Introduction to the Ecology of Written Language*. Oxford: Blackwell.

Barton, D. (2001) Directions for literacy research: analysing language and social practices in a textually mediated world, *Language and Education: An International Journal*, 15(2/3): 92–104.

Barton, D. and Hamilton, M. (1998) *Local Literacies: Reading and Writing in Context*. London: Routledge.

Baynham, M. and Prinsloo, M. (2001) New directions in literacy research, *Language and Education*, 15(2/3): 83–92.

Bearne, E. (2003) Introduction, in M. Styles and E. Bearne (eds) *Art, Narrative and Childhood*. Stoke on Trent: Trentham.

Bearne, E. and Farrow, C. (1991) *Writing Policy in Action*. Buckingham: Open University Press.

Bearne, E. and Kress, G. (2001) Editorial, *Reading, Literacy and Language*, November, 35(3): 89–93.

Bennett, N. (1993) Knowledge bases for learning to teach, in N. Bennett and C. Carre (eds) *Learning To Teach*. London: Routledge.

Bereiter, C. (1980) Development in writing, in L.W. Gregg, L.W. Steinberg and E.R. Steinberg (eds) *Cognitive Processes in Writing*. Hillsdale, NJ: Lawrence Erlbaum Associates.

Bereiter, C. and Scardamalia, M. (1987) *The Psychology of Written Composition*. Hillsdale, NJ: Lawrence Erlbaum Associates.

Bernstein, B. (1971) On the classification and framing of educational knowledge, in M. Young (ed.) *Knowledge and Control*. London: Collier-Macmillan.

Bernstein, B. (1996) *Pedagogy, Symbolic Control and Identity*. London: Taylor & Francis.

Boahl, A. (1979) *Theatre of the Oppressed*. London: Pluto.

Bolton, G. (1984) *Drama as Education*. London: Longman.

Bond, E. (1995) Commentary on the war plays, in R. Drain (ed.) *Twentieth Century Theatre*. London: Routledge.

Booth, D. (1989) Imaginary gardens with real toads: reading and drama in education, *Theory into Practice*, XXIV(3): 193–8.

Booth, D. (1996) *Story Drama: Reading, Writing and Role Playing Across the Curriculum*. Markham: Pembroke Publishers.

Bourdieu, P. (1977) *Outline of a Theory of Practice* (trans. R. Nice). Cambridge: Cambridge University Press.

Bourne, J. (2002) Home languages in the Literacy Hour, *Supporting Pupils Learning English as an Additional Language* (Appendix). Annesley: DfES Publications.

Brice Heath, S. (1982) Protean strategies in literacy events: ever-shifting oral and literate traditions, in D. Tannen (ed.) *Spoken and Written Language: Exploring Orality and Literacy*. Norwood, NJ: Ablex.

Brice Heath, S. (1983) *Ways with Words: Language, Life and Work in Communities and Classrooms*. Cambridge: Cambridge University Press.

Brice Heath, S. (2000) 'Seeing our way into learning', *Cambridge Journal of Education*, 30(1): 121–32.

Bromley, H. (2003) Putting yourself in the picture: a question of talk, in E. Arizpe and M. Styles (eds) *Children Reading Pictures: Interpreting Visual Texts*. London: Routledge.

Brooker, L. (2002) *Starting School – Young Children Learning Cultures*. Buckingham: Open University Press.

Brown, M., Askew, M., Baker, D., Denvir, H. and Millett, A. (1998) Is the national numeracy strategy research-based? *British Journal of Educational Studies*, 46(4): 362–85.

Browne, A. (1994) *Zoo*. London: Red Fox.

Bruce, B.C. (1999) Response: speaking the unspeakable about 21st century technologies, in G.E Hawisher and C.L. Selfe (eds) *Passions, Pedagogies and 21st Century Technologies*. Logan, UT: Utah State University Press and National Council of Teachers of English.

Bruner, J. (1966) *Towards a Theory of Instruction*. Cambridge, MA: Harvard University Press.

Bruner, J. (1983) *Child's Talk: Learning to Use Language*. Oxford: Oxford University Press.

Bruner, J. (1985) Vygotsky: a historical and conceptual perspective, in J. Wertsch (ed.) *Culture, Communication and Cognition: Vygotskian Perspectives*. Cambridge: Cambridge University Press.

Bruner, J.S. (1986) *Actual Minds, Possible Worlds*. London: Harvard University Press.

Bruner, J. (1987) The transactional self, in J.S. Bruner and H.E. Haste (eds) *Making Sense: The Child's Construction of the World*. London: Routledge.

Bruner, J. (1990) *Acts of Meaning*. Cambridge, MA: Harvard University Press.

Bruner, J. (1996) *The Culture of Education*. Cambridge, MA: Harvard University Press.

Bruner, J.S. and Haste, H.E. (eds) (1987) *Making Sense: The Child's Construction of the World*. London: Routledge.

Burgess-Macey, C. (1999) *Classroom Literacies: Young Children's Explorations in Meaning Making in the Age of the Literacy Hour*. Oxford: Blackwell.

Calderhead, J. (1988) The development of knowledge structures in learning to teach, in J. Calderhead (ed.) *Teachers' Professional Learning*. Basingstoke: Falmer.

Calkins, L. (1984) *The Art of Teaching Writing*. Portsmouth, NH: Heinemann.

Cameron, D. (2003) Schooling spoken language: beyond 'communication', in QCA (ed.) *New Perspectives on Spoken English*. London: QCA.

Carnegie Forum on Education (1986) *A Nation Prepared: Teachers For the Twenty-first Century*. New York: Carnegie Forum on Education.

Carter, R. (1997) *Investigating English Discourse: Language, Literacy and Literature*. London: Routledge.

Castells, M. (2001) *The Internet Galaxy: Reflections on the Internet, Business and Society*. Oxford: Oxford University Press.

Chambers, A. (1993) *Tell Me: Children Reading and Talk*. Stroud: The Thimble Press.

Cherryholmes, C. (1987) A social project for curriculum: post-structural perspectives, *Journal of Curriculum Studies*, 19(4): 295–316.

Chi, M.T.H., Feltovich, J.P. and Glaser, R. (1981) Categorization and representation of physics problems by experts and novices, *Cognitive Science*, 5(2): 121–52.

Chi, M., Glaser, R. and Rees, E. (1982) Expertise in problem solving, in R. Sternberg (ed.) *Advances in the Psychology of Human Intelligence*, Vol. 1. New Jersey: Erlbaum.

CILT (Centre for Information on Language Teaching and Research) (2002) *European Language Portfolio*. London: CILT.

Claxton, G. (2000) in Watkins *et al.* (eds) *Tomorrow's Schools: Towards Integration*. London: Routledge.

Cochran-Smith, M. and Lytle, S. (1999) Relationships of knowledge and practice: teachers' learning in communities, *Review of Research in Education*, 24: 249–305.

Codling, R.M. and Gambrell, L.B. (1997) *The Motivation to Write Profile: An Assessment Tool for Elementary Teachers*. College Park: University of Maryland.

Cole, M. (1996) *Cultural Psychology*. Cambridge, MA: Harvard University Press.

Cole, G. and LCHC (1987) *Contextual Factors in Education*. Madison, WI: Wisconsin Center for Education Research.

Cole, M. and Engestrom, Y. (1993) A cultural-historical approach to distributed cognition, in G. Salomon (ed.) *Distributed Cognitions: Psychological and Educational Considerations*. Cambridge: Cambridge University Press.

Collins, J. and Collins, K. (eds) (1997) *The Handbook of Strategic Writing Lessons*. University of Buffalo, NY: GSE Publications.

Connolly, F.M., Clandinin, D.J. and He, M.F. (1997) Teachers' personal practical knowledge and the professional knowledge landscape, *Teaching and Teacher Education*, 13(7): 665–74.

Corden, R. (2000) *Literacy and Learning Through Talk*. Buckingham: Open University Press.

Corden, R. (2002) Developing reflective writers in primary schools: findings from partnership research, *Educational Review*, 54(3): 249–76.

Craft, A. (2000) *Creativity Across the Primary Curriculum: Framing and Developing Practice*. London: Routledge.

Cremin, M. (2003) The role of the imagination in drama. Thesis submitted for a doctoral examination, University of Kent, Canterbury.

D'Andrade, R. (1995) *The Development of Cognitive Anthropology*. Cambridge: Cambridge University Press.

D'Arcy, P. (1999) *Two Contrasting Paradigms in the Teaching of Writing*. Sheffield: National Association for the Teaching of English.

Dadds, M. (1999) Teachers' values and the Literacy Hour, *Cambridge Journal of Education*, March, 29(1): 7–20.

Datta, M. (2000) *Bilinguality and Literacy: Principles and Practice*. London: Continuum.

Denmaine, J. (1999) *Education Policy and Contemporary Politics*. London: Macmillan.

DfEE (Department for Education and Employment) (1998a) *The National Literacy Strategy: Framework for Teaching*. London: HMSO.

DfEE (Department for Education and Employment) (1998b) *ITT National Curriculum for Primary English*. London: DfEE.

DfEE (Department for Education and Employment) (1998c) *Teaching: High Status; High Standards – Requirements for Courses of Initial Teacher Training*. Circular 4/98. London: HMSO.

DfEE (Department for Education and Employment) (1999a) *The National Curriculum for England and Wales*. London: HMSO.

DfEE (Department for Education and Employment) (1999b) *All Our Futures: Creativity Culture and Education*. Report of the National Advisory Committee on Creative and Cultural Education. Sudbury: DfEE.

DfES (Department for Education and Skills) (2002a) *Supporting Pupils Learning English as an Additional Language*. Annesley: DfES Publications.

DfES (Department for Education and Skills) (2002b) *Languages for All, Languages for Life: A Strategy for England*. Annesley: DfES.

DfES (Department for Education and Skills) (2002c) *The National Literacy and Numeracy Strategies: Building on Improvement*. London: DfES.

Dillard, A. (1989) *The Writing Life*. New York: Harper & Row.

Dillon, J.T. (1990) *The Practice of Questioning*. London: Routledge.

Dombey, H. (1988) Partners in the Telling, in M. Meek and C. Mills (eds) *Language and Literacy in the Primary School*. Barcombe: Falmer Press.

Dombey, H. (2003) Interactions between teachers, children and texts in three primary classrooms in England, *Journal of Early Childhood Literacy*, 3(1): 37–58.

Donald, M. (1991) *Origins of the Modern Mind: Three Stages in the Evolution of Culture and Cognition*. Cambridge, MA: Harvard University Press.

Donoahue, Z. (1997) Giving children control: fourth graders initiate and sustain discussions after teacher read-alouds, *Networks, 1* http://www.oise. utoronto.ca/ ~ctd/ networks/

Doonan, J. (1993) *Looking at Pictures in Picture Books*. Exeter: Thimble Press.

Doyle, W. (1983) Academic work, *Review of Educational Research*, 53(2): 159–99.

Doyle, W. and Carter, K. (1984) Academic tasks in the classroom, *Curriculum Inquiry*, 14(2): 129–49.

Earl, L., Levin, B., Leithwood, K. *et al.* (2001) *Watching and Learning 2: OISE/UT Evaluation of the Implementation of the National Literacy and Numeracy Strategies*. Toronto: University of Toronto, Ontario Institute for Studies in Education.

Edwards, A.D. (1992) Teacher talk and pupil competence, in K. Norman (ed.) *Thinking Voices: The Work of the National Oracy Project*. London: Hodder and Stoughton.

Edwards, V. (1998) *The Power of Babel: Teaching and Learning in Multilingual Classrooms*. Stoke-on-Trent: Trentham Books.

Edwards, D. and Mercer, N. (1987) *Common Knowledge: The Development of Understanding in the Classroom*. London: Methuen.

Edwards, A. and Ogden, L. (1998) Constructing curriculum subject knowledge in primary school teacher training, *Teaching and Teacher Education*, 14(7): 735–47.

Edwards, A.D. and Westgate, D.P.G. (1992) *Investigating Classroom Talk*. London: Falmer Press.

Emig, J. (1983) *The Web of Meaning: Essays on Writing, Teaching, Learning and Thinking*. Upper Montclair, NJ: Boynton/Cook.

English, E., Hargreaves, L. and Hislam, J. (2002) Pedagogical dilemmas in the national literacy strategy: primary teachers' perceptions, reflections and classroom behaviour, *Cambridge Journal of Education*, 32(1): 1–25.

Faigley, L. (1999) Beyond imagination: the Internet and global digital literacy, in G.E. Hawisher and C.L. Selfe (eds) *Passions, Pedagogies and 21st Century Technologies*. Logan, UT: Utah State University Press and National Council of Teachers of English.

Feiman-Nemser, S. and Flodden, R.E. (1986) The cultures of teaching, in M. Wittrock (ed.) *Handbook of Research on Teaching* (3rd edn). New York: Macmillan.

Feldman, C.F. (1987) Thought from language: the linguistic construction of cognitive representations, in J. Bruner and H. Haste (eds) (1987) *Making Sense: The Child's Construction of the World*. London: Routledge.

Feldman, A. (1997) Varieties of wisdom in the practice of teachers, *Teaching and Teacher Education*, 3(7): 757–74.

Fenstermacher, G.D. (1994) The knower and the known: the nature of knowledge in research on teaching, *Review of Research in Education*, 20: 3–56.

Filer, A. and Pollard, A. (2000) *The Social World of Pupil Assessment*. London: Cassell.

Fish, S. (1980) *Is There a Text in this Class?* Harvard, MA: Harvard University Press.

Flanders, N. (1970) *Analyzing Teacher Behavior*. Reading, MA: Addison-Wesley.

Flower, L. and Hayes, J. (1981) A cognitive theory process of writing, *College Composition and Communication*, 32: 365–87.

Fox, M. (1993) *Radical Reflections: Passionate Opinions on Teaching, Learning and Living.* New York: Harcourt Brace and Company.

Fox, R. (2000) *Assessing Writing at KS1. Some Problems and Solutions.* UKRA: Blackwell.

Freebody, P. and Freiberg, J. (2001) Re-discovering practical reading activities in homes and schools, *Journal of Research in Reading,* 24(3): 222–34.

Freeman, W.G. (1995) *Societies of Brains: A Study in the Neuroscience of Love and Hate.* Hillsdale, NJ: Erlbaum.

Freire, P. (1970) *Pedagogy of the Oppressed.* New York: Herder & Herder.

Furlong, J. and Maynard, T. (1995) *Mentoring Student Teachers: The Growth of Professional Knowledge.* London: Routledge.

Galton, M., Simon, B. and Croll, P. (1980) *Inside the Primary Classroom.* London: Routledge and Kegan Paul.

Galton, M., Hargreaves, L., Comber, C., Wall, D. and Pell, A. (1999) *Inside the Primary Classroom: 20 Years On.* London: Routledge.

Gardner, H. (1993) *Multiple Intelligences: The Theory in Practice.* New York: Basic Books.

Gee, J. (1996) *Social Linguistics and Literacies* (2nd edn). London: Falmer Press.

Gee, J.P. (2000) The new literacy studies: from 'socially situated' to the work of the social, in D. Barton, M. Hamilton and R. Ivanic (eds) *Situated Literacies: Reading and Writing in Context.* London: Routledge.

Gilster, P. (1997) *Digital Literacy.* New York: John Wiley & Sons.

Giroux, H.A. (1987) Introduction: literacy and the pedagogy of political empowerment, in P. Freire and D. Macedo (eds) *Literacy: Reading the Word and the World.* London: Routledge and Kegan Paul.

Goldberg, N. (1986) *Writing Down the Bones: Freeing the Writer Within.* Boston, MA: Shambhaha Publications.

Goleman, D. (1995) *Emotional Intelligence.* New York: Bantam Books.

Goodman, S. and Graddol, D. (1996) *Redesigning English: New Texts, New Identities.* London: Routledge.

Goody, J. (1993) *The Interface Between the Written and the Oral.* Cambridge: Cambridge University Press.

Graff, H. (1991) *The Legacies of Literacy: Continuities and Contradictions in Western Culture and Society.* Bloomington, IN: Indiana University Press.

Grainger, T. (2001) Drama and writing, *Primary English Magazine,* April.

Grainger, T. (2002) Drama and writing: passion on the page, *Secondary English Magazine,* 5(4): 16–22.

Grainger, T. and Cremin, M. (2001) *Resourcing Classroom Drama.* Sheffield: NATE.

Grainger, T., Goouch, K. and Lambirth, A. (2003) Playing the game called writing: children's views and voices, *English in Education,* 36(1).

Gravelle, M. (2000) *Planning for Bilingual Learners: An Inclusive Curriculum.* Stoke-on-Trent: Trentham Books.

Graves, D. (1983) *Writing: Teachers and Children at Work.* Portsmouth, NH: Heinnemann.

Green, B. (1998) Teaching for difference: learning theory and post-critical pedagogy, in D. Buckingham (ed.) *Teaching Popular Culture: Beyond Radical Pedagogy.* London: UCL Press.

Greene, M. (1995) *Releasing the Imagination: Essays on Education, the Arts and Social Change.* San Francisco: Jossey Bass Publications.

Greeno, J.G. (1997) On claims that answer the wrong question, *Educational Researcher*, 26(1): 5–17.

Grice, H.P. (1975) Logic and conversation, in P. Cole and J. Morgan (eds) *Syntax and Semantics*, Volume 3, *Speech Acts.* New York: Academic Press.

Grossman, P.L., Wilson, S.M. and Shulman, L.E. (1989) Teachers of substance: subject matter knowledge for teaching, in M.C. Reynolds (ed.) *Knowledge Base For The Beginning Teacher.* New York: Pergamon.

Halliday, M.A.K. (1975) *Learning How to Mean. Explorations in the Development of Language.* London: Edward Arnold.

Halliday, M.A.K. (1978) *Language as Social Semiotic: The Social Interpretation of Language and Meaning.* London: Arnold.

Harding, D.W. (1977) Psychological processes in the reading of fiction, in M. Meek, A. Warlow and G. Bolton (eds) *The Cool Web: The Pattern of Children's Reading.* London: The Bodley Head.

Hardman, F., Smith, F. and Wall, K. (2003) 'Interactive whole class teaching' in the National Literary Strategy, *Cambridge Journal of Education*, 33(2): 197–215.

Hardy, B. (1977) Towards a poetics of fiction: an approach through narrative, in M. Meek, A. Warlow and G. Bolton (eds) *The Cool Web: The Pattern of Children's Reading.* London: The Bodley Head.

Hargreaves, A. (1978) The significance of teachers' coping strategies, in L. Barton and R. Meighan (eds) *Sociological Interpretations of Schooling and Classrooms: A Reappraisal.* Driffield: Nafferton Books.

Hargreaves, A., Lieberman, A., Fullan, M. and Hopkins, D. (eds) (1998) *The International Handbook of Educational Change.* Dordrecht: the Netherlands: Kluwer Press.

Hargreaves, L. *et al.* (2002) How do elementary school teachers define and implement 'interactive teaching' in the National Literacy Hour in England? AERA Conference Paper.

Harré, R. (1978) Accounts, actions and meanings: the practice of participatory psychology, in M. Brenner and P. Marsh (eds) *The Social Contexts of Method.* London: Croom Helm.

Harré, R. (1995) Discursive psychology, in J. Smith, J. Harré and L. Van Langenhove (eds) *Rethinking Psychology.* London: Sage Publications.

Harré, R. and Gillet, G. (1994) *The Discursive Mind.* London: Sage.

Hayes, J. and Flower, L. (1980) Identifying the organisation of writing processes, in L. Gregg and E. Steinberg (eds) *Cognitive Processes in Writing.* Hillsdale, NJ: Lawrence Erlbaum Associates.

Heathcote, D. (1980) *Drama as Context.* Sheffield: NATE.

Henry, M. (2000) Drama's ways of learning, *Research in Drama Education*, 5(1): 45–62.

Hirst, P.H. (1974) *Knowledge and the Curriculum: A Collection of Philosophical Papers.* London: Routledge and Kegan Paul.

HMI (2000) *Writing: Could Do Better, HMI Discussion Paper.* London: DfES.

Hume, A. (1983) Research on the Composing Process, *Review of Educational Research*, 53(2): 210–16.

Iser, W. (1978) *The Act of Reading: A Theory of Aesthetic Response.* Baltimore, MD: John Hopkins University Press and Routledge Kegan Paul.

Jackson, P.W. (1968) *Life in Classrooms.* New York: Holt, Rinehart and Winston.

Johnson, M. (1987) *The Body in the Mind: The Bodily Basis of Meaning, Imagination and Reason.* Chicago: University of Chicago Press.

Kenner, C. (2000) *Home Pages: Literacy Links for Bilingual Children.* Stoke-on-Trent: Trentham Books.

Kenner, C., Kress, G., Al-Khatib, H., Kam, R. and Tsai, K-C. (forthcoming) Finding the keys to biliteracy: how young children interpret different writing systems, *Language and Education*.

Kiefer, B. (1995) *The Potential of Picture Books: From Visual Literacy to Aesthetic Understanding.* Englewood Cliff, NJ: Merrill.

King, S. (2000) *On Writing: A Memoir of the Craft.* New York: Scribner.

Knobel, M. and Healey, A. (1998) Critical literacies: an introduction, in M. Knobel and A. Healey (eds) *Critical Literacies in the Primary Classroom.* Newtown, NSW: Primary English Teaching Association.

Korthagen, F. and Lagerwerf, B. (1996) Reframing the relationship between teacher thinking and teacher behaviour: levels in learning about teaching, *Teachers and Teaching*, 2(2): 161–90.

Krechevsky, M. and Stork, J. (2000) Challenging educational assumptions: lessons from an Italian American collaboration, *Cambridge Journal of Education*, 30(1).

Kress, G. (1997) *Before Writing: Rethinking the Paths to Literacy.* London: Routledge.

Lamott, A. (1995) *Bird by Bird: Some Instructions on Writing and Life.* New York: Anchor.

Lanham, R. (2001) What's next for text? *Education, Communication & Information*, 1(1).

Lankshear, C and Knobel, M. (1997) Literacies, texts and differences in the electronic age, in C. Lankshear (ed.) *Changing Literacies.* Buckingham: Open University Press.

Lankshear, C., and Snyder, I. (2000) *Teachers and Technoliteracy: Managing Literacy, Technology and Learning in Schools.* Sydney: Allen & Unwin.

Larkin, J., McDermott, J., Simon D. and Simon, A. (1980) Expert and novice performance in solving physics problems, *Science*, 208: 1335–42.

Laurillard, D. (1993) *Rethinking University Teaching: A Framework for the Effective Use of Educational Technology.* London: Routledge.

Lave, J. (1988) *Cognition in Practice: Mind, Mathematics and Culture in Everyday Life.* Cambridge: Cambridge University Press.

Lave, J. and Wenger, E. (1991) *Situated Learning: Legitimate Peripheral Participation*. Cambridge: Cambridge University Press.

Lee, A. (1997) Questioning the critical: linguistics, literacy and pedagogy, in G. Clachan and I. Reid (eds) *Framing and Interpretation*. Melbourne: Melbourne University Press.

Leinhardt, G. (1988) Situated knowledge and expertise in teaching, in J. Calderhead (ed.) *Teachers' Professional Learning*. London: Falmer Press.

Lemke, J. (1995) *Textual Politics*. London: Taylor & Francis.

Levin, B. (1998) An epidemic of education policy: what can we learn from each other? *Comparative Education*, 34: 131–41.

Levin, B. and Riffel, J.A. (1997) Schools and the changing world, *Journal of Educational Administration*, 31: 4–21.

Levine, J. (1992) Pedagogy: the case of the missing concept, in K. Kimberley, M. Meek and J. Miller (eds) *New Readings: Contributions to an Understanding of Literacy*. London: A. & C. Black.

Li, W. (1994) *Three Generations, Two Languages, One Family*. Clevedon: Multilingual Matters.

Little, W., Fowler, H.W. and Coulson, J. (1973) *The Shorter Oxford English Dictionary on Historical Principles*, 3rd edn. Oxford: Oxford University Press.

Luke, A. (1998) *Getting Over Method: Literacy Teaching as Work in New Times*. London: Language Arts.

Luke, A. and Freebody, P. (1997) Critical literacy and the question of normativity: an introduction, in S. Muspratt, A. Luke and P. Freebody (eds) *Constructing Critical Literacies: Teaching and Learning Textual Practice*. Cresskill, NJ: Hampton Press.

Lundvall, B. and Johnson, B. (1994) The learning economy, *Journal of Industry Studies*, 1: 23–42.

Lusted, D. (1986) Why pedagogy?, *Screen* 27, 5: 2–14.

Mackey, M. (2002) *Literacies Across Media: Playing the Text*. London: Routledge/Falmer.

Manovich, L. (2001) *The Language of New Media*. Cambridge, MA: The MIT Press.

Marsh, J. (2001) One-way traffic? Connections between literacy practices at home and in the nursery. Paper presented at BERA Conference, University of Leeds, September.

Martin, J.R. and Rothery, J. (1986) What a functional approach to the writing task can show teachers about 'good writing', in B. Couture (ed.) *Functional Approaches to Writing: Research Perspectives*. London: Frances Pinter.

Maynard, T. (1997) The limits of mentoring: the contribution of the Higher Education tutor to primary students' school-based learning, in J. Furlong and R. Smith (eds) *The Role of Higher Education in Initial Teacher Training*. London: Kogan Page.

Maynard, T. and Furlong, J. (1993) Learning to teach and models of mentoring, in D. McIntyre and H. Hagger (eds) *Mentoring Perspectives on School-based Teacher Education*. London: Kogan Page.

McMahon, S. I., Raphael, T. E. with Goatley, V. J. and Pardo, L. S. (1997) *The Book Club Connection: Literacy Learning and Classroom Talk*. New York: Teachers College Press.

McWilliam, N. (1998) *What's in a Word? Vocabulary Development in Multilingual Classrooms*. Stoke-on-Trent: Trentham Books.

Medwell, J., Wray, D., Poulson, L. and Fox, R. (1998) *Effective Teachers of Literacy*. London: Teacher Training Agency.

Meek, M. (1988) *How Texts Teach What Readers Learn*. Stroud: Thimble Press.

Meek, M. (1991) *On Being Literate*. London: The Bodley Head.

Mercer, N. (1995) *The Guided Construction of Knowledge: Talk Among Teachers and Learners*. Clevedon: Multilingual Matters.

Mercer, N. (2000) *Words and Minds*. London: Routledge.

Messenheimer, T. and Packwood, A. (2002a) Writing: the state of the state vs. the state of the art in English and American schools, *Reading, Literacy and Language*, 3: 11–15.

Messenheimer, T. and Packwood, A. (2002b) Reading like a writer, 38th UK Reading Association International Conference: Reaching Out, Moving Forward: Developing Literacies Through Interaction, University College Chester, 12th–14th July.

Middleton, D. and Edwards, D. (eds) (1990) *Collective Remembering*. London: Sage.

Millard, E. (2003) Towards a literacy of fusion: new times, new teaching and learning? *Reading Literacy and Language*, April 37(1).

Mines, H. (2000) The relationship between children's cultural literacies and their readings of literary texts. Unpublished PhD thesis, University of Brighton.

Ministère de l'Education Nationale (1995) *Programmes de l'école primaire*. Paris: Ministère de l'Education Nationale.

Moffett, J. (1968) *Teaching the Universe of Discourse*. Boston, MA: Houghton Mifflin and Co.

Mortimore, P. (1999) *Understanding Pedagogy and its Impact on Learning*. London: Paul Chapman.

Moss, P. (2001) The otherness of Reggio, in L. Abbott and C. Nutbrown (eds) *Experiencing Reggio Emilia: Implications for Preschool Provision*. Buckingham: Oxford University Press.

Moyles, J. (1994) *The Excellence of Play*. Buckingham: Open University Press.

Moyles, J., Hargreaves, L. *et al.* (2003) *Interactive Teaching in the Primary School*, Maidenhead: Open University Press.

Mroz, M. and Wall, K. (2002) Unpublished paper presented at the International Reading Association World Conference, Edinburgh.

Mroz, M., Smith, F. and Hardman, F. (2000) The discourse of the Literacy Hour, *Cambridge Journal of Education*, 30(3): 379–90.

Murray, D. (1982) The teaching craft: telling, listening, revealing, *Learning by Teaching: Selected Articles on Writing and Teaching*. Portsmouth, NH: Boynton/Cook.

Murray, D. (1990) *Shoptalk: Learning to Write with Writers*. Portsmouth, NH: Boynton/Cook.

Neelands, J. (2000) Drama – it sets you free or does it?, in J. Davison and J. Moss (eds) *Issues in English Teaching*. London: Routledge.

Nelson, K. (1996) *Language in Cognitive Development: The Emergence of the Mediated Mind*. Cambridge: Cambridge University Press.

Nicholson, H. (2000) Drama, literacies and difference, in E. Bearne and V. Watson (eds) *Where Texts and Children Meet*. London: Routledge.

Norman, K. (ed.) (1992) *Thinking Voices: The Work of the National Oracy Project*. London: Hodder and Stoughton.

Noschis, K. (1992) Children's changing access to public places, *Children's Environments*, 9(2): 3–9.

Nystrand, M. with A. Gamoran, R. Kachur and C. Prendergast (1997) *Opening Dialogue: Understanding the Dynamics of Language and Learning in the English Classroom*. New York: Teachers' College Press.

O'Neill, C. (1995) *Drama Worlds: A Framework for Process Drama*. New Hampshire: Heinemann.

Ofsted (Office for Standards in Education) (1994) *Science and Mathematics in Schools: A Review*. London: HMSO.

Ofsted (2000) *The National Literacy Strategy: the second year*. London: Nelson.

Ofsted (2002) *National Literacy Strategy: the first four years*. 1998–2002 London: Arkle Print.

Olson, D. (1996) *The World on Paper: The Conceptual and Cognitive Implications of Writing and Reading*. Cambridge: Cambridge University Press.

Packwood, A. and Messenheimer, T. (2002) The secret to being a writer is to read, World Reading Conference, Edinburgh, 28 July – 1 August.

Poulson, L. and Avramidis, E. (2003) Pathways and possibilities in professional development: case studies of effective teachers of literacy, *British Educational Research Journal*, 29(4), 527–44.

Poulson, L., Avramidis, E., Fox, R., Medwell, J. and Wray, D. (2001) The theoretical beliefs of effective teachers of literacy in primary school: an exploratory study of orientations to reading and writing, *Research Papers in Education*, 16(3): 271–92.

Prentice, R. (2000) Creativity: a reaffirmation of its place in early childhood education, *The Curriculum Journal*, 11(2): 145–158.

Putnam, D. and Borko, H. (2000) What do new views of knowledge and thinking have to say about research on teacher learning? *Educational Researcher*, 29(1): 4–15.

QCA (Qualifications and Curriculum Authority) (2000) *Curriculum Guidance for the Foundation Stage*. London: QCA.

QCA (2002) *The arts, creativity and cultural education: An international perspective*. National Foundation for Educational Research/QCA: London.

Reboul-Sherrer, F. (1989) *Les premiers instituteurs, 1833–1882*. Paris: Hachette.

Reid, I. (1992) *Narrative Exchanges*. London: Routledge.

Reid, I. (2001) *What is Needed to Make Australia a Knowledge-driven and Learning-driven Society?* B-HERT Position Paper No. 5. Melbourne: Business/Higher Education Round Table CAN 050 207 942.

Robinson, K. (2001) *Out of Our Minds*. Oxford: Capstone Press.

Rogoff, B. (1990) *Apprenticeship in Thinking: Cognitive Development in Social Context*, New York: Oxford University Press.

Rosenblatt, L. (1938) *Literature as Exploration*. New York: Appleton-Century.

Rosenblatt, L. (1978) *The Reader, the Text and the Poem*. Carbondale, IL: Southern Illinois University Press.

Roth, P. (1998) *I Married a Communist*. Boston, MA: Houghton Mifflin.

Sainsbury, M. (1998) *Literacy Hours: A Survey of the National Picture in the Spring Term 1998*. Slough: NFER.

Schwab, J.J. (1964) The structure of the disciplines: meanings and significance, in G.L. Ford and L. Purgo (eds) *The Structure of Knowledge and the Curriculum*. Chicago: Rand McNally.

Schwab, J.J. (1978) in I. Westbury and N.J. Wilkof (eds) *Science, Curriculum and Liberal Education*. Chicago: University of Chicago Press.

Shulman, L.S. (1986) Those who understand: knowledge growth in teaching, *Educational Researcher*, 15(2): 4–14.

Shulman, L.S. (1987) Knowledge and teaching: foundations of the new reform, *Harvard Educational Review*, 57(1): 1–22.

Shulman, L.S. (1998) Theory, Practice and the Education of Professionals, *Elementary School Journal*, 98(5): 511–26.

Sinclair, J.McH. and Coulthard, M. (1975) *Towards an Analysis of Discourse*. Oxford: Oxford University Press.

Skidmore, D. (2002) Unpublished paper from ESRC project on teacher–pupil dialogue and the comprehension of literary texts, University of Reading.

Skidmore, D., Perez-Parent, M. and Arnfield, S. (2003) Teacher–pupil dialogue in the guided reading session, *Reading, Literacy and Language*, 37(2).

Smith, F. (1983) *Essays Into Literacy*. Portsmouth, NH: Heinemann.

Sneddon, R. (1993) Beyond the national curriculum: a community project to support bilingualism, *Journal of Multilingual and Multicultural Development*, 4(3): 237–45.

Snyder, I. (1996) *Hypertext: The Electronic Labyrinth*. Melbourne: Melbourne University Press.

Snyder, I. (2001) The new communication order, in C. Durrant and C. Beavis (eds) *P)ict)ures of English: Teachers, Learners and Technology*. Adelaide: Wakefield Press and Australian Association for the Teaching of English.

Snyder, I. (ed.) (2002) *Silicon Literacies: Communication, Innovation and Education in the Electronic Age*. London: Routledge.

Sorenson, E.R. (1979) Early tactical communication and the patterning of human organization: a New Guinea case study, in M. Bullowa (ed.) *Before Speech: The*

Beginning of Interpersonal Communication. Cambridge: Cambridge University Press.

Standards and Effectiveness Unit (1998) *The National Literacy Strategy: Framework for Teaching*. London: Department for Education and Employment.

Sternberg, R. (1997) *Successful Intelligence*. New York: Plume.

Sternberg, R. and Horvath, J. (1995) A prototype view of expert teaching, *Educational Researcher*, 24(6): 9–17.

Stine, R.L. (1997) *It Came from Ohio! My Life as a Writer*. New York: Scholastic.

Street, B. V. (ed.) (1993) *Cross Cultural Approaches to Literacy*. Cambridge: Cambridge University Press.

Street, B. (1995) *Social Literacies: Critical Approaches to Literacy in Development, Ethnography and Education*. London: Longman.

Street, B.V. (1997) The implication of the new literacy studies for literacy education, *English in Education*, 32(3): 45–59.

Styles, M. and Arizpe, E. (2001) 'A gorilla with grandpa's eyes': how children interpret visual texts – a case study of Anthony Browne's *Zoo*, *Children's Literature in Education*, 32: 261–81.

Sutton-Smith, B. (1997) *The Ambiguity of Play*. Cambridge, MA: Harvard University Press.

Taylor, P. (2000) *The Drama Classroom: Action, Reflection Transformation*. London: Routledge/Falmer.

Taylor, P. (1995) *Pre–Text and Story Drama: The Artistry of Cecily O'Neill and David Booth*. Research Monograph Series. Australia: NADIE.

Tharp, R.G. and Gallimore, R. (1988) *Rousing Minds to Life: Teaching, Learning and Schooling in Social Context*. Cambridge: Cambridge University Press.

Tochon, F. and Munby, H. (1993) Novice and expert teachers' time epistemology: a wave function from didactics to pedagogy, *Teaching and Teacher Education*, 2: 205–18.

Twiselton, S. (1999) 'Literacy activities – purposeful tasks or ways of keeping busy?' in *Children's Perceptions of their Learning with Trainee Teachers*, London: Routledge.

Twiselton, S. (2000) 'Seeing the Wood for the Trees: the National Literacy Strategy and Initial Teacher Education; pedagogical content knowledge and the structure of subjects', *The Cambridge Journal of Education*, 30(3), 391–403.

Unsworth, L. (2001) *Teaching Multiliteracies Across the Curriculum*. Buckingham: Open University Press.

Van Tassell, M.A. and Galbraith, B. (1997) Seeds and webs. Unpublished paper, OISE/University of Toronto.

Volosinov, V.N. (1973) *Marxism and the Philosophy of Language*. New York: Seminar Press.

Vygotsky, L. ([1962] 1986) in A. Kozulin (ed.) *Thought and Language*. Cambridge, MA: MIT Press.

Vygotsky, L.S. (1978) *Mind in Society*. Cambridge, MA: Harvard University Press.

Vygotsky, L.S. (1981) The genesis of higher mental functions, in J.V. Wertsch (ed.) *The Concept of Activity in Soviet Psychology*. Armonk, NY: Sharpe.

Warwick, P. and Maloch, B. (2003) Scaffolding speech and writing in the primary classroom: a consideration of work with literature and science pupil groups in the USA and UK, *Reading, Literacy and Language*, 37(2).

Wattenberg, B. (1991) *The First Universal Nation*. New York: The Free Press.

Webster, N. (1975) *Webster's New Twentieth Century Dictionary of the English Language Unabridged*, 2nd edn. United States: William Collins & World Publishing.

Wells, G. (1982) *Language, Learning and Education*. Bristol: Centre for the Study of Language and Communication, Bristol University.

Wells, G. (1986) *The Meaning Makers: Children Learning Language and Using Language to Learn*. London: Hodder and Stoughton.

Wells, G. (1999) *Dialogic inquiry: Towards a Sociocultural Practice and Theory of Education*. Cambridge: Cambridge University Press.

Wells, G. (ed.) (2001) *Action, Talk, and Text: Developing Communities of Inquiry*. New York: Teachers College Press.

Wells, G. (2002) Learning and teaching for understanding: the key role of collaborative knowledge building, in J. Brophy (ed.) *Social Constructivist Teaching: Affordances and Constraints*. Advances in Research on Teaching, Vol. 9. London: Elsevier/JAI.

Williams, R. (1976) *Keywords: A Vocabulary of Culture and Society*. London: Fontana Press.

Williams, R. ([1958] 1983) *Culture and Society: 1780–1950*. New York: Columbia University Press.

Wilson, S.M. and Berne, J. (1999) Teacher learning and the acquisition of professional knowledge: an examination of research on contemporary professional development, *Review of Research in Education*, 24: 173–209.

Wilson, S.M., Shulman, L.S. and Richert, A.E. (1987) 150 different ways of knowing: representations of knowledge in teaching, in J. Calderhead (ed.) *Exploring Teachers' Thinking*. London: Cassell.

Winokur, J. (1986) *Writers on Writing*. Philadelphia: Running Press.

Winston, J. (1998) *Drama, Narrative and Moral Education*. London: The Falmer Press.

Wittrock, M.C. (1986) *Handbook of Research on Teaching* (3rd edn). New York: Macmillan.

Wood, D. (1988) *How Children Think and Learn*, London: Blackwell.

Woods, P. (1996) *Researching the Art of Teaching: Ethnography for Educational Use*. London: Routledge.

Woods, P. (1997) *Restructuring Schools, Reconstructing Teachers: Responding to Change in the Primary School*. Buckingham: Open University Press.

Wragg, E.C., Bennett, S.N. and Carre, C. (1989) Primary teachers and the national curriculum, *Research Papers in Education*, 4: 17–45.

Wray, D. (1994) *Language and Awareness*. London: Hodder and Stoughton.

Wray, D., Medwell, J., Poulson, L. and Fox, R. (2002) *Teaching Literacy Effectively in the Primary School*. London: Routledge Falmer.

Wright, P. (1999) The thought of doing drama scares me to death, *Research in Drama Education*, 4(2): 227–37.

Wyse, D. and Jones, R. (2001) *Teaching English, Language and Literacy*. London: Routledge Falmer.

Young, M.D.F. (1998) *Curriculum of the Future. From the 'New Sociology of Education' to a Critical Theory of Learning*. London: Falmer Press.

Author index

Subject index

LITERACY AND LEARNING THROUGH TALK

STRATEGIES FOR THE PRIMARY CLASSROOM

Roy Corden

This book focuses on the inter-relationship between reading, writing, speaking and listening. Psychologists and educationalists, influenced by the work of Vygotsky, have emphasized the importance of social interaction in learning, and the National Writing, Oracy and LINC Projects highlighted the need for quality interactive pupil discourse and effective pupil–teacher interaction. However, although the DfEE claims that the successful teaching of literacy is characterized by good quality oral work, speaking and listening is not included in the National Literacy Strategy Framework and the Literacy Training Pack does not address the issue.

Literacy and Learning through Talk blends theory, research and practice to show how an integrated programme of work can be developed to ensure that literacy is taught in a vibrant and stimulating way. Strategies for developing successful group work and whole class, interactive discourse are examined, and effective teaching roles and questioning techniques are explored. Transcripts of group discussions and examples of children's work illustrate various points and work plans and practical classroom activities are described.

Contents
Introduction – Talking, learning and literacy – The discourse of literacy – Planning for talk – Group work – The role of the teacher – Exploratory talk – Speaking and listening to reading and writing: story making, story telling – Children's literature – References – Index.

204pp   0 335 20450 3 (Paperback)   0 335 20451 1 (Hardback)

LISTENING TO STEPHEN READ
MULTIPLE PERSPECTIVES ON LITERACY
Kathy Hall

- How do different reading experts interpret evidence about one child as a reader?
- What perspectives can be brought to bear on reading in the classroom?
- How can a rich notion of literacy be promoted in the regular primary classroom?

In this book Kathy Hall invites you to extend your perspective on reading by considering the responses of well known reading scholars (e.g. Barbara Comber, Henrietta Dombey, Laura Huxford and David Wray) to evidence of one child as a reader. Reading evidence from 8-year-old Stephen, who is 'under-achieving' in reading, together with the suggestions of various experts about how his teacher could support him provide a vehicle for discussing different perspectives on reading in the primary classroom. The various approaches to literacy analysed include psycho-linguistic, cognitive-psychological, socio-cultural and socio-political. The book aims to guide your choice of teaching strategies and to support your rationale for those choices. Acknowledging the complexity and the richness of the field of research on literacy, the book demonstrates the futility of searching for a single right method of literacy development. Rather we should search for multiple perspectives, guided by the diverse needs of learners.

Contents
Introduction – Part one: A psycho-linguistic perspective – Ann Browne's observations, suggestions and theoretical perspectives – Teresa Grainger's observations, suggestions and theoretical perspectives – Reading as a problem-solving activity – Part two: A cognitive-psychological perspective – Laura Huxford's observations, suggestions and theoretical perspectives – David Wray's observations, suggestions and theoretical perspectives – Words matter – Part three: A socio-cultural perspective – Henrietta Dombey's observations, suggestions and theoretical perspectives – Mary Hilton's observations, suggestions and theoretical perspectives – Reading and communities of practice – Part four: A socio-political perspective – Barbara Comber's observations, suggestions and theoretical perspectives – Jackie Marsh's observations, suggestions and theoretical perspectives – Reading the word and the world – Conclusion – Bibliography – Index.

224pp   0 335 20758 8 (Paperback)   0 335 20759 6 (Hardback)

TEACHING MULTILITERACIES ACROSS THE CURRICULUM
CHANGING CONTEXTS OF TEXT AND IMAGE IN CLASSROOM PRACTICE

Len Unsworth

Teaching literacy in today's primary and junior secondary schools involves both teaching children what people understand as traditional literacy and also teaching children how to read and produce the kinds of texts typical of the current and emerging information age. This still means understanding grammar as a functional tool in reading and writing but it also now necessarily entails explicit knowledge about how images and layout can be structured in different ways to make different kinds of meanings and how both text and image are used in electronic formats. This major new textbook outlines the basic theoretical knowledge teachers need to have about visual and verbal grammar and the nature of computer-based texts in school learning. In doing so it:

- addresses both the present demands in literacy teaching and the emerging demands for teaching the multiliteracies of the information age;
- provides accessible, integrative, classroom oriented coverage of the complex range of current and emerging issues (like teaching grammar, visual literacy, the role of computer-based information and communication technology, critical literacy, literacies and learning in English and other curriculum areas);
- includes both theoretical frameworks and detailed practical guidelines with examples of classroom work;
- deals with the continuities and differences in the teaching of infants, children in the primary school and the transition to the first years of secondary education.

Contents
Introduction – Changing dimensions of school literacies – Learning about language as a resource for literacy development – Describing visual literacies – Distinguishing the literacies of school science and humanities – Exploring multimodal meaning-making in literature for children – Developing multiliteracies in the early school years – Developing multiliteracies in content area teaching – Teaching multiliteracies in the English classroom – References – Index.

320pp   0 335 20604 2 (Paperback)   0 335 20605 0 (Hardback)

NEW LITERACIES
CHANGING KNOWLEDGE AND CLASSROOM LEARNING
Colin Lankshear and Michele Knobel

An intriguing book which argues why the use of new media is transforming ways of knowing and making meaning in the digital age. Essential reading for anyone who cares about literacy education.

Associate Professor Ilana Snyder, Monash University

A good book opens a window onto new vistas; an excellent one, on the other hand, pulls readers through the opening and beyond, inviting critical dialogue at every turn. *New Literacies* belongs in the excellent category.

Donna Alvermann, University of Georgia

Literacy education continues to be dominated by a mindset that has passed its use-by date. Education has failed to take account of how much the world has changed during the information technology revolution. It proceeds as though the world is the same as before – just somewhat more technologised. This is the hallmark of an 'outsider' mindset. In fact, qualitatively new literacies and new kinds of knowledge associated with digitally saturated social practices abound. 'Insiders' understand this, 'outsiders' do not. Yet 'outsider' perspectives still dominate educational directions. Meanwhile, student 'insiders' endure learning experiences that mystify, bemuse, alienate and miseducate them.

This book describes new social practices and new literacies, along with kinds of knowledge associated with them. It shows what is at stake between 'outsider' and 'insider' mindsets, argues that education requires a shift in mindset, and suggests how and where pursuit of progressive change might begin.

Contents
Foreword – Part one: What's new? – From 'reading' to the 'new literacy studies' – The 'new literacy studies' and the study of new literacies – Atoms and bits: Literacy and the challenge of mindsets – Part two: Staring at the future – Faking it: The national grid for learning – Attention economics, information and new literacies – The ratings game: From eBay to Plastic – Part three: Changing knowledge – Digital epistemologies: Rethinking knowledge for classroom learning – New ways of knowing: Learning at the margins – Bibliography – Index.

240pp   0 335 21066 X (Paperback)   0 335 21067 8 (Hardback)